* *

YOUNG IRELAND

**GLUCKSMAN
IRISH DIASPORA**

* *

Young Ireland

A Global Afterlife

Christopher Morash

* * *

NEW YORK UNIVERSITY PRESS
New York

* *

NEW YORK UNIVERSITY PRESS
New York
www.nyupress.org

Library of Congress Cataloging-in-Publication Data
Names: Morash, Chris, 1963–   author.
Title: Young Ireland : a global afterlife / Christopher Morash.
Other titles: Global Ireland
Description: New York : New York University Press, [2023] | Series: Glucksman Irish diaspora
series | Includes bibliographical references and index. | Summary: "This book offers new
insights on the integration of Irish diasporic communities into the fledgling democracies
of Australia, Canada, and the United States to which they offered a significant ideological
contribution as they engaged with key debates about nationalism, democracy, citizenship,
and minority rights"—Provided by publisher.
Identifiers: LCCN 2022051826 | ISBN 9781479822218 (hardback) | ISBN 9781479822232 (ebook)
| ISBN 9781479822256 (ebook other)
Subjects: LCSH: Irish—Political activity—Foreign countries—History—19th century. |
Young Ireland movement. | Irish—Foreign countries—Intellectual life. | Irish diaspora—
History—19th century. | Nationalists—Ireland—History—19th century. | Ireland—Politics
and government—19th century. | Transnationalism.
Classification: LCC DA928 .M67 2023 | DDC 909/.0491628I—dc23/eng/20221117
LC record available at https://lccn.loc.gov/2022051826

This book is printed on acid-free paper, and its binding materials are chosen for strength and
durability. We strive to use environmentally responsible suppliers and materials to the greatest
extent possible in publishing our books.

Manufactured in the United States of America

10 9 8 7 6 5 4 3 2 1

Also available as an ebook

CONTENTS

LIST OF FIGURES

Introduction

The Young Ireland Generation

Speaking in Dublin on 4 July 2017, the prime minister of Canada, Justin Trudeau, evoked the memory of the Young Ireland leader Thomas D'Arcy McGee, describing him as "equal parts proud Canadian and proud Irishman" and aligned himself with McGee as an advocate "for an open and diverse society."[1] Later that same year, while on a state visit to Australia, the president of Ireland, Michael D. Higgins, spoke of the Australian "impulse to build here a new and better world, to bend the destiny of this land towards a more humane and egalitarian future."[2] In his speech, President Higgins evoked the memory of yet another Young Irelander, Charles Gavan Duffy, who "arrived in Australia as an emigrant and, as a politician and later Premier of Victoria became an advocate for Federation as the vehicle for the creation of a new nation."[3] In claiming Irish figures from the 1840s for a liberal democratic politics in the twenty-first century, Trudeau and Higgins were not alone. When the US president, Barack Obama, addressed an Irish audience in Dublin in 2011, he spoke of how, "when Abraham Lincoln struggled to preserve our young union, more than 100,000 Irish and Irish Americans joined the cause, with units like the Irish Brigade charging into battle—green flags with gold harp waving alongside our star-spangled banner."[4] Perhaps the most recognizable figure in the ranks of that Irish Brigade was, once again, a Young Irelander: Thomas Francis Meagher.

On one level, there is nothing remarkable about visiting heads of state reminding their hosts of the historical ties binding their respective countries. There is something else going on here, however. While Trudeau, Higgins, and Obama are paying the host the compliments expected of a guest, they are also laying down a marker for their own credentials, and those of their countries, whether that be as "an open and diverse society" (Trudeau), leaning toward "a more humane and egalitarian future" (Higgins), or redressing the legacy of slavery and strengthening American institutions (Obama). For our purposes, what is particularly significant is that all three leaders find historical exemplars for the cause of twenty-first-century liberal democratic politics among the ranks of the Young Ireland movement of the 1840s: McGee, Duffy, and (at least implicitly) Meagher.

This book seeks to explain why Trudeau, Higgins and Obama might feel comfortable in the historical company of these Young Irelanders. It is a study of how some of the more significant ideas concerning democracy, state formation, nationalism, and liberalism were forged in Ireland in the 1840s and later rippled throughout the world when the Young Irelanders were exiled in 1848. It begins with that intense period of political activity in Ireland in the mid-1840s, focused around political writing in the newspaper *The Nation* and culminating in a series of minor military actions in 1848, the most well-known example of which was the not unfairly derided "battle for widow McCormack's cabbage patch" in Ballingarry County Tipperary.[5] From that point, the Young Irelanders whom Trudeau, Obama, and Higgins would remember almost 170 years later had indeed "been scattered all over the world," as Sir Charles Gavan Duffy put it in 1880.[6]

Indeed, the careers of many of the Young Irelanders lasted much longer—and, arguably, had more impact—than the few years during which they had been active in Ireland. In 1856 Duffy himself emigrated to Australia, where he advocated large-scale land reform, which in turn encouraged the colonization of Victoria, a state of which he would become the premier in 1871. Likewise, Thomas D'Arcy McGee emigrated to the United States following the failure of the 1848 rebellion and by 1857 had moved to Canada, where he rapidly ascended in the political world, ultimately becoming a driving force behind Canadian Confederation in 1867. In those same years, after being transported to Van Diemen's Land following the 1848 rebellion, Thomas Francis Meagher escaped to the United States, where he would become a brigadier general in the Union Army and, subsequently, acting governor of the Territory of Montana, where, among other initiatives, he argued that "the Black heroes of the Union Army" were entitled to settle.[7]

If, in the twenty-first century, Trudeau, Higgins, and Obama can broadly be considered an ideologically aligned transnational grouping,

Duffy, McGee, and Meagher may well in some respects be considered their nineteenth-century equivalents. We need to keep in mind, however, that John Mitchel, who became one of the American South's most vociferous supporters of slavery during the Civil War (and not likely to be name-checked by Trudeau, Higgins, or Obama), was also transported to Van Diemen's Land. While Mitchel's influence on militant nationalism in Ireland would be considerable, his attitudes to race were at odds with many of his contemporaries in the Young Ireland movement (and, indeed, with O'Connellite nationalism). And yet, even while Young Irelanders like Duffy, McGee, and Meagher espoused certain liberal values, they actively promoted policies of settler colonialism that involved the subjugation of other races. This, of course, was not unique to the Young Irelanders; as Duncan Bell has argued, nineteenth-century liberalism saw settler colonialism as the key to the world order.[8] It is in this wider frame of an increasingly globalized liberalism that we need to view Young Irelanders after 1848, rather than confining them to the comparatively few years during which they were active in Irish nationalist politics. At the same time, we can recognize that their political formation in Ireland always formed a context for the ideas they developed and the policies they pursued in the societies in which they found themselves.

Therefore, this book concerns itself with tracing the continual transnational reimagining of a particular iteration of concepts of democracy, state-building, nationalism, liberty, and settler colonialism through key individuals in the Young Ireland movement. As such, it is a work of global intellectual history, which studies the circulation of intellectual concepts in a global space.[9] These ideas were forged in a national context in Ireland in the 1840s, but transformed in the transnational context of the Australian colonies, Canada, and the United States in the 1850s and 1860s, at pivotal junctures in the emergence of new national communities and new states. At the same time, the Young Irelanders never lost their sense of Ireland as their political touchstone. For some, their commitment to Irish nationalism became more entrenched, developing into a much more militarily aggressive and republican Fenianism; for others, the movement went in the opposite direction, becoming less radical and more reconciled to the aims of the British Empire. However, as their political positions and ideas evolved outside of Ireland, they continued to use many of the same methodologies they had employed there, such as the shaping of public opinion through newspapers, speeches, and letters, to which they added newer technologies, notably the telegraph. In the process, the Young Ireland generation abroad crafted an Irish nation not contained by the physical boundaries of the island of Ireland, and it was through this complex flow of ideas and narratives that Irish diasporic communities in Canada, Australia, and the United States integrated themselves into the political life of their fledgling democracies.

In focusing on the Young Irelanders' engagement with the processes of both imagining and working to form new states, this book moves away from the common perception of them as primarily cultural nationalists.[10] While that work in Ireland in the 1840s remained a point of reference, after they left many of the Young Ireland leaders spent far more time and energy conceptualizing and building. The first was a practical, quotidian process involving fiscal, administrative, and military matters; the Young Irelanders' participation in the Union Army, in the negotiations for Confederation, or in colonization in Australia all provide evidence of this kind of activity. While some of the conceptual work they carried out after leaving Ireland involved some of their better-known literary and cultural productions, it more often took the form of political theory, often in response to situations in which they found themselves. For instance, an identifiable body of Young Ireland political writing emerged out of the context of Van Diemen's Land, just as a body of writing that contributes to the shaping of the idea of a national culture exists in Canada, and to a particular formulation of the American idea of manifest destiny.

Formation

Not the least remarkable aspect of this body of work is that figures such as Duffy, McGee, and Meagher continued to think of themselves as a group years or even decades after they had actually been together in the same room (or even on the same continent). And yet we find Thomas Francis Meagher writing to his former Young Ireland colleague John Blake Dillon fifteen years after they had both left Ireland to say, "Young Ireland looks up finely in the mild autumn of his days."[11] By then, the Young Irelanders were long past the point at which they could be described as an active movement, which, arguably, passed in the spring of 1848. However, as Meagher's letter suggests, many of them still thought of themselves as Young Irelanders and spoke of "Young Ireland" as an entity with a continuing existence. This suggests, at the very least, that we need to find different means of describing them than as a political movement.

Charles Gavan Duffy once retrospectively characterized the Irish nationalists of 1848 as "the generation of men with whom it was said a new soul came into Ireland."[12] This richly suggestive description presents us with a means of studying their impact outside of Ireland. Moreover, Duffy's generational conception would not have been unfamiliar in the 1840s, for the idea of generational difference as an agent of change was a nineteenth-century one, first explored by Auguste Comte in the 1830s and 1840s.[13] Indeed, the "Young" in "Young Ireland" was an expression of self-conscious generational distancing, and the term "Young Ireland" was in use as early as 1843, when it was coined by Daniel Owen Madden in *Ireland and Its Rulers since 1829*, only a year after *The Nation* first saw publication.[14] And, in the early 1840s, most of them were young, and part of the same generation.[15] Duffy was born in 1816, Meagher in 1823, and McGee in 1825, which meant that when *The Nation* was founded, they were all in their twenties. The vast majority were educated and from the upper and middle classes, and they moved in similar vocational and social circles.[16] Beyond this, it has been argued that at the core of a sociological understanding of generational identity is a collective response to a catastrophe and a collective memory of such an event; in the case of the Young Ireland generation, that catastrophe was writ large in the Great Famine (1845–52), which profoundly influenced their understanding of the world.[17]

Much of this formation, and the public sphere in which it occurred, centered on *The Nation*, which was run mainly by middle-class men who believed that "every nation had an undeniable right to self-rule."[18] Although not initially founded in response to the Famine (the first issue was published in 1842, three years before the first crop failure), what is astonishing about *The Nation* is the extent to which, in the midst of mass starvation and the effective collapse of large sections of rural society, it held that the path to nationality lay through the writing of Irish history, the advancement of Irish music and art, and the creation of an Irish literature. If a distinctive Irish culture could make its presence felt, they argued, the right to self-government would become self-evident.[19] Driving their enterprise was deep frustration with British administrators and politicians, for whom the Young Irelanders' logic of "self-evident" nationality was far from evident, as well as with the previous generation of Irish nationalists, epitomized by Daniel O'Connell, whose gradualist approach to repealing the Act of Union they saw as timid. In response, a faction within the Young Irelanders became increasingly willing to use violence to agitate for Irish self-government. Admittedly, in comparison with their precursors and successors—the United Irishmen in the 1790s, or the Fenians in the 1860s, who assembled uniforms and arsenals and took part in military drills—the Young Irelanders were comparative civilians. What they shared was conviction in the need for immediate and effective political transformation. While, at the time, this may have marked them out from the mainstream of Irish nationalism, it inevitably drew comparisons with other nationalist organizations in countries as diverse as the territories of partitioned Poland, Italy, Germany, and Mexico, among others.[20] What additionally distinguished Young Ireland from the Repeal Association was the fact that Young Ireland was never really a formal organization, but, rather, a group of men and women who shared certain ideals, attitudes, and a newspaper (and, eventually, several newspapers). In some respects, because of this lack of any formal organizational structure, there was no structure to collapse when their political activities in Ireland came to an end in the late 1840s; as a "generation," however, they could carry on for the rest of their lives.

Legacies

Accounts of Young Ireland's lasting influence almost always centers around their literary production, particularly the poems published in *The Nation* and later anthologized in collections such as *The Spirit of the Nation*. Indeed, if one is looking for shorthand for an Irish nationalist creed in the nineteenth century, it is difficult to beat a poem such as Thomas Davis's "A Nation Once Again" (but if one is looking for great literature, that might be a different matter):

So, as I grew from boy to man,
I bent me to that bidding
My spirit of each selfish plan
And cruel passion ridding;
For, thus I hoped someday to aid,
Oh, can such hope be vain?
When my dear country shall be made
A Nation once again![21]

Thus, there is much truth to the common view. In spite of the concerted efforts of such figures as W. B. Yeats during the Irish Literary Revival to replace Young Ireland's literature (largely predicated on not unfair assessments of its quality), the poems published in *The Nation* remained stubbornly influential for a broad spectrum of Irish nationalists.[22] By the same token, Peter Hart, in work based on extensive interviews, has remarked that the texts most commonly read by Young IRA Volunteers in Co. Cork at the time of the War of Independence were John Mitchel's *Jail Journal* and the writing of another former Young Irelander, Cork-born Alexander Martin Sullivan. Hart writes that "the young men of 1917 and 1918 read these works with passion and imbued them with revolutionary meaning but they were nevertheless a familiar part of mainstream Irish literature, read equally by large numbers of non-Volunteers."[23] That the writings of Young Irelanders became popular among such a wide variety of Irish people ensured Young Ireland's influence on Irish politics long after their activity in Ireland as a political organization. Moreover, because Young Ireland's nationalism was built upon the malleable idea of the spirit of the nation, later generations of Irish nationalists could impress their own meanings and interpretation onto the writings of Young Ireland, as the concept of "spirit" could accommodate many kinds of content. In this respect, the Young Irelanders provided "Irish nationalist writing" with what Roy Foster has called a "powerfully mobilizing rhetoric for the next century."[24] Paradoxically, however, the effectiveness of the very rhetoric that ensured their enduring influence would also serve to obscure Young Ireland's political thought.

At the core of this rhetoric was an idea born of the kind of shared experience that makes the concept of a "generation" so indispensable here:

the existence of a shared trauma, which in turn produces its own theorization. For the young men and women of the Young Ireland generation, born in the 1820s and coming of age in the 1840s, that experience was the Irish Famine. As members of the middle class, however, it was not the experience of hunger and disease per se that was so formative—at least in terms of political theory—but the impression of passive suffering to which it gave rise. If the defining image of the Famine was of a woman holding her starving child, its counterimage was a young male rebel springing into action. In such a reading of the rebellion, strongly encoded in gendered terms, what mattered most was not the outcome, but the resistance of those who rebelled and were willing to make sacrifices to resist Ireland's emasculation. In this way, Young Ireland neatly fits within a long-standing narrative of Irish history, connecting the republicanism of the 1790s with the Rising of 1916 and leaving a long radioactive thread in some strands of subsequent Irish republicanism.[25]

What is not widely recognized is that, in Young Ireland's political writing, involvement was more crucial than sacrifice—an attitude that can be traced to one of the foundational ideas shared by almost all the key figures associated with *The Nation*: that the right to citizenship, and the rights it conferred, was contingent on participation in the political process. To put it simply, the Young Irelanders did not believe that rights were intrinsic, but instead they believed that rights needed to be claimed. Half a century later, this concept would be elastic enough to accommodate ideas of sacrifice and martyrdom, most memorably in the writings of Pádraig Pearse. For the Young Irelanders, however, the core idea was not principally about the justification of armed rebellion; rather, it was the nature and origin of political rights. Unlike, for instance, the Chartists or American liberals, who argued for the universality of white-male political rights, the Young Irelanders adopted the nineteenth-century British liberal view that rights were "qualified" and, hence, must be earned.[26] This meant that the Young Irelanders felt differently than those in Britain, Australia, British North America, and elsewhere who argued that the qualifications for the rights of citizenship (particularly the right to vote) should be based on property ownership. Although the view would, ultimately, contain a liberal politics, it does not sit neatly in the spectrum of nineteenth-century political thought as usually understood.

As it was held by the Young Irelanders, the idea that rights were earned stemmed in part from what might seem like an unlikely source: the British philosopher Thomas Carlyle, of whom many of the Young Irelanders were forthright in their admiration. What makes this affinity all the stranger is that much of Carlyle's political thought was directed toward justification of the empire from which, as Irish nationalists, the Young Irelanders aimed to detach their nation. In ultimately launching a rebellion on the principle that "right equals might"—to use Carlyle's well-known formulation—the Younger Irelanders were "accepting the terms (but not the conclusions) of the argument behind the moral justification for colonialism."[27] Where Young Ireland pushed beyond Carlyle, however, was in their belief that the rights earned through active participation were not limited by race or religion—lines that Carlyle drew very firmly in his writing. Hence, extending this principle to minority groups brought the Young Irelanders (perhaps unexpectedly) into the ambit of liberal political thought. Therefore, when Young Irelanders found themselves engaging with aboriginal peoples in Australia, African Americans in Montana, or Catholics in Canada, they advocated policies that would protect—to varying degrees—the rights of these groups, to allow them to become active in civil life. As the philosopher Will Kymlicka reminds us, "Minority rights were an important part of liberal theory and practice in the nineteenth century, and these rights were seen to be vested in national, religious, and ethnic groups."[28]

While "liberalism" might not seem like an obvious political label for a group who admired Carlyle (who was perhaps the very antithesis of liberalism), in fact the uses to which the Young Irelanders put some of his ideas harmonized surprisingly well with many of the key precepts of liberalism. One measure of this can be found in Sean Farrell's observation that the Young Irelanders tended (with a few notable exceptions) to gravitate toward societies that were developing a strong liberal ethos, even when they were not sent there by illiberal force.[29] In the United States, for instance, political liberalism had been at the core of the political thought of the revolutionary generation of the 1770s and remained a feature in political debate throughout the nineteenth century,[30] while in the settler empire, including Canada and Australia, liberalism was deeply imbricated in arguments for European migration.[31] Indeed, Duncan Bell has argued that for British political thinkers "imagining colonies as semi-autonomous, collectively self-governing communities, free of the feudal vestiges of British society, and populated overwhelmingly by energetic 'civilised' white people, aligned them with liberal visions of political progress"—a view shared, to a large extent, by most of the Young Ireland generation.[32] In addition, the basic liberal premise that the people conferred legitimacy on government became a central part of their worldview.

At the same time, it must be remembered that liberalism was not accepted by everyone in the Young Ireland generation. John Mitchel rejected liberalism completely, calling "British civilization . . . the most base and horrible tyranny that has ever scandalized the earth,"[33] at one point referring to "Habeas Corpus, Trial by Jury, and other Palladia of the British Constitution" as tools of the "ameliorative enemy."[34] His move toward the Confederate states during the US Civil War stands as one of the shining counterexamples to the drift of figures such as Duffy and McGee toward the emerging liberal democracies in Australia and Canada. For his part, Mitchel chose antebellum Tennessee precisely because it seemed to him a bastion of anti-liberalism. Mitchel was something of an exception, however, and the vast majority of the Young Ireland generation, once outside of Ireland, increasingly confirmed their liberalism of the 1840s in their political choices.

The key correlative to the Young Ireland belief that rights were earned through political participation was that an effective liberal state made political participation possible, and that existential threats to the existence of such a state could be defended against through nation-building. For a group who, in Ireland, rebelled against the state, this may seem like a contradiction. However, there the state was inextricably linked with the United Kingdom of Great Britain and Ireland, which Young Ireland saw as incompatible with Irish nation-building. In Australia, Canada, and the United States, on the other hand, the situation was quite different. In the settler colonies (and, to a lesser extent, in the United States), they saw the state as precarious rather than stable and, hence, thought that its role as a shield against the dominance of majority groups needed strengthening. In Ireland, there was a need both to delegitimize the British state (the tendency that dominates in Mitchel's writing) and to legitimize a future Irish state through establishing historical precedent (which dominates, for instance, in McGee's work).

Once outside of Ireland, the imperative to delegitimize fell away, but so too did the appeal to a legitimizing history. Thus, while the Young Irelanders maintained the imperative for nation-building, they had to search for new means of accomplishing it in the new states in which they found themselves. This, in many ways, sparked the most forward-looking elements of their view of the world.

Of course, when we speak of "state-building," we need to acknowledge that the developmental stages of the nation-state in Canada and Australia in the 1860s, as well as that of the United States in those same years, were very different. Nonetheless, in the United States, Young Ireland found something of a counterpart in Young America: a national movement mirroring some of the features of similar European movements, as a means of buttressing a state that was nearly a century old, but that many felt was under threat.[35] In this respect, then, just as the Young Irelanders in Australia and Canada played a key role in the development of nationalism that would aid state development in completely new political entities, so too, in the otherwise very different context of the United States, did the Young Irelanders become participants in a pivotal moment in American political life. Of particular importance here, we can note that Canada, Australia, and the United States were all actively involved in settler colonialism in the second half of the nineteenth century, where the Young Irelanders also played a role. By examining the Young Ireland generation's contributions to—and criticisms of—settler colonialism, we can broaden our understanding of the complexities at the heart of the relationship between Irish nationalism and the mid-nineteenth-century developments of empire.[36]

There is more to it than this, however. Although David Dwan has written of "Young Ireland's nervous fascination with democracy" in an Irish context, once they moved beyond Ireland any nerves quickly settled.[37] A further critical point of commonality between Canada, Australia, and the United States in years after 1848—during which the Young Ireland leaders were active in these countries—was an intense debate about the nature of democracy. In Australia (particularly in Victoria), the 1850s saw a major expansion of democratic rights as universal adult male suffrage by secret ballot was enacted in 1856, the year in which Charles Gavan Duffy arrived in Melbourne. In 1857, the requirement that members of the Legislative Assembly of Victoria be property owners was abolished, followed by other democratic reforms.[38] With respect to this, Ann Curthoys and Jessie Mitchell have argued that debates about democracy and radicalism were instrumental in the development of the state of Victoria.[39] Likewise, in Canada, Confederation came about in part as a response to demands for representation by population,[40] which is why Elisabeth Heaman and Janet Ajzenstat and others have placed debates about democracy and liberty at the core of the process of Confederation.[41] Meanwhile, in the United States, contested visions of the relative powers of the various arms of the state, as well as of the individual citizen, contributed to the Civil War—so much so that Sean Wilentz has argued that the Civil War was a "revolution caused by the rise of American democracy."[42]

To put it simply, in each instance members of the Young Ireland generation settled into the political lives of societies in which states were being built and contributed to debates over the nature of democracy in those states. While this is more obvious in Canada and Australia in the latter decades of the nineteenth century, it is equally true in the United States. Whereas the traditional interpretation suggests a relatively straightforward transition from a weak federalist to a strong centralized state during and directly after the Civil War, work by recent historians has emphasized that the antebellum state was much stronger than historians have believed, in two senses.[43] First, the individual states deployed their police power extensively to regulate public health, safety, and welfare in the name of producing a just and well-ordered society.[44] Of particular interest to Irish people in the United States were the strict laws that individual states used in an attempt to regulate immigration.[45] Second, the federal government deployed subtle forms of power that made it much stronger than it appeared in quotidian life— for example, in the realms of indirect taxation, communication and transportation, the judicial system, territorial acquisition, conflict with Native Americans, and fugitive slave policy. Indeed, it has been suggested that the antebellum federal state might be most usefully seen as imperial, with a distant center exerting considerable power in the peripheries (through the acquisition of territories and the subjugation of Native Americans) even as the national government remained inconspicuous in the everyday lives of its citizenry.[46] Thus, while the United States in the 1860s was unquestionably at a different point in its development as a state when compared to Australia or Canada, many of the issues at the heart of political debate were not without parallel.

If we then place within this constellation of evolving nation-states a set of individuals with established political skills, and—this is the key point—a perspective that overarches any individual circumstance in which they might have found themselves, something illuminating emerges. Thought of in this way, the study of the Young Ireland generation after 1848 becomes more than simply an extended chapter in Irish history, or a new development in Irish diasporic history. The fact that the Young Ireland generation continued to see themselves *as a generation* long after they ceased to have any but the most oblique involvement in Irish politics meant that they considered themselves a part of transnational network with a common point of reference outside of the particulars of Australia or Canada or the United States. Thus, even as figures such as Duffy, McGee, and Meagher became immersed in the political debates and campaigns of the countries in which they found themselves, they brought to those contexts a wider, networked perspective, capable of transcending local concerns due to the fact that their political vision was always grounded in another context. Most often, this other perspective expressed itself simply as Irishness, whose visual emblems were the shamrocks and harps that adorned the ceremonial encomia with which they were regularly presented. Today, however, we can begin to see this perspective for what it was: a true transnationalism, capable of being simultaneously rooted in local circumstances and of taking the wider perspective.

1

Ireland, 1842–1848

On 15 October 1842, the first issue of *The Nation* was published at 12 Trinity Street in Dublin. The front page—which consisted primarily of a list of subscribers to a tribute to O'Connell and an advertisement for the collection of the "O'Connell Compensation Fund"—did not indicate that the newspaper would serve as the foundation for a new direction in nineteenth-century Irish politics.[1] It was not until page 8, after reports on topics such as the "Lancashire Special Commission," "Municipal Revision in the Provinces," and "India, Afghanistan, and China," that the reader might note that *The Nation* represented a new approach. Here, the editors explained their reasons for publishing the paper and introduced its motto: "To create and foster public opinion and make it racy of the soil."[2] From the outset, *The Nation*'s editors lay down a marker that their project concerned what Irish people thought and felt as much as economic policy or the actions of government. "National feelings, National habits, and National government," they declared, "are indispensable to individual prosperity."[3] From its title to its manifesto, *The Nation* left little doubt of its status as an agent of nationalism.

There was, however, a problem: What did the paper's proprietors mean by "nationalism"? If pressed, they would have likely said, "Ireland must be free," as Eva of *The Nation* (Mary Anne Kelly), who started contributing to the paper in 1844, asserted in 1848.[4] Nevertheless, the Young Irelanders did not always clearly articulate—nor did they always agree on—their idea of "free" Ireland. In order to understand what they thought freedom meant in an Irish context, how they believed that they could bring it about, and what Ireland would look like once it was free, we must first examine the social and cultural contexts in which Young Irelanders operated—contexts shaped by the communications technology that they employed to disseminate an Irish national narrative. Typically, scholars have argued that this narrative was crafted by means of their cultural output; yet, as their reaction to the Famine demonstrates, their political thought was more complicated, and notions such as "shame" and "masculinity" played a key role in shaping Young Ireland's understanding of citizenship and rights as earned.

Young Ireland

The context in which the Young Ireland movement developed and operated is essential to grasping its political and cultural impact. As, in the words of Davis, "an organisation, centring in Dublin," examining the Dublin cultural and social worlds in which Young Irelanders operated will help us to better understand their nationalism.[5] The prospectus released to advertise *The Nation* before its first issue was published introduces us to some of the movement's key figures, including Charles Gavan Duffy, John O'Connell, Thomas Davis, and James Clarence Mangan.[6] As *The Nation* grew in popularity, it would make famous other figures who will become more familiar to us as we proceed: for instance, writers Thomas Francis Meagher, John Mitchel, William Smith O'Brien, Thomas Chisholm Anstey, Thomas D'Arcy McGee, Richard O'Gorman, Terrence Bellew McManus, Thomas Antisell, Mary Anne Kelly, Jane Elgee, and Kevin Izod O'Doherty. By noting how these contributors to *The Nation* came together, we can begin to see more clearly the development of Young Ireland's nationalism. As Helen Ting has highlighted, "The significance (indeed the existence) of cultural worlds in our lives as well as nation-views for that matter, does not derive from holding them 'in mind' as some whole image (we may or may not do this), but from recreating them through work and in interactions with others."[7] Essentially, a social sphere that fostered a particular outlook, in which a certain set of values was collectively accepted, was an essential precondition.

Integral to this development was the world of educated, middle-class Dublin that coalesced around noted Dublin institutions: for example, Trinity College, Dublin, located in the city center, its front gate only a few meters from the old Parliament, and attended toward the end of the 1830s by a number of the prominent members of the Young Ireland generation who would later travel abroad, including John Mitchel, John Blake Dillon, John O'Mahony, Richard O'Gorman, Bryan O'Loghlen,

Gerald Henry Supple, Charles Stanley Monck, John O'Leary, and Moses Wilson Gray. Indeed, given the relatively small size of the college at the time (when the total student population was between 1,500 and 1,600) it is likely that at the very least some of them crossed paths.[8] Thomas Davis, the movement's intellectual driving force, who studied there between 1831 and 1836, would later vacillate between proclaiming that he had "not one sad or angry reminiscence of old Trinity," and that "Dublin University is the laughing-stock of the literary world, and an obstacle to the nation's march."[9] Yet Davis's connection to Trinity—in particular, its student societies—was a strong one; he was elected to the position of auditor, the highest executive office, of the Historical Society (known as "Hist"), a debating organization at the heart of Trinity student life for the discussion of political ideas.[10] It was here where "Trinity College, permeated by prejudice and with manifest social and intellectual failings, was none the less the seedbed wherein matured the most powerful, cogent, and developed ideal of modern Ireland."[11] Of course, other institutions and forces would shape their thinking; however, it needs to be recognized that Trinity provided a forum through which some of their key members could shape their ideas of Irish nationalism.

This ideal of a national Irish future articulated at Trinity found particular purchase among a group of young Irish men and women in Dublin, predominantly the children of the middle classes from outside the city who had moved there from elsewhere in Ireland. Indeed, of the twenty-six Young Irelanders who would end up having significant careers abroad, only five were born in or grew up in Dublin. This marked them as different—in Dublin city in 1841, 79 percent of the residents had been born there—and arguably contributed to their national viewpoint, as it forced them to merge their respective regional viewpoints.[12] In other words, these were members of an ambitious middle class who had come to Dublin to pursue professional careers. Many of them were recently qualified barristers. The clubbishness of the law library and of King Inn's (the training institution for barristers in Ireland), and the practice whereby barristers would pick up cases by standing in the lobby of the courts, meant that the law as a profession entailed a certain enforced sociability.[13] Years later Duffy would recount that "I met Dillon in the Hall of the Four Courts; he made me acquainted with

THE BIRTH OF "THE NATION"

Figure 1.1. *The Birth of the Nation*, T. F. O'Sullivan, *The Young Irelanders*. 2nd ed. Tralee: Kerryman, 1945, 42.

Davis."[14] Likewise, those Young Irelanders who became professional journalists belonged to a relatively small professional circle where networking was essential, and, naturally, as the worlds of the courts and the pressrooms overlapped, news, gossip, and ideas flowed freely back and forth.[15] In short, the relatively small size of Dublin's educational and professional circles created the necessary social sphere in which a view of an Irish national future could be developed.

Why, then, did Davis, Duffy, Dillon, and the other future Young Irelanders articulate a nationalist vision of an Irish future? Here, again, Dublin is important. In the 1830s, a distinctive culture emerged there, largely through its active press, which differentiated it from the rest of Ireland.[16] This press was supported by a population that was increasingly literate; by 1841, 84.5 percent of Dubliners between the ages of sixteen and twenty-five were literate.[17] This literate public created a market for affordable newspapers and magazines, such as the weekly *Dublin Penny Journal* and the *Irish Penny Journal*, which, at their apex, had circulation figures of up to 50,000 a week (a considerable number, given that the population of Dublin City in 1841 was only 212,275).[18] Affordable popular publications also included literary magazines like the *Dublin Magazine*, the *Irish Catholic Magazine*, the *Dublin University Magazine*, and the *Dublin Literary Gazette*.[19] These periodicals fit into the category described by Jürgen Habermas as "literary journalism" in their intention to educate their reader and to provide an outlet for critical expression.[20] In the first instance, they offered a space in which Young Irelanders could learn the publishing business; for example, the *Citizen* (1839–41), a monthly journal of literature and art, offered an early venue for the work of Charles Gavan Duffy and Thomas Davis.[21]

Dublin was also the ideal place for the nationalism espoused in the many periodicals produced during the 1830s to combine with political action, and it was in this environment that Young Ireland would emerge from Daniel O'Connell's political organizations. Both O'Connell's successful movement for Catholic Emancipation and his campaign for Repeal of the Act of Union were headquartered in Dublin, which created an active political scene in which Irish self-government played a large role.[22] The editors of *The Nation* were careful to emphasize that "JOHN O'CONNELL, ESQ., M.P.," O'Connell's favorite son, was one of the paper's first contributors; indeed, his name is the only one that is written in all capital letters in its prospectus. Moreover, Young Irelanders, in the early days of the movement, were not only active within O'Connell's campaign for Repeal of the Act of Union, but enthusiastic supporters of it. Writing from Boston (but later to join the paper's staff in 1845), in *Historical Sketches of O'Connell and His Friends* Thomas D'Arcy McGee claimed—in typically hyperbolic fashion—that "the name of my immortal subject has been familiar to the civilized world for nearly forty years. The free of the earth venerate it—the tyrants and task-masters of men hate its utterance, so ominous of the annihilation of their unhallowed caste. Were those who have been benefited by the labors of his life, to assemble in congress, at the call of gratitude, an assembly would be formed without a parallel in all past history."[23]

McGee was not unique among the Young Irelanders in venerating O'Connell early on. For instance, *The Nation* reported favorably on "The Liberator" and his "monster" repeal meetings.[24] Moreover, Davis (who joined the Repeal Association in April 1841), Duffy (who organized O'Connell's visits to Belfast), and O'Brien (who joined the Repeal Association in 1843)—among many others who would ascend to the leadership of Young Ireland—started their political careers within O'Connell's Repeal movement.

The fact that the Young Irelanders served their political apprentice-ships in O'Connell's Repeal Association sheds light on their future po-litical careers. O'Connell, a barrister, had built a reputation as a shrewd politician by the time his Catholic Association achieved Catholic Emancipation in 1829.[25] The association used large public meetings to galvanize public support as well as to demonstrate that O'Connell had the capacity to mobilize a large number of people.[26] This convinced the majority of the Irish public and the British government that his demands should be acceded to through a series of reforms of the Act of Union.[27]

Once O'Connell had achieved Catholic emancipation, he began to earnestly advocate for the Act of Union's repeal—a long-term goal. As early as 1810, he argued that "the Union was . . . a manifest injustice— and it continues to be unjust at this day; it was a crime, and must be still criminal."[28] In order to remedy this, O'Connell established the Repeal Association. O'Connell's strongest argument for Ireland's inde-pendence was based on the question of rights. At a "monster" meeting in Mullaghmast in 1843, he told the audience "that no portion of the empire had the power to traffic on the rights and liberties of the Irish people."[29] Focusing on the political and constitutional elements of re-peal made sense for O'Connell; after all, he was an experienced lawyer who had run a successful campaign for Catholic emancipation based on the argument that it was, in his own words, "a right which was my due."[30] Yet his campaign for repeal of the Act of Union was less effec-tive, and it was partly in that failure that the Young Irelanders came to recognize that the case for repeal had to be based, at least in part, on a different argument. This, combined with disputes about O'Connell's management of money, his declining health, and a number of other dis-putes, meant that the Young Irelanders soon became disillusioned with O'Connell, leading them to denounce what they saw as "the corruption and imbecility of Conciliation Hall," which was his headquarters.[31]

Moreover, one of the main consequences of the legislation that had enabled Catholic emancipation in 1829 would militate against O'Connell successfully repealing the Act of Union: the raising of the property qualification required for voting in county elections from forty shillings to ten pounds.[32] Although the measure had been intended to ensure that the Irish franchise was brought into line with the rest of the Union, it did not have the desired effect. The reforms meant that "in 1829 the Irish proportion of the enfranchised within the United Kingdom, already relatively small, fell drastically."[33] Thus, in Ireland, only 1 in 26 borough dwellers had a vote, and, in county constituencies, only 1 in 116 had one compared to 1 in 17 borough dwellers in England and Wales, and 1 in 26 in those who lived in the countryside.[34] Among the disenfranchised Irish middle classes, this cultivated animosity toward the Union. Indeed, although many Irish had been active in political campaigning through O'Connell's organizations, and, as such, it would be argued that "on the eve of the Famine the Irish population was one of the most politicised in Europe . . . involvement in the parliamentary process, however, was recent and small scale."[35] Therefore, it is possible to speculate that this state of affairs would have encouraged Young Ireland to pursue a course of action largely outside the realm of parliamentary politics, as many of the petty bourgeois who made up the movement would have been excluded from that arena anyway.

The Young Ireland generation embraced "democracy, which we advocate."[36] In 1848, Mitchel wrote that "democracy, I believe, is the destiny of the world."[37] However, like many other European nationalists, they feared that democracy could lead to the oppression of minority groups, especially in Ireland, where sectarian and class divisions were so apparent. "Young Ireland," as David Dwan suggests, was haunted by a "distressingly perceptive account of these shortcomings."[38] Likewise, Davis argued, in advocating for democracy they had "to guard against a tyranny over the majority or by the majority."[39] The Young Irelanders' response to this remained remarkably consistent throughout their careers: their conviction that nationalism could counter the perceived ill effects effects of democracy. In 1848, Meagher told an assembled audience: "Nor do I wish that this movement should become a mere democratic movement. I desire that it should continue to be what it has been, a national movement—a movement not of any one class, but of all classes. (Hear, hear.) Narrow it to one class—decide that it shall be a democratic movement and nothing else—what, then? You augment the power that is opposed to you."[40] For Meagher, and for Young Ireland more broadly, nationalism could overcome the class and sectarian divisions, which, they believed, made elements of democracy dangerous to Ireland.

It was in this context that *The Nation* was founded in 1842, growing out of a Repeal movement with which some younger members were rapidly losing patience. The *Nation* group took up the phrase "Young Ireland," which quickly gained traction.[41] Madden used the term to describe the nationalist writers who wrote for *The Nation* and other nationalist publications, telling his readers that "Young Ireland, like Young England, aspires after the speculative and ideal."[42] "Young Ireland," then, was a broad descriptive term that can be subdivided into a number of overlapping groups, some more formal than others. The most prominent of these was the Irish Confederation, described by T. W. Moody as "the official organisation of Young Ireland."[43] Established in 1847 at a meeting in the Rotunda in Dublin, it ran three candidates in the general election of that year: Richard O'Gorman in Limerick City, William Smith O'Brien in Limerick County, and Thomas Chisholm Anstey in Youghal. Of those candidates, both O'Brien and Anstey were elected as MPs, although this did not mean that there was a Young Ireland political party yet as such.[44] Instead, we might more accurately think of the movement as being organized around *The Nation*; hence, as the group splintered over key issues, the conflicts within the organization can be traced through the press.

These fissures were most apparent in the debate within the Confederate Clubs over the legitimacy of armed resistance, which was opposed by many who were convinced that an Irish nation could be established through parliamentary means. The debate intensified in the mid-1840s, to the point at which John Mitchel, who supported armed conflict, left *The Nation* to establish the *United Irishman* in February 1848, declaring: "The world is weary of old Ireland and also of Young Ireland."[45] Not all Young Irelanders agreed with Mitchel, however, and a majority of the movement remained united behind the *Nation*'s editor, Charles Gavan Duffy, who continued to argue for a parliamentary path to statehood. However, as 1848 progressed, and the "February Revolution" in France was followed by the "March Revolution" in the German-speaking states, talk of revolution in Ireland alarmed the British authorities, who responded by suspending habeas corpus.[46] Rather than calming matters, this convinced some of the more moderate Young Irelanders that armed revolution was the only option.[47] Thus, by the beginning of the summer of 1848, this particular ideological gap among the Young Irelanders had narrowed, and the rebellion that followed came to be known as the "Young Ireland rebellion," which would subsequently be claimed by almost everyone associated with the movement, in spite of the wide disagreement on the matter in the years leading up to it.

Technology and Generational Change

One of the things that separated the world in which Daniel O'Connell brought about Catholic Emancipation in 1829 from the world of the Repeal movement in the 1840s was a change in communications technology. From the beginning, the group who came to be known as "Young Ireland" saw that an Irish national movement had to encompass the entire country, both quickly and efficiently, and they were the first generation who had the technologies available to make this happen. In order to transmit their idea of an Irish nation across Ireland, they relied on newspapers with a national distribution and a national focus. The centrality of the newspaper to their political project was, effectively, the articulation of an idea that would later become central to studies of nationalism: that the construction of a nation depends on the creation of a shared national history.[48] This wholesale embrace of print culture was one of the points that differentiated the Young Irelanders from their immediate predecessors. Admittedly, O'Connell did cultivate a supportive press (notably the *Pilot*), as had various political parties in the eighteenth century, but, as Joep Leerseen has pointed out, "the successor generation to O'Connell significantly used newspapers, pamphlets and other print media to spread its message (whereas O'Connell himself had largely relied on physical gatherings, fundraising networks and mass meetings)."[49]

A partial explanation for this lies outside the realm of communications technology per se. The introduction of a national system of education in 1831 gave a greater number of people the skills necessary to access printed materials. Nevertheless, communications technology made a major impact on the preference of the Young Ireland generation for printed media over oral communication. Here the work of Benedict

Anderson proves useful: in *Imagined Communities*, he argues that print capitalism was responsible for spreading and creating an "imagined community" where people felt that they shared common experiences with others whom they had never met, a phenomenon that he locates in the latter part of the eighteenth century.[50]

By the time Davis, Duffy, and Mitchel were meeting in debating societies and outside courthouses, developments in communications technology that improved the profitability and ease of printing had effectively created a print revolution. The first steam-powered mechanical press had been introduced in Dublin in 1833, marking a distinct advance over its predecessors, and was therefore a new but established means of producing newsprint more quickly and more cheaply than ever before by the time *The Nation* was published for the first time in 1842. Indeed, even in the nine years between the first operation of the steam press in Dublin and the launch of *The Nation*, a dynamic was set in motion that would continue well into the next century, where less expensive production costs leading to lower prices, combined with higher literacy rates, produced a spiral of increased demand for newspapers.[51]

It was in an expanding market for newspapers, therefore, that the Young Ireland generation would begin their careers in journalism, which consolidated the sense of themselves as a "generation." For instance, "the founders of the new journal [*The Nation*] were all under thirty years of age," Charles Gavan Duffy would recall, who himself "spent the interval between my twentieth and six-and-twentieth year in newspaper offices."[52] Duffy's experience, like that of others in the Young Ireland generation, came about because of the opportunities afforded by the expansion of communications technologies.

Conversely, by this point O'Connell had already established his personal networks and made use mainly of physical gatherings to communicate with the Irish public sphere, attempting to repeat the strategy that had worked for the Catholic Emancipation campaign in the 1820s. Consequently, he saw little reason to whole-heartedly embrace newspapers, against which he sometimes had an antagonistic relationship, leading him to declare in 1833 (after suing the *Times*): "I have succeeded against the Press."[53] This is not to say that O'Connell did not engage with them; his cultivation of Catholic newspapers like the *Pilot* demonstrated that he was aware of their importance.[54] However, because his choice of which press to engage with and when was so often "arbitrary," O'Connell was unable and unwilling to utilize it to its full extent.[55] In this respect, at least, he differed both from the generation of Irish nationalists who preceded him and those who would succeed him. Nevertheless, it should be acknowledged that O'Connell played a critical role in creating the conditions necessary for the development of Irish nationalism through *The Nation*. The continued civic and political campaign for Catholic Emancipation led by O'Connell in its later years had ensured the presence of an active public sphere in Ireland; deployed as it was by the Young Irelanders, print simply provided a way of influencing that public sphere (which, in turn, made newspaper publishing a viable enterprise).[56]

A national press—at least in the sense of a press that covered the geographical expanse of Ireland—required faster and more sophisticated forms of transport to function. Without an adequate network, newspapers would never reach their readership. Although underdevelopment was symptomatic of the Irish economy in general, Ireland at the beginning of the Famine had one of the most comprehensive road transportation systems in Europe.[57] In both geographical and imaginative terms, this facilitated the development of a national press: information could travel to Dublin relatively quickly, and that information could then be published in a newspaper within a short space of time. This created a sense of the Irish Confederation as a national movement, as *The Nation* was able to print reports on the "progress of the organisation" based on the results of meetings held across the country the day after they took place.[58] News from Ballina, Enniscorthy, Kerry, Navan, Middleton, Newry, and Nenagh were regularly displayed alongside one other, and, although the reports that a "Confederate Club is being formed" in Enniscorthy and Navan were not exactly earth shattering, the visual impact of displaying the meetings together on the same page gave a tangible form to the claim that the Young Ireland movement spanned the Irish nation.[59] Furthermore, because no reader could attend a meeting in Nenagh and Newry at the same time, it was only through the mediation of print that they could learn of the proceedings of each of the meetings at the same time. This, it could be argued, takes Anderson's concept of "community in anonymity" a step further.[60] It was one thing for readers to consider themselves anonymous, vicarious members of a community; it was a different relationship entirely for readers who had attended one of the local meetings recorded in the pages of *The Nation* to see how that meeting connected with others across the island. At the very least, we can say that the press was crucial to the expansion of the Irish public sphere. However, once this expansion had occurred, it had no clear geographical limit; by that point, the Irish public sphere could conceivably be extended to anywhere that news could travel to and from Ireland.

The reshaping of the Irish public sphere through an expanded print culture was enabled by the rapid expansion of the Irish railway system between 1845 and 1853, when the total track mileage increased from seventy to seven hundred miles.[61] The Young Irelanders, who saw the potential for change to be wrought through this expansion, reported on and editorialized about "the general subject of Railways, and the material, almost incalculable, changes which the portentous development of the Railway system is destined to create in the whole social and political state of the world."[62] Reports would often explain that news had arrived by train, making the mechanism by which news was transmitted a topic for news in its own right. In the instance of the trial of William Smith O'Brien following the 1848 rebellion, *The Nation* told its readers that "the glad tidings of O'Brien's jury having been discharged reached town by the 11 o'clock train."[63] In a case like this, the newspaper made the experience of the collapse of O'Brien's trial (not just the facts of the trial itself) a national experience that encompassed the communications technology that made it possible. To return to Anderson's influential paradigm, here we see an "imagined community" taking form, as an event experienced by a small number of individuals in one part of the country becomes a simultaneous national event in which everyone who reads of it is not simply a witness, but also, in the act of witnessing, a participant.[64]

The Nation took further steps to ensure that the act of reading a newspaper was experienced by readers as taking part in forming a national community. The Confederate Clubs established around Ireland what were known as "Repeal reading rooms," and *The Nation* regaled its readers with accounts of "the cultural activity of reading out loud," which meant that the information in the newspapers reached a wider audience than it otherwise would have, had it relied solely upon the literate population.[65] The myth of groups of illiterate peasants gathering to have *The Nation* read to them became a central part of the narrative that people could engage with Irish nationalism simply by reading or listening to Irish nationalist literature. Behind this cozy image of *The Nation* settling into a traditional folk culture, however, was a recent history of rapid technological change.

What is more, the successful focus of the Young Ireland generation on the use of technology to spread their conception of an Irish nation had a significant but unintended consequence: it triggered the process of separating Irish nationalism from the physical island of Ireland, as the principal mode of communication became print rather than large public gatherings. Printed materials transported by the railways allowed for speedy communication of information over space. Newspapers in particular were, as a material good, light and easy to transport.[66] Because of this, as the Young Ireland generation dispersed throughout the world, newspapers could travel with them, and the exiles could continue to participate in a public sphere from which they were physically remote. Moreover, as communications technology improved and its reach extended, so, too, did the Irish public sphere and the reach of Irish nationalism.

The Nationalism of Young Ireland

By 1842, then, there was in Ireland a group of men and women, well educated, capable, and impatient with the status quo, with access to communications technology that mapped onto the national territory with historically unprecedented effectiveness, who defined themselves as "nationalists." Again, this begs the question: What did the Young Irelanders mean by "nationalism"? The answer is less obvious than it might appear. To start with, we can turn to the prospectus to *The Nation*, written largely by Thomas Davis. In one particularly long sentence, he imparts a vision of an Irish nationalism:

Nationality is their first object—a nationality which will not only raise our people from their poverty, by securing to them the blessings of a domestic legislature, but inflame and purify them with a lofty and heroic love of country; a nationality of the spirit as well as the letter; a nationality which may come to be stamped upon our manners, our literature, and our deeds; a nationality which may embrace Protestant, Catholic, and Dissenter, Milesian and Cromwellian, the Irishman of a hundred generations, and the stranger who is within our gates; not a nationality which would preclude civil war, but which would establish internal union and external independence; a nationality which would be recognized by the world, and sanctified by wisdom, virtue, and time.[67]

The prospectus's opening lines tell us that Young Ireland's nationalism was explicitly political (and pragmatic) and had an independent Irish Parliament as its end goal. To this extent, their nationalism was primarily political, premised on their belief that the political and national unit should be the same.[68] However, what precisely is constituted by the "nationality" that this legislature would serve is more elusive. Young Ireland's national unit was pluralist, did not define itself by religion or by language, and accommodated new migrants. It was, in the simplest terms, liberal. What is remarkable about the prospectus, however, is that it makes no mention of self-evident, immanent criteria for nationality; there is not even an insistence on geographical copresence—which is just as well for a culture in which diaspora would feature so strongly. What is more remarkable is the implicit assumption in Davis's statement that national characteristics do not yet exist among the Irish people; instead, "nationality may come to be stamped upon our manners, our literature, and our deeds"—which implies that they are not immanent. In other words, they have yet to create what Anderson describes as an "imagined political community."[69] When we consider this document in detail, we find a remarkable contrast between the inspirational lift of its rhetoric, and the conceptual gap at the heart of its political project.

It was to fill this gap that the Young Irelanders committed so much of their energy to culture as a tool for achieving political independence. They saw themselves as a group who could educate the Irish people and instill within them the benefits of nationhood, such as courage, glory, and virtue. To this end, they engaged in a deliberate project to cultivate an Irish nationality through education. In a letter from 1841, O'Brien told Davis that "either you or I, or someone, should compile a short account of the geography, history, and statistics of Ireland, to be printed in fifty or sixty pages of a report, accompanied by a map, and circulated extensively. We must do more to educate the people. This is the only moral force in which I have any faith."[70] The last line of this letter is of vital importance. The Young Irelanders believed that nationality had a role in shaping the behavior of a people, and vice versa: that "moral force" would bring the nation as a political unit into being. Furthermore, they believed that the nation did not preexist its creation, even if it must exist to justify the foundation of the national state. Hence, we see their focus on defining the geographic boundaries with a map and on using history to demonstrate the distinctiveness of the Irish experience, all bound up in a larger educational project that was not the same as the formal system of education for spreading literacy and numeracy; otherwise, the national school system that had been created in 1831 would have sufficed. Rather, it was about making Irish people aware of their unique identity, about educating Irish people to be Irish. "We wrote the *Nation* less as a paper of news than of education," wrote Charles Gavan Duffy in 1843. "We did not seek to gratify people by hot intelligence, but to preach to them the gospel of nationality."[71] At the very least, this meant imagining that there had once been a secure Irish nationality, which, somewhere back in time, had been lost, and the role of "education"—in the special sense in which it was used by the writers in *The Nation*—was to make "the Irish aware again of Irish national identity, and then to make them aware that there was a world outside, beyond England."[72]

A particularly important part of this world outside of England was Germany. It was most often to its example that the Young Irelanders turned when they sought to explain how a new Irish nation might be developed. In many ways this made sense. In the first instance, Germany offered an example of nationalism overcoming sectarian divides.[73] Moreover, many of the influences of the cultural nationalism embraced by Young Ireland came from Germany; discussion of such work appeared in Dublin periodicals in the first half of the nineteenth century.[74] Whereas other scholars—largely using circumstantial evidence—have based this understanding on an Irish embrace of romantic Herderian nationalism, the facts weigh far more heavily for the German influence on the importance of the state in the development of nationalism.[75] The German connection made most explicit by Young

Irelanders was with Prussia. This was surprising, in that Prussia was not actually a nation. As Christopher Clark has argued, "No modern state more strikingly vindicates" the argument that states and nations are "constructed or invented" and that "collective identities" are "forged by acts of will" than Prussia.[76] It was "an assemblage of disparate territorial fragments lacking natural boundaries or a distinct national culture, dialect of cuisine," and, as such, an unusual place for a group of aspiring nationalists to admire.[77] Yet it was in the very incoherence of the Prussian claim to sovereign statehood that appealed to the Young Irelanders. Davis in particular admired Prussia; he wrote: "Does Ireland now differ from Prussia? Why can Prussia wave her flag among the proudest in Europe, while Ireland is a farm? . . . The difference is in Knowledge."[78] What impressed him was the notion that the Prussians had created one of Europe's most modern states primarily through education, and it was this example that led him to declare: "Educate, that you may be free."[79]

Yet the focus on making the Irish people aware of "the spirit" of the Irish nation presented a major problem. As Erica Benner has put it in a wider context, at the core of the nationalist thought underlying Young Ireland's arguments for the existence of an Irish nation was the idea that nations "were constituted by common bonds of language, which drew legitimating force not from acts of consent but from nature and historical evolution."[80] Indeed, Herder had asserted that "each language has its particular national character," and that this unique character was proof of "the peculiar character of the nation's manner of thought" and, therefore, its rationale for existing.[81] Thomas Davis held a similar view. "The language," he wrote, "which grows up with a people, is conformed to their organs, descriptive of their climate, constitution, and manners, mingled inseparably with their history and their soil, fitted beyond any other language to express their prevalent thoughts in the most natural and efficient way."[82] He went even further: "The language of a nation's youth is the only easy and full speech for its manhood and for its age. And when the language of its cradle goes, itself craves a tomb"—effectively stating that it would only be through the revival that Ireland would become a nation.[83] This argument that linguistic boundaries should define political boundaries was adopted by most other European nationalist movements in the 1840s for whom language—in particular, the presence of a unique local language—had been the primary means through which nationality was expressed. For instance, in Hungary, the notion that people had a "moral obligation" to speak their native language was seized upon by Hungarian nationalists in the 1840s to encourage support for the revival of Hungarian.[84] At the same time, German nationalists argued that a moral civic community required its own language.[85] Each of these nationalist movements, among others, drew extensively from the work of Herder, who had asked in 1772: "Has a nation anything more precious than the language of its fathers?"[86] Like the Hungarian and German nationalists during the 1840s, Davis famously argued that "a people without a language of its own is only half a nation. A nation should guard its language more than its territories—'tis a surer barrier, and more important frontier, than fortress or river."[87]

In reality, the *idea* of the Irish language was more important to the Young Irelanders than the language itself, and Young Ireland's actual attempts to use the Irish language were few and far between. Many of them may have "claimed that there was an indissoluble link between the Irish nation and the Irish language"; however, "Irish was seen to be a goal to be pursued, but the linguistic means they employed were English."[88] Duffy had faced vehement objections when he tried to organize Irish language classes through Young Ireland, and the use of Irish-language names in *The Nation* was also opposed.[89] These objections, though, were portrayed by the Young Irelanders (after the fact, in any case), as practical rather than ideological, and it would seem that Irish was seen by some as a lost cause.[90] Although its decline would be accelerated by the Famine in the second half of the 1840s, by the early 1800s it had already been supplanted by English as the preferred language of most Irish people.[91] The pace of anglicization had been exacerbated in 1831 by the introduction of the national primary school system, where English was the sole language of instruction.[92] In this case, the existence of a national education system hindered Young Ireland's efforts to educate the people and make the spirit of the nation visible. The practical fact of the matter was that if *The Nation* was going to appeal to a broad section of the public, it had to do so through English. This was a position accepted even by the most enthusiastic defender of the Irish language, Davis, who believed that the reintroduction of Irish should be a long-term goal of Irish nationalism.

In the absence of a clear linguistic basis for Irish nationalism, history became the primary means through which the Irish nation was legitimized. In this respect, Young Ireland's writing made an instrumental use of history; as James Quinn has identified, they thus portrayed Irish history as "no haphazard series of events, but a coherent narrative that traced the evolution of a unique national community."[93] A "sense of history" could become an effective substitute for a widely spoken indigenous language, an act of substitution that David Dwan has strongly argued "was central to Young Ireland's understanding of political discourse, practice and right," informing their attempts to educate the Irish people and imbue them with a sense of national spirit.[94] To this end, they wrote prolifically on the subject, not least through *The Nation*, which, published at various points (in "the habit of French journals"), serialized works of Irish history. Indeed, they seem to have understood intuitively Anderson's suggestion that "the newspaper is an 'extreme form' of the book," because, in distrusting book-length histories, through *The Nation* they made those histories more accessible.[95] Readers were treated to the double spectacle of history unfolding in the past and in the present, side by side on the same page. "The Book that Irishmen most want is a National History," the *Nation* announced in 1847.[96] "That book, all other means of procuring it failing, we propose giving them through *The Nation*, in the course of the ensuing year—and afterwards in a more enduring form."[97] Even excluding *The Nation*, we can count at least thirty-three separate publications on the history of Ireland by Young Irelanders before the 1848 rebellion, including Michael J. Barry's *Ireland As She Was, As She Is, and As She Shall Be*; Thomas Davis's *Literary and Historical Essays*; and Thomas D'Arcy McGee's *A Memoir of the Life and Consequences of Art MacMurrough*.[98]

At the center of Young Ireland's writing of history was the idea that history was meant to have an effect in the present. Here again we see the influence of the philosopher Thomas Carlyle, who, in spite of his antipathy toward both Ireland and nationalism, majorly influenced many Young Irelanders.[99] Mitchel, for instance, "absorbed and repeated Carlyle's views on a number of matters," and Duffy published *Conversations with Carlyle* about his dealings with the book's namesake over forty years.[100] He would recount a visit by a number of Young Irelanders to Carlyle in London in 1845, reporting that "the Young Irishmen were greatly impressed by the philosopher and his wife."[101] They were particularly drawn to his musings on heroism and liberty; Carlyle was fascinated by the role played by "the Heroic in human affairs," which he felt was essential to our understanding of history. "The history of what man has accomplished in this world," he wrote, "is at bottom the History of the Great Men who have worked here."[102] His use of the term "Great Men" was not casual, and it had a gender-specific message; to Carlyle, and to many of his admirers, "the heroic" was a masculine trait.[103] This reading of history proved attractive to Young Ireland, whose literary output venerated Irish heroes. Thomas D'Arcy McGee, one of the movement's most prolific writers of history, produced a number of works that venerated Irishmen. His *Irish Writers of the Seventeenth Century*, published in 1846, focused on a number of Gaelic Irish exiles, including Phillip O'Sullivan Beare, who had written their own histories of Ireland.[104] That Beare had written histories was important: through writing he was educating the nation, which was in itself heroic, thus suggesting a tunnel of receding mirrors, of heroic historians achieving heroic status by writing about their own predecessors. For McGee, then, O'Sullivan Beare's life was more than simply instructional; writing (and reading) Irish history was a form of political action. It was also character forming. He wrote: "Let it not escape the young men of Ireland. His life teaches a lesson which is as rare amongst authors as his works are in the libraries. Both are national and elevating in character full of candour and fervency."[105] What is more, underlying the moral lessons of McGee's history is a Herderian principle, in which "the literary perpetuation (or creation) of morally exemplary individuals" could be used to shape the nation in the present.[106]

Squaring the writing of Irish history with *The Nation*'s aspiration to "embrace Protestant, Catholic, and Dissenter, Milesian and Cromwellian" (to use the language of its 1842 prospectus) and the fractured reality of the Irish past was always going to be problematic. The extent to which, for instance, a hagiography of a seventeenth-century Gaelic Catholic chieftain such as Aodh O'Neill could constitute the basis for a shared history was always going to be in doubt. John Mitchel acknowledged this in the opening lines of his own *Life and Times of Aodh O'Neill, Prince of Ulster*, first published in 1845, in which he laments that "perhaps in no country, but only Ireland, would a plain narrative of wars and revolutions that are past and gone two centuries and a half ago, run any risk of being construed as an attempt to foster enmity between the descendants of two races that fought so long since for mastery in the land."[107] Mitchel attempted to navigate around the issue by telling his readers that the consequences of Protestant Plantation was that "once more new blood was infused into old Ireland; the very undertakers that planted Ulster grew racy of the soil; and their children's children became, thank God not only Irish, but united Irish—became 'eighty-two' Volunteers—anti-Union patriots—in every struggle of Irish nationhood against English domination."[108] Via historical narrative, Mitchel connected the Ulster Planters, through eighteenth-century Patriot politics, with Irish nationalism in the 1840s, using the United Irishmen as the implied link. Mitchel went on to tell his readers that the present struggle for Irish nationality "shall not be an exception," and that the Ulster Protestants would continue to be "more Irish than the Irish."[109] At the core of Mitchel's argument is the claim that "the several races that now occupy Irish soil, and are known to all the world besides, as Irishmen," could claim the history of Ireland as their own, even if it involved reaching across the confessional and racial divides that in the early nineteenth century were often conflated with national as much as ethnic divides.[110] In this particular case, Mitchel subsumed the racial narrative of Irish nationalism into a larger historical narrative, and, by writing in English, he implicitly rejected the concept of Irish nationalism as linguistic. Instead, the nation's "spirit" could be found in the narrative of its history, through which linguistic, ethnic, and religious differences were ironed out. Therefore, Aodh O'Neill, who, for Mitchel, "was the first, for many a century, to conceive, and almost to realize the grand thought of creating a new Irish Nation" became central to inspiring a new generation of Irish nationalists.[111] Mitchel's histories, like those of McGee and others, fit neatly into the pedagogic model adopted by Young Ireland in its writing of history. As such, "Irish nationalist historiography looked both to the past and the future; back to a long tradition of resistance and forwards to the achievement of independence, creating a continuum in which Irish history and mission reinforced each other."[112]

Young Ireland clearly articulated in *The Nation* their vision of the purpose of writing Irish history:

Of course, the first object of the work we project will be to make Irish History familiar to the minds, pleasant to the ears dear to the passions, and powerful over the taste and conduct of the Irish people in times to come. More *events* could be put into a prose history. Exact dates, subtle plots, minute connexions and motives, rarely appear in Ballads, and for these ends the worst prose history is superior to the best Ballad series; but these are not the highest ends of history.

The Young Irelanders divided history into two forms. Prose history was to be used to give accounts of the past. However, for their purposes, the goal of history was not to tell the story of the past. Rather, it was

to hallow or accurse the scenes of glory and honor, or of shame and sorrow; to give to the imagination the arms, and homes, and senates, and battles of other days; to route, and soften, and strengthen, and enlarge us with the passions of great periods; to lead us into love of self-denial, of justice, of beauty, of valour, of generous life and proud death; and to set up in our souls the memory of great men, who shall then be as models and judges of our actions these are the highest duties of history, and these are best taught by a Ballad History.[113]

It is clear from this extract that Young Ireland's understanding of history intended to awaken the spirit of the Irish nation. The nuance and subtlety that Mitchel had sought in the opening pages of his work on Aodh O'Neill was not what Young Ireland were searching for in their history. For them, the writing of history centered around its emotional impact. Therefore, the way they told the story and why had more importance for them than its accuracy.

To be truly effective as public history, history requires an audience. Here, too, the use of ballads is important: as John Hutchinson has argued, for cultural nationalists "the past had also to become a living experience," and to this end, ballads had a clear instrumental significance.[114] In translating Irish history into something that was sung around the country, the Young Irelanders made history part of the Irish people's everyday experience. As Joep Leersen puts it, "*The Nation* almost willed itself into a virtual historical and social concourse."[115] Ballad history allowed them to reach beyond the literate population who could afford newspapers and the leisure to read them and thus offered, as Shaun Richards and David Cairns note, "a means of communicating, directly and regularly, with audiences of the same size as those who attended O'Connell's mass rallies," which they used to present their vision of Irish nationality.[116] *The Nation* had a broad appeal across all sections of sections of Irish society, and, as such, it played an important role as part of the wider political press in Dublin.[117]

This broad appeal was evident in the introduction to *The Spirit of the Nation*, a collection of ballads in which Davis declared that "we care not into how many or how few of the drawing-rooms of England or America this book of ours will reach. It will have done its work, and entered into the heart of Ireland, for good and for ever."[118] Not only were ballads seen as a form that could reach a wide audience; because they were designed to be sung, they were also regarded as a form of literature meant to enter into oral culture. This reversed the usual flow from oral to written culture, which manifested in the collecting and writing down of oral and folk culture that Timothy Baycroft has identified as typical of so many nationalists across Europe in the nineteenth century.[119] Moreover, ballads disseminated "a sense of Irishness at an emotional, not an intellectual, level, intimating that a sense of self is something which is felt rather than understood."[120] This further strengthened their appeal to a group seeking to rouse the spirit of the nation. As is well known, people like Thomas Crofton Croker earlier in the century, and Sir William Wilde in the 1840s, were collecting Irish folklore. Here, however, the problem of language rears its head again, for much of this existed in the Irish language. Therefore, one might view the ballads written by Young Ireland as an attempt to circumvent this issue; the extent to which this freshly minted folklore was intended to work in tandem with longer prose histories can be measured by the fact that the topics covered by Charles Gavan Duffy's *The Ballad Poetry of Ireland* focused both on historical topics like those seen in the prose works of McGee and Mitchel, including the "Dirge of O'Sullivan Beare" by J. J. Callanan, and on works that dealt with the lived experience in contemporary Ireland such as the "Lament of the Irish Emigrant" by Lady Dufferin, Helen Sheridan.[121] The ballad brings the past of two centuries ago into dialogue with the present, coating both with the thick patina of tradition, to be presented as the voice of "the people."

As the Young Ireland movement became more militant from about 1846, their poetry reflected this change, partly manifesting itself as anti-Englishness. It must be acknowledged that part of Young Ireland's understanding of Irish nationalism had long been defined in opposition to England. This is certainly true in, for instance, Thomas Davis's influential 1843 poem "The West's Asleep!," in which he instructs the reader to "sing, Oh! Hurrah! Let England quake! We'll fight till death for Ireland's sake."[122] This can be attributed in part to the challenges faced by Irish nationalists: if the spirit of the nation is so elusive—not language, not race, not religion—then one of the few options left was to define it in negative terms, as that which it is not (or, at least, that to which it is opposed). This much, at least, can be defined precisely, and in a single word: England. However, an increased anti-Englishness in Young Ireland's cultural production after Davis's death in 1845 is also clear. If we take for instance, some of the work by Mary Anne Kelly (Eva of *The Nation*), we can see it come increasingly to the fore of Young Ireland's writings. In 1847 she wrote:

> For Ireland all, is the thunder call,
> For Ireland and her salvation: . . .
> Every rank and shade, be ye soon arrayed,
> For that end to help each other.
> 'Gainst England all, 'gainst England all.[123]

In 1848 she made a similar argument in the self-explanatory "Down, Britannia, Down!"[124] Kelly was not the only writer whose work took on an aggressively anti-English tone; indeed, her work can be seen as part of a clear movement by Young Irelanders toward a more radical understanding of Irish nationalism, as was evident when Young Ireland briefly split in 1848. Mitchel's advocacy of a more militant approach led him to set up a new newspaper, the *United Irishman*, which, in turn, was suppressed and then followed by the *Irish Tribune* and the *Irish Felon*, successively. Nonetheless, they were to reconcile, for a few years anyway, in exile. Moreover, in Ireland, it would not just be Kelly and Mitchel who would advocate a more militant path, as we can see in the speech given by Thomas Francis Meagher in 1846 in which he declared: "I look upon the sword as a sacred weapon."[125]

Class and the Economy

An analysis of the Irish economy formed a key part of Young Ireland's nationalist endeavor, even if this was not always entirely coherent. A brief reminder of their backgrounds tells us why they had reason to be interested in the economy. Almost the entire leadership of Young Ireland were part of a relatively new (dating to the eighteenth century) aspiring Irish middle class.[126] This Irish middle class existed in a condition of relative affluence during the years of the Famine. For Young Ireland, the middle-class nature of their leadership was essential to understanding their ideas, and it would not be unfair to suppose that "nationalism like theirs [was] an ideology of a small middle-class or petty bourgeois elite'"[127] For instance, Meagher was the son of a Waterford merchant, Mitchel was the son of a dissenting clergyman, and Duffy the son of a shopkeeper; in this regard, the aristocratic William Smith O'Brien, the son of a baronet, was the exception, whereas a generation earlier he would have been the norm (and, indeed, his own father was an MP for many years).[128] They believed, as *The Nation* stated in 1845, that the middle classes "are emphatically the nation."[129] The middle-class Young Irelanders were thus socially aspirant, but they came of age at a time when the wider economic conditions of the 1840s posed a challenge to social aspiration of all kinds. This was true even before the Famine, for, as Cormac Ó Gráda has shown, "the period 1839–44 seems to have been particularly depressed," mostly the result of bad harvests and a downturn in the American and British economies that affected Irish exports like linen.[130] Therefore, it is not unreasonable to suspect that this decline in future economic prospects helped the Young Irelanders to become, to use Malcolm Brown's phrase, "the militant wing of the Irish middle class."[131]

With this in mind, it makes sense that they should have published and spoken extensively on economic matters throughout the 1840s, with *The Nation* reporting regularly on international markets, and Mitchel publishing a book, *Irish Political Economy*, that featured extracts from the work of Jonathan Swift and George Berkeley.[132] One of the best examples of Young Ireland's economic nationalism can be found in the Linen Hall in Belfast in November 1847, where Thomas Francis Meagher argued for a policy of selective protectionism:

That the taxes of this island may be levied and applied by its own decrees, for its own particular use and benefit; that the produce of the soil may be at our own free and full disposal, and be dealt with precisely as the national necessities require; that the commerce of the island, protected by native laws, may spring into strenuous activity, and cease to be a mere channel trade, . . . on these grounds, sir, we insist that Ireland shall be exempt from foreign rule.[133]

This focus on protectionism and taxation could be seen as a means of giving Ireland the freedom to find its own destiny. Indeed, a number of the Young Irelanders professed admiration of the German economist Friedrich List, whose "national system" of political economy can be viewed in contrast to the universalist economics of, say, Adam Smith. "Great, independent nations," List argued, possessed "a commercial system of their own, a national system of agriculture and industry, national system of money and credit." List was the architect of the *Zollverein*, which was a customs union of German-speaking states.[134] This view was much admired by many Young Irelanders, who used List's ideas to construct a shared, cross-confessional national state-building narrative.[135] In fact, *The Nation* favorably referenced the *Zollverein* many times.[136]

Thomas D'Arcy McGee added a further dimension to the argument, making the case that free trade between Ireland and the rest of the United Kingdom had damaged Ireland's manufacturing economy. He was speaking to a room full of people deeply invested in Ulster's linen industry at a time when, as part of a larger legislative package of reforms that would have reduced the cost of importing food, duties on the importation of raw cotton were also being repealed. This was seen to pose a very real threat to Ulster's linen industry; McGee argued that "many weavers have not, at this time, when their web is sold, more than one shilling for their week's work."[137] Speaking of manufacturing more broadly, "in 1800," he told the crowd (citing some somewhat dubious statistics), "with a population of less than 6,000,000, about 1,400,000 were . . . engaged in manufacturing occupations; but in 1839, no more than 14,870 were thus employed"; in fact, the census of 1841 indicated that 1,097,900 people were employed in manufacturing industries.[138] For McGee, the accuracy of the figures was not important; he sought to argue a narrative of economic decline that he felt would be well received by a broad audience. Meagher tried to do likewise, contending that the Orange Order were actually wayward nationalists, born of the Volunteers of 1778, of which the Belfast Company had been the foundation for the United Irishmen. "Why have you forsworn the faith," he demanded of a room filled with Ulster merchants, "of which your fathers were the intrepid missionaries?"[139] This was not well received. When Thomas D'Arcy McGee rose to speak again, "the confusion became so great, that it was utterly impossible for him to proceed; some blackguards in the centre of the room exploded several squibs of gunpowder, which created a smoke that rendered the gallery and hall altogether invisible, and almost suffocated the audience."[140] Although this evening may have ended in "confusion," the basic point is worth underlining: that the Young Irelanders saw that a common economic cause could be the foundation of a national self-interest—even if that recognition was not mutual. It also tells us that, when the occasion required it, they were more than happy to allow national unity to trump economic justice.

Having said this, there were those associated with Young Ireland for whom the extreme poverty that followed from the failure of the potato crop in 1845 would lead to more radical economic analyses. Of particular significance in this regard was James Fintan Lalor, who in 1847 radically proclaimed: "I acknowledge no right of property in a small class which goes to abrogate the rights of a numerous people."[141] Lalor argued that he acknowledged "no right of property in eight thousand persons, be they noble or ignoble, which takes away all rights of property, security, independence, and existence itself, from a population of eight millions, and stands in bar to all the political rights of the island, and all the social rights of its inhabitants."[142] We can see here the extent to which nationalism formed a sort of ideological adhesive, in that Lalor's proto-Marxism coexisted with a wider political movement that embraced the "socially conservative approach" of Charles Gavan Duffy and William Smith O'Brien, whose family were large landowners.[143] O'Brien himself wrote to Irish landlords in 1846 to say that "I am disposed to hope that you will listen in no unfriendly spirit to one belonging to your own class"; O'Brien continued by contending that the "happiest day of your lives will be that in which the nobility and gentry of Ireland shall assume their natural position as the friends, protectors and leaders of the Irish people, strong in their attachment."[144] For O'Brien, landlords were an essential part of the Irish nation; for Lalor, it was only through the abolition of large estates that Ireland would become a nation, declaring that "had the people of Ireland been the landlords of Ireland, not a human creature would have died for hunger, nor the failure of the potato been considered a matter of consequence."[145] And yet, while the Young Irelanders clearly differed on fundamental economic issues, this was rarely the cause of disputes within the movement. Essentially, a spirit of the nation, based on a narrative of history, could accommodate contradiction, just as it could sectarian and ethnic difference. For example, the third issue of the *Irish Felon*, of which Lalor was the editor, included "a striking likeness of W.M. Smith O'Brien Esq., M.P."—hardly the pin-up that most proponents of abolishing landlordism would be expected to put on their walls.[146]

Shame, the Famine, and Nationalism

When the Young Irelanders first started formulating their inclusive narrative of Irish national identity in 1842, it seemed possible that, in spite of a general economic malaise, a new beginning could be made in Irish politics. In August 1845, however, when the potato crop was hit by blight, everything changed. Only a few months earlier, Charles Gavan Duffy had written in his preface to *The Spirit of the Nation* that the literature and ballads within it were "seized on by Ireland's friends as the first bud of a new season, when manhood, union, and nationality, would replace submission, hatred, and provincialism. It was paraded by our foes as the most alarming sign of the decision and confidence of the national party."[147] Only a few months later, those words must have seemed bitterly ironic. In 1847, Thomas D'Arcy McGee presented a very different picture: "The peasant, with his wife and little ones, is driven to seek the shelter of some roadside shed, not fit to be a kennel for dogs—and when, perhaps, the wife of his heart lies dying in the slow agony of starvation, and some demonical agent of a prodigal absentee strips.the wretched covering from above her head, and leaves her there to perish in the face of heaven?"[148]

Rather than creating a manly and vigorous nation, the Young Irelanders were living through a tragedy of epic proportions that would drastically alter Irish society. In purely demographic terms, in the estimates of John Fitzgerald and Peter Gray, Ireland lost approximately one-quarter of the population it was expected to have by the 1851 census, largely due to emigration and death by disease and starvation.[149] It is no exaggeration to say that the Great Famine "ranks among the most severe" famines to have occurred in the Western World.[150] The societal upheaval caused by what Enda Delaney has called "the descent into chaos in the middle of the nineteenth century" could not but play a central role in the radicalization of Young Ireland.[151] In 1845, at the beginning of the Famine, John Mitchel wrote: "In the history of mankind there has been no such powerful agent, no such irresistible force to sway, this way or that, the fate of nations as dearness and scarcity of food." He went on to argue that famine "convulsed the whole frame of society; and the agony of one season of famine and disease has given birth to revolutions which might otherwise be postponed for a generation."[152] Mitchel's premonition would prove to be accurate.

In order to understand how the Famine radicalized the Young Irelanders, we must first understand how they saw it. This is no easy task. It is undoubtedly true that, as Kerby Miller has argued about Irish people more generally, "the Great Famine seared its survivors with vivid, imperishable memories," and that the Famine became a key part of how they saw the world.[153] However, the Young Irelanders in turn played a key role in shaping those memories. Niall Ó Cíosáin has described John Mitchel's *Jail Journal*, first published in 1854, and *The Last Conquest of Ireland (Perhaps)*, first published in 1861, as the "most influential nationalist treatment of the Famine" that would come to have a "major influence on subsequent writing about the Famine."[154] Mitchel was responsible for the oft-quoted line that laid the blame for the Famine squarely on the English state: "The Almighty, indeed, sent the potato blight, but the English created the famine."[155] Works by other Young Irelanders employed visceral imagery in their description of the Famine. For instance, Duffy wrote in 1898 that "men fell dead daily in the streets and by the wayside, and were flung coffinless into the earth. Whole districts were swept bare as a desert of human life. Men fled from it into exile, dying in multitudes on the sea, or perishing in foreign countries, till a new plague sprung from the stench of their unburied corpses."[156] Furthermore, he emphasized the extent to which the famine was a man-made tragedy by speaking of "inhuman deaths."[157]

There was, however, a sharp contrast between how Young Ireland presented the Famine *after* 1848 and how they understood it *in* the 1840s. At the core of the Young Irelanders' contemporary response to the Famine was the challenge it presented to their nationalism. In their conception of Irish nationality, they had given a central position to the idea of heroic resistance, which meant that their central narrative was radically undermined by the "unheroic" moral consequences of the Famine and of Famine relief. In 1847, one of the worst years of the Famine, Mitchel complained in a speech given in Dublin's Music Hall about the reliance of many victims on poor relief, no matter how in-adequate, exclaiming that they were "crying out piteously: Justice to Ireland! Food, food! Money, money!" Mitchel then argued that many in Ireland "are tired of the attitude of the beggar."[158] His criticism echoed a wider Young Ireland belief that "such appeals would in themselves indicate Ireland's unfitness for self-governance."[159] At the same meeting, Meagher was similarly critical of the moral degradation he thought had been brought about by the Famine; he told the crowd, "Heaven forbid that the blight which putrefied your food should infect your souls! Heaven forbid that the Famine should tame you into debase-ment, and the spirit which has triumphed over the prison and the scaf-fold, should surrender to corruption."[160] Both Mitchel and Meagher saw the Famine—and, even more, Famine relief—as something with the potential to make Irish people submissive in the face of British at-tempts at cultural as well as political domination. These speeches were part of a gendered Young Ireland narrative concerned with the belief that the Famine and famine relief would emasculate the Irish people by creating a race of beggars.

At the core of Meagher's complaints about the Famine was this idea of submission. In a similar style, Mitchel wrote in *The Last Conquest of Ireland (Perhaps)* that, "as for us expatriated and exterminated Irish . . . our enemy pursues us . . . until Ireland shall become, as Scotland is, a contented province of the British Empire, thoroughly subdued, civi-lized, emasculated, and ameliorated."[161] For Mitchel, as for many of the other Young Irelanders, the notion of submissiveness lay at the core of their understanding of the impact of the Famine on the Irish people. As David Lloyd has argued, "For Young Ireland nationalists in the 1840s, 'manliness' as an ethical and political disposition of the subject was defined properly opposed not to womanliness but to slavery, the ultimate index of subjugation."[162] Because the Famine further subjugated the Irish people, it presented an affront to Ireland's masculine pride. If, as Mitchel and others believed, Ireland had been feminized by the lack of response to the Famine, then, for Young Ireland, the nationalist resistance to that subjugation, even if unsuccessful, would have the effect of countering shame with masculine resistance. In this respect, they were not unlike other European nationalist movements of the time. Lucy Riall has identified similar self-fashioning in relation to Giuseppe Garibaldi in Italy, who presented himself as a masculine savior of Italian pride, a role model for the Young Italy generation, and an alternative to the then-established perception of the Italian "national character." Like the Young Irelanders, Garibaldi had an active afterlife, and from the 1840s onward he deliberately cultivated this heroic image of himself, as the man who "helped mastermind the heroic, if doomed, defence of the Roman Republic against the French army sent to restore the Pope in the summer of 1849," which made him a crucial character in the Italian national origin story.[163]

The connection made by the Young Irelanders between the Famine and subjugation meant that one of their key questions for their followers was "Will you submit to this?"[164] The responses varied. For instance, in *The Last Conquest of Ireland (Perhaps)*, Mitchel recounted an evening in Dublin at the height of the Famine:

> The band of friends, known to the outside world as "Young Ireland," now all scattered, exiled, or dead, at that time, over and above all the ordinary appliances of pleasure offered by a great city, met weekly at the house of one or the other; and there were nights and suppers of the gods, when the reckless gaiety of Irish temperament bore fullest sway. Like the Florentines in plague-time, they would at least live while it was yet day; and that fiery life, if it must soon burn out, should burn brightly to the last.[165]

Mitchel intended this story as an example of Young Ireland's refusal to submit to the horrors of the Famine and, as a consequence, British attempts at subjugating Ireland. For him, at least, it was a story of heroic resistance. Although written in 1876 and part of Young Ireland's self-representation as heroic during the Famine, it might be read as an example of the extent to which their concerns were not directed at the starving poor. The class prejudice and harshness displayed by Mitchel was breathtaking, given that, as late as 1876, he maintained that banqueting, in the midst of the Famine, while his fellow Irish people were starving, was a heroic act. Indeed, the Young Irelanders would be reproached by the ardent O'Connellite Richard Barrett, who was critical of them in general, after the 1848 rebellion for this very reason. "I could not help regretting," he wrote, "that when so much was urged about the sympathy which ought to be felt for the leaders, the same sympathy was not claimed by themselves, or their partisans, for the poor whom these leaders involved in their suffering."[166] As with their attitudes to economic protectionism, the fostering of an Irish national spirit would always outweigh other concerns.

Young Ireland's most direct response to the supposed moral crisis brought about by the Famine came about on 29 July 1848, when a group of its most radical supporters, including Meagher, staged a rebellion, later dubbed as that of the "Widow McCormack's Cabbage Patch," in Ballingarry, Co. Tipperary.[167] The rebellion, led by men with no military experience, was poorly planned, inadequately supported, and, unsurprisingly, failed to achieve its goal of the establishment an independent Irish state, or, indeed, even to mobilize any substantial interest in the revolutionary cause.[168] Yet the reasoning behind it can be traced in part back to Young Ireland's admiration for Thomas Carlyle and an acceptance of "Carlyle's doctrine that basic human rights and freedoms are not intrinsic but earned through force—'right equals might,'" even if in an Irish context that meant "accepting the terms (but not the conclusions) of the argument behind the moral justification for colonialism."[169] Thus, in taking dramatic action to assert Ireland's right to independence and in turn resist English subjugation, the Young Irelanders made a statement about the Irish nation's right to exist. For his part, Carlyle saw the tribute to his own concept of heroism, but read the result merely as further proof of his own racialized convictions about the general moral failure of the Irish population as a whole: "The generous young men who last bore the heat of the contest have received the wages that oftenest pay heroic toil. They stood in the front rank, nearest the danger, and they have been struck down. They are now pining in exile or seething in prison-ships, and Ireland, it is said, is slavishly indifferent to their fate."[170]

The Young Irelanders drew different conclusions about the rebellion. In their narrative what mattered most was not its outcome, but the fact that those who rebelled made sacrifices to resist what they regarded as the emasculation of Ireland. Their struggle was about "cleansing" the nation's honor "in blood"—an idea that would be echoed later in the century and beyond, most famously in Pádraig Pearse's belief in "redemption through sacrifice."[171] As had happened in Germany, France, Italy, and elsewhere, the presentation of the rebellion as a masculine intervention in response to national shame allowed the Young Irelanders to further politicize gender and institute masculine violence as an essential part of the state-building process.[172] Young Ireland used their participation in the rebellion to cultivate an image of themselves as the group who had saved Ireland's honor during the Famine, thereby ensuring that, "far from damaging their reputation, the events of 1848 helped to serve them, and they were praised by later nationalists for having asserted in arms Ireland's right to independence."[173] It allowed them to claim, as Charles Gavan Duffy noted in his 1880 reflections, that they had been "the generation of men with whom it was said a new soul came into Ireland."[174] Last but not least, the rebellion counted as the most dramatic manifestation of a belief that Young Ireland had developed during the Famine, which was that the right to citizenship was contingent on participation in the political process—and there could be no more vivid commitment to participation in politics than armed rebellion.

Conclusion

The aftermath of the 1848 rebellion was also the end of the Young Ireland movement as a distinct political grouping. The response of the state was to try its leaders for a variety of crimes, including high treason and treason felony. Of those convicted, Thomas Francis Meagher and William Smith O'Brien were sentenced to death by hanging, drawing, and quartering; however, their sentences were soon commuted to transportation to Van Diemen's Land. John Mitchel was sent to Bermuda and then to Van Diemen's Land; after a chase through Ireland, Thomas D'Arcy McGee would escape to the United States and later move to Canada. Other Young Irelanders who played a relatively minor role in the movement in Ireland, like John O'Mahony and James Stephens, escaped initially to France and then to the United States, where they continued to be involved in militant Irish politics, including in the Fenian movement and the Irish Republican Brotherhood. Others, like Charles Gavan Duffy, who had been tried for and acquitted of treason felony three times, and who then served as an MP for New Ross from 1852, left Ireland in 1856 for economic reasons, to take part in the gold rush in Australia. Others, who are outside of the scope of this work like Martin McDermott, who had gone to Paris in the 1840s to build support for Young Ireland, spent a period in Egypt after 1848; both Moses Grey Wilson and John Robert Godley, who spent significant amounts of time in New Zealand; and Thomas Antisell, who would live in New York and California and then come to spend the years 1871–76 in Japan as a scientific advisor, for which he was awarded the Order of the Rising Sun by Emperor Meiji, are all indicative of a global Young Ireland generation. Their dispersal made it appear as if 1848 had been a failure; however, the nationalism that they had sought to cultivate would endure, symbolized, with all of its contradictions, in the tricolor brought to Ireland by Thomas Francis Meagher in 1848. It was nonsectarian, nonethnic, not linguistically based, and its capacity for accommodating economic and ideological contradiction would prove to be a strength rather than a weakness. Built on the development of a coherent, often historical, narrative that is then claimed as the spirit of the nation, it offered a place within this narrative to anyone willing to embrace it. In this, it was distinctive. It was neither civic nationalism, because it did not rely upon institutions or adherence to political ideals, nor was it an ethnic nationalism relying on race and language, although elements of both imbued it, and it was this openness of form that would become important as the Young Irelanders moved abroad.

2

Van Diemen's Land, 1848–1856

Writing of Van Diemen's Land in his *Jail Journal*, John Mitchel claimed: "There is no action, no living, properly to speak, in a country so remote from all the great centres of this world's business: Whatever is done here can only be said to be inchoate, provisional, and not a perfect act, until news of it go to England, and an answer return."[1] This passage captures the Young Irelanders' sense of being transported not only to the other side of the world but also to a place where they would be isolated from any events of consequence. However, even as Mitchel wrote this, a transnational network was developing around the Young Irelanders in Van Diemen's Land. Their formative time there provided a foundation for their careers, and they, in turn, would come to play an important role in Van Diemonian politics at a crucial stage in the colony's history. As early as 1852, Patrick O'Donohoe, one of the less prominent of those transported, was already proclaiming that the former Young Irelanders would prove important figures "in this incipient stage on the highway to future greatness and renown . . . laying the foundation of great, free, and united states in the Southern Hemisphere."[2]

In the years that followed, the Young Irelanders who found themselves in Australia would set forth proposals for a new constitution and engage in the vigorous debate over transportation at the center of the colony's politics. Once extracted from the deep historical roots of division in Ireland, they came to think about Van Diemen's Land in a similar manner as other colonists: as an empty stage upon which new, experimental forms of government could be erected, while at the same time never losing the anti-imperial element of their thinking. This, of course, would lead to certain complications, in that they would be effectively engaged in a colonial enterprise while at the same time highlighting some of the contradictions of the British Empire. Nonetheless, Van Diemen's Land was essential to the development of a globalized Young Ireland generation, both because of its importance as one of the first centers of a global network, and because of the opportunity it gave the Young Irelanders to engage with politics outside of Ireland.

Van Diemen's Land, now known as Tasmania, is an island situated about 240 kilometers south of Australia where, in 1803, a penal colony was established.[3] In the early 1800s, the capital, Hobart, and the northern town of Launceston were founded; both would become the primary urban settlements on the island. While the penal system that newly arrived convicts encountered varied throughout the period in which transportation operated, by the time the Young Irelanders came most of those who arrived in Van Diemen's Land would have been subject to the probation system: a series of graduated steps through which they earned greater independence. Upon arrival, convicts were confined either to penal stations or to probation stations. As they progressed through the system, they worked in labor gangs on public works, followed by a period in which those granted a probation pass could be hired out to settlers. Good conduct while in possession of this pass eventually led to a ticket of leave, which allowed convicts to depart, either with some restrictions or with a pardon.[4] As a consequence of the transportation system, approximately seventy-six thousand convicts were sent to Van Diemen's Land between 1803 and 1853, when the practice of transporting convicts to the colony was ended forever.[5]

Arrival in Van Diemen's Land

The Young Irelanders who had been sentenced to transportation arrived in Van Diemen's Land between October 1849 and April 1850. Of the leadership of Young Ireland, eight were sent there: Kevin Izod O'Doherty, John Martin, Patrick O'Donohoe, Terence Bellew MacManus, Thomas Francis Meagher, William Smith O'Brien, and John Mitchel. Although he was transported to the island for his role in the Chartist movement, William Paul Dowling can still be considered a Young Irelander; his association with the Chartists was due to the fact that he had traveled from Ireland to London in 1846 to organize the Davis Club, a chapter of the Confederate Club, with a view to affiliation with the Chartists,[6] which resulted in his being drafted into their "Ulterior Committee."[7]

These eight men were joined by seven others: Richard Bryan, James Casey, Thomas Donovan, James Lyon, Edward Tobin, Thomas Wall, and John Walsh, all of them semi-illiterate laborers, except for Wall, who was listed as a "top sawyer."[8] This latter group had been sentenced to transportation for seven to fourteen years for their participation in an attack led by the Young Irelander James Fintan Lalor on the Cappoquin Police Barracks in County Waterford. While all of the leadership (with the exception of Dowling) would leave Van Diemen's Land when pardoned by the Crown in 1856, their time in the Southern Hemisphere is essential to our understanding of how the Young Ireland generation defined themselves outside of Ireland. It was arguably in Australia that the exiles first developed the idea of an Irish nation separate from the physical boundaries of the island of Ireland. Moreover, the early engagement of the Young Irelanders with local anti-transportation politics in Van Diemen's Land served as the first time they successfully merged local political concerns with their own aims.

Before the Young Ireland exiles became involved with local politics, they had to come to terms with their new home. In his *Jail Journal*, John Mitchel wrote of his disorienting arrival in April 1850. "I respect the Southern Cross," he told his readers, "but pray that my own destiny may be cast under Arcturus and his suns." Mitchel spoke of Van Diemen's Land as a place in which "all the traditions and associations of times and seasons are reversed and confounded . . . think of May morning falling at Hallowmas!—and instead of turning a yule-log, . . . hiding from the flagrant sun at Christmas! What becomes of St. Swithin and his showers? Of Candlemas and his ice?"[9] Mitchel's sense of the seasons turned upside-down provides him with a metaphor for the magnitude of the change wrought by transportation on the lives of the Young Irelanders. The convicts, and the family members who joined some of them, remarked upon the unfamiliar landscape. John Mitchel's wife, Jenny, wrote to her mother: "Such a drive I had through the bush. Minnie, [their daughter], was quite frightened at the sight of all the great trees and mountains, no houses and no road, only a track, but I was greatly delighted and excited and so were the boys."[10] Jenny Mitchel's remarks about the emptiness of Van Diemen's Land are typical of the responses of many Europeans who arrived in Australia—both forcibly and by choice—in those years.

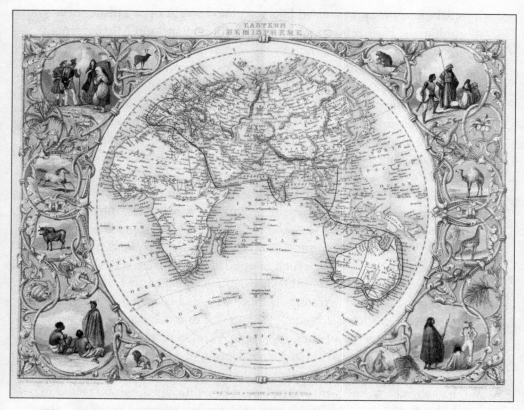

Figure 2.1. *Eastern Hemisphere*, J. Rapkin, J. Rogers, and H. Warren, in *Tallis's Illustrated Atlas and Modern History of the World*. London: John Tallis, 1851. National Library of Australia, MAP NK 2456/11.

However, this land that appeared empty was the product of what numerous scholars, including Tom Lawson, Colin Martin Tatz, and Ben Kiernan, have come to recognize as a genocide of the Aboriginal population by British colonists.[11] The aboriginal population of Van Diemen's Land has been estimated at between three thousand and fifteen thousand persons prior to the beginning of British colonization in 1803; by 1847, only forty-seven Aboriginal Tasmanians survived.[12] In place of the Aboriginal population, British "imperial policy was designed to create a structured, hierarchical society modelled on rural Britain, necessarily lacking an ancient aristocracy but with a wealthy, educated gentry who could exercise local authority."[13] The social structure of the colonial society meant that Van Diemen's Land was at once a place entirely unlike the British Isles and yet uncannily similar. John Mitchel would refer to it as "a bastard, transported, misshapen England."[14]

In this system, the Young Irelanders were an odd fit. They were well-educated public figures, most from prosperous middle-class families; William Smith O'Brien's father was a baronet and a former MP. At the same time, they were convicted criminals. This meant that they presented a challenge to both colonial and imperial officials. It would have destabilized the already uncertain class structure of the colony to treat them the same as the predominantly working-class convicts that populated it, but neither could they be welcomed into the colony's governing elite.[15] As a pragmatic middle way through this dilemma, the lieutenant-governor of the colony, William Denison, had been given explicit instructions to immediately offer the Irish prisoners upon their arrival a ticket of leave, which allowed them to live freely within defined, separate districts.[16] This instruction came directly from London, where the colonial secretary, Henry Grey, had confided to the prime minister, Lord John Russell: "I am minded to think that we had better send Mitchel with a ticket of leave to Van Diemen's Land as soon as possible."[17] He worried that the perception of Mitchel as being poorly treated, in light of the fact that his long voyage to Van Diemen's Land had already caused controversy, would be politically disadvantageous in Ireland. As Grey told Parliament, this was not standard practice: "The Government, wishing to act with as much indulgence in this case as was consistent with their public duty, had departed from the usual practice pursued towards ordinary convicts, and issued instructions to the Governor of Van Diemen's Land . . . to offer them [the Young Irelanders] tickets of leave immediately, provided they would give an engagement that they would not avail themselves of the indulgence in attempting to escape."[18]

All of the transported Young Irelanders acceded to this arrangement except for O'Brien, who provides us with a vignette of the role played by the notion of heroic honor in Young Ireland thinking. Upon arrival O'Brien announced that he planned to give himself "the indulgence in attempting to escape"; therefore, he could not honorably accept the attached conditions of a ticket. Announcing his escape was perhaps not the most cunning move, and when he did make a break for freedom, the captain of the schooner he hired for the purpose turned him in. It was only after receiving a significant number of letters encouraging him to accept a ticket of leave that he felt able to write in his journal that "the considerations which originally induced me to refuse my parole have to a great extent ceased to operate upon my judgement. It seems to me that it would be very ungracious to refuse to yield to such an appeal merely for the sake of indulging caprice or pride."[19]

In their professional lives in Ireland, many of the Young Irelanders picked up where they had left off. Patrick O'Donohoe, a law clerk was given leave to live in Hobart from the beginning, largely because O'Brien had argued forcibly on his behalf that to send him anywhere else would mean that he could not practice, which would "consign him to starvation."[20] As it turned out, there was not much call for law clerks in Hobart either, and, in O'Donohoe's own words, "we altogether failed in procuring employment in our own profession."[21] In Hobart, he established a weekly newspaper, the *Irish Exile and Freedom's Advocate*, which published its first issue on 26 January 1850 and would continue publishing until April 1851.[22] In its first edition O'Donohoe states that "we were driven by sheer necessity into this arena; and we cannot conceive that the Lieutenant-Governor would prevent us to earn, in an Editor's room, writing fair and legitimate comments on public matters."[23] Ironically, the fact that O'Donohoe could establish a newspaper, given that a number of the Young Irelanders were in Van Diemen's Land because they had been convicted of treason felony due to their writings in *The Nation*, suggests that, in some respects, they were freer in the convict colony than they had been in Ireland. This was not lost on the Young Irelanders, who set about transplanting ideas about independence and the right to self-government that the state had sought to vanquish from Ireland and exported them to the new colonies. Yet, as Dowling remarked in a letter to his sister, O'Donohoe had to strike a fine balance in his writings, because "if he comes out too strong the government will pounce on him and if not strong enough the people won't buy his paper."[24] Indeed, some of the Young Irelanders, hopeful of returning to Ireland, tried to discourage O'Donohoe from establishing the *Irish Exile*.[25]

The *Irish Exile and Freedom's Advocate* traded on the Young Irelanders' narrative. By making clear that his newspaper was the work of a Young

Ireland exile, O'Donohoe sought to appeal not only to Irish readers in Van Diemen's Land but also sought to appeal to Irish readers in other parts of Australia and New Zealand. The newspaper regularly published the number of subscribers from outside the island, listing sixty-eight in Melbourne, sixty-seven in Sydney, and forty-two in Geelong.[26] The first issue opened with an article containing an evocative description of the circumstances in which the Young Irelanders found themselves, replete with the archaic, purple diction that marks so much Young Ireland poetry. Using language that echoed Young Ireland's earlier emphasis on shame, O'Donohoe told his readers that "we have already endured almost every pang which legalized cruelty could inflict—we were sentenced to an ignominious death, because we would release an enslaved and famished race of bondsmen. We were immured in filthy dungeons for twelve months, and then torn from family, friends, and native land, transported for life 16,000 miles."[27] O'Donohue's employment of vivid imagery in his writing in the *Irish Exile and Freedom's Advocate* enhanced precisely the narrative of martyred patriots that the government hoped to avoid by sending the Young Irelanders to Van Diemen's Land. Moreover, it foreshadowed the extent to which the newspaper would seek to translate a criticism of imperialism that had been developed in Ireland by the Young Irelanders to Van Diemen's Land.

Even though O'Donohoe had the initial freedom to run his newspaper, restrictions were placed on the liberty of the transported Young Irelanders. As 1850 progressed, O'Donohoe began to publish arguments against the system of transportation, which he had initially supported, albeit not for the Irish exiles. Richard Davis argued that O'Donohoe's early support for transportation came from an unspoken quid pro quo with Denison, the lieutenant-governor, who faced a press almost completely hostile to transportation and thus allowed the publication of a radical paper only because it did not object to transportation.[28] This is supported by Denison's decision to revoke O'Donohoe's ticket of leave in December 1850, after the newspaper had come out strongly against transportation. Additionally, the system of tickets of leave intended to require them to live in separate police districts and not to meet one another—a condition they largely ignored. This was not without risk, as tickets of leave could be revoked by the lieutenant-governor for breaches of the conditions upon which they were granted. Nevertheless, the Young Irelanders regularly met at places like Lake Sorrell, in the middle of Van Diemen's Land, where a number of the districts to which they had been confined converged.[29] These meetings, conducted in secret, allowed the Young Irelanders to discuss their situation and contributed to their ability to produce a relatively cohesive account of their experience in Van Diemen's Land.

The Global Influence of Young Ireland

The Young Irelanders—William Smith O'Brien in particular—had a number of supporters in the House of Commons. O'Brien's brother, Lucius, was an MP who worked with Sir Colman O'Loghlen, a barrister and baronet who had written for *The Nation*, to seek a pardon for the exiled Young Ireland leader.[30] So, too, did Henry Grattan, an MP for Meath (whose father, the famous orator Sir Henry Grattan, had been so influential in the eighteenth-century Irish Parliament that it became known as "Grattan's Parliament"), who argued that "he knew of no law of this country that imposed torture," but that the continued imprisonment of O'Brien was tantamount to it.[31] Thomas Chisholm Anstey, then the MP for Youghal, who had spent a considerable part of his childhood in Van Diemen's Land, where his parents had been among the first voluntary settlers, was another member of Parliament who raised questions about the conditions in which the Young Irelanders were being held.[32] He sought to "call the attention of the House to the conduct of Sir William Denison, lieutenant-governor of Van Diemen's Land, in the matter of the revocation of the tickets of leave lately held by Messrs. M'Manus, O'Doherty, and O'Donohoe, who had been transported to Van Diemen's Land for political offences committed in Ireland in 1848."[33] Their tickets of leave had been withdrawn in January 1851 because they had left their districts to visit O'Brien, which, although typically unofficially permitted, had particularly irritated Denison in this instance.[34]

Perhaps because he was motivated by family ties rather than any more easily discounted political reason, Lucius O'Brien offered the most forceful argument in the House of Commons for leniency toward the Young Irelanders. He stated that "he (Sir L. O'Brien) thought him [William Smith O'Brien] very wrong and injudicious, and never by word, sign, or otherwise, had his brother received any encouragement from him."[35] Notwithstanding, he believed it to be in the government's best interests to treat the Irish prisoners well. He told the House on 14 June 1850 that "his brother had fallen into so bad a state of health that his life was despaired of." Having refused a ticket of leave, William Smith O'Brien was at this point being held at a probation station on Maria Island. His brother astutely argued that "if by any treatment that was designedly harsh, or if by not taking what might appear to be only the ordinary precautions, his brother's life should be lost, or his reason become impaired, the Government would incur a severe responsibility. It would be used as a handle against them, and in Ireland a fatal use might be made of it, which the Government, as public men, might well wish to avert."[36] Lucius's contention was based on two premises. The first was that the harsh treatment of his brother "was not in accordance with the mild spirit of the British constitution. His brother thought he was engaged in a good cause."[37] The second (and more interesting, for our purposes) premise was that the Young Irelanders maintained a sufficient hold over the Irish public imagination that the death of one of them could inflame public opinion in Ireland. In this, Lucius O'Brien's argument reflected a view already widespread in Westminster, where there was anxiety about turning prisoners into martyrs.

Part of the care with which the British government acted with regard to the transported convicts was a product of the Young Irelanders' ability to continue speaking through the Irish press, even from abroad. Although the dispersal of the Young Ireland generation weakened it, *The Nation* remained a popular and influential newspaper until it ceased publication in 1900. Charles Gavan Duffy, who was not transported in 1848, stayed on as editor until he left Ireland voluntarily in the 1850s. The more radical Young Ireland newspapers—Mitchel's *United Irishman*, and its successor, the *Irish Felon*—closed down in 1848, and most of the figures associated with them, including Mitchel, Kevin Izod O'Doherty, and John Martin, were transported. That left Duffy in Ireland, telling readers that his absent colleagues were being "persecuted by Sir William Denison."[38] Other Irish newspapers took particular umbrage at the suggestion that the Young Irelanders had reneged on the terms of their tickets of leave, and that they deserved punishment. The

Kerry Evening Post, for instance, accused Denison of "wantonly provoking" the exiles and of being "oppressive."[39]

The Irish press based their coverage of the Young Irelanders on the transported leaders' own accounts. As was common practice at the time, a letter sent by William Smith O'Brien to Duffy in 1851 that appeared in *The Nation* was reprinted by the *Belfast Newsletter*. The letter, written after O'Brien had been released from solitary confinement following his attempted escape from Maria Island, contained a blistering critique of British efforts to present their treatment of the Young Irelanders as benign: "I set no value whatever upon the sort of liberty which I now enjoy and would return to my cell to-morrow without feeling that I had made any sacrifice in surrendering the boasted indulgences which are paraded to the world as illustrative of British clemency and magnanimity."[40] In creating outlets for them, the Irish press allowed the Young Irelanders in Van Diemen's Land and their colleagues at home to shape a narrative that portrayed them as Irish heroes, supported by statements such as O'Brien's, who declared from his exile: "My attachment to my native land continues unaltered and unalterable."[41]

In writing from abroad, the Young Irelanders had begun to establish a globalized Irish national community, shaped outside the island of Ireland. Newspapers in the United States played a key role in that process, helped by the fact that a number of those involved in Young Ireland in the 1840s fled there after 1848.[42] In May 1850, the *Boston Pilot*, a Boston Irish Catholic newspaper (briefly edited by McGee from 1842 to 1844), wrote that "we have the pleasure of presenting to his troops of friends, a long, detailed, and most interesting letter from Meagher."[43] The letter had originally been published in *The Nation*, but its reproduction in Boston was indicative of the globalizing nature of the Irish nationalist community in the 1850s and the concern outside of Ireland for the fate of the Young Irelanders. Even outside of the press that specifically targeted Irish diaspora, such were the numbers of Irish people among the American population that the plight of the Young Irelanders was of interest to the American press more generally. For instance, readers of the *New York Times* in October 1851 would have heard about the suppression of O'Donohoe's *Irish Exile and Freedom's Advocate*.[44] The point here is that an emerging transnational media network rendered one of the key motivations for transportation ineffective. Transportation was based on a geographical paradigm: if you were shipped someone off to the other side of the planet, they were beyond influence, as good as dead. Young Ireland's use of the media subverted this arrangement: in transporting them to Van Diemen's Land, the government simply made their cause even more transnational.

The integration of a globalized version of Irish nationalism into the narratives that other political groups sought to promote in countries like the United States meant that Irish nationalism was backed by genuine political power. News of O'Brien's treatment, for example, caused consternation in America.[45] This was deliberately cultivated by the Young Irelanders, who believed that, by making their cause a possible source of diplomatic tension between Britain and the United States, they could leverage American power to secure their release.[46] In June 1852, O'Brien expressed to his wife his intentions in this regard: "I am also beginning to hope something from the movement in America in favour of the Irish Exiles."[47] O'Brien and the deported Young Irelanders met with some success in their plan, at least insofar with the number of resolutions passed by the US Senate supporting them. On 4 December 1851, "Mr. Foote of Mississippi, asked and obtained leave to bring in a joint resolution (S.2) expressive of sympathy of Congress for the exiled Irish patriots Smith O'Brien and Thomas T. Meagher [sic] and their associates."[48] The idea that the 1848 rebellion had been an act of patriotism that was part of a global movement toward independence from empires was further reinforced by other resolutions presented to the Senate at the same time as Senator Foote's motion and can be understood, for instance, in the context of a Senate resolution passed in preparation for the arrival in the United States of Louis Kossuth, one of the heroes of the Hungarian rebellion of 1848.[49] At the very least, it would suggest an implicit connection being made in some quarters in the United States that linked American political values with the European Forty-Eighters, including the Young Irelanders.[50]

Furthermore, through public meetings, supporters of the Young Irelanders in the United States encouraged their public representatives to lobby the American government on their behalf. This meant that politicians like Senator Cass of Michigan "presented the proceedings of a public meeting held at Detroit, in the State of Michigan, in favour of an application by the US to the government of Great Britain for the liberation of Smith O'Brien, Thomas T. Meagher [sic], and their associates; which were read."[51] Like the press in Ireland, lobbying by American supporters of the Young Irelanders helped to create a globalized Irish nationalist community capable of mustering considerable political support. As such, the mid-nineteenth-century newspaper press —and, as Jürgen Osterhammel argues, developments in communications technology—did not bring about the predicted collapse of the category of the nation, which had previously been understood in defined geographical terms. Instead, in opening up larger "spaces of communication," communications technology increased "the capacities of nationalist movements" by allowing them to use information, language, and networks outside the geographical borders of the nation.[52]

In arguing for their release, the Young Irelanders and their supporters were keen to emphasize that what Anstey referred to as the "political offences" of which the Young Irelanders had been convicted made them different than ordinary prisoners. Relying upon his connections to Van Diemen's Land, Anstey argued that "there was not a respectable person in the island who did not see and understand the immense distinction between the offences of these gentlemen and the vulgar offences of the ordinary convicts"—"gentlemen" being the key word in the sentence.[53] Thus, Anstey contended, there would not be a backlash in the colony if the Young Irelanders were treated with leniency,[54] a conclusion that a quick examination of newspapers in Van Diemen's Land would vindicate.[55] He called upon the House "not to allow these three gentlemen to be punished with undue severity."[56] John Mitchel's wife, Jenny, made a similar point: "The servants who are nearly all convicts, are sad plagues, and the women far worse than the men. I have a Tipperary woman who was convicted at Clonmel at the time of O'Brien's trial was proceeding (of course her crime was theft or some such thing), but she, I can perceive, is quite proud of being convicted at the same time he was!"[57] Aside from illustrating the class position of the Young Ireland leadership, Jenny Mitchel's account indicates that Young Irelanders saw themselves as morally superior to other convicts who had been sent to Van Diemen's Land for other crimes; at the same time, this did not prevent them from becoming involved in a political debate about the matter of transportation per se.

The Campaign against Transportation

Concurrent with the global campaign intended to secure their release, the exiled Irish leaders began to engage with colonial politics in Van Diemen's Land. The very reason that they found themselves in the Southern Hemisphere—the penal system of transportation—meant that they had been thrust into the center of the most important political question in Van Diemen's Land at a time when a majority of the islanders were seeking transportation's end.[58] From the outset, their relative success in presenting their situation as morally unjust made the cause of the Young Irelanders attractive to the anti-transportationists as another example of the failings of the policy. In a wider context, arguments for the abolition of transportation were gaining support across the British Empire. In the Cape Colony, "agitation reached a pitch" when the Boers, who had long opposed the practice and whose loyalty to the imperial authorities was questionable, protested against "the arrival of the Neptune" carrying Mitchel. Their protest ended transportation there.[59] The same was true of Australia, where "by 1849 the colonies were in uproar over the issue."[60] A combination of increased free immigration to Van Diemen's Land and New South Wales had brought with it "a more balanced sex ratio, increased marriage rate and a growing desire for respectability and political representation."[61] The people of Van Diemen's Land were watching these developments carefully, and the arrival of the Young Irelanders came at a critical moment, when transportation had been reintroduced in the colony in 1848 after a brief suspension in 1846. As Hilary M. Carey has written, "The voyage of the Neptune, with its cargo of Irish pauper and political prisoners, became the catalyst for an outpouring of cross-colonial, anti-convict agitation that was qualitatively different to the earlier phases of the anti-transportation movement."[62] For instance, John West, a prominent advocate for abolishing transportation, dates a turning point in the campaign as the arrival of the Neptune: "From this time the colonists continued to protest, especially against the violation of public faith whenever a convict vessel anchored on their shores."[63]

Aware of the negative sentiment in the colony toward transportation, some among the Young Ireland generation in Van Diemen's Land quickly attached themselves to the campaign. In a letter to Mary

Thompson, Jenny Mitchel wrote that "the settlers and free inhabitants of this country are most anxious . . . to get rid of transportation to these colonies, and hold occasionally great league meetings on the subject."[64] The settlers felt that transportation prevented the development of Van Diemen's Land. Their two main arguments centered around the damage done by criminals to the colony's moral fabric, and the economic impacts of cheap convict labor.

Opposing transportation was a cause with significant popular support in opposition to a government policy. This was familiar territory for the Young Irelanders, and their involvement in anti-transportation politics gives us cause to dispute Malcolm Campbell's assertion that "conditions of life in Tasmania provided little nourishment either for Young Ireland's political activism or any local manifestation of fervent Irish nationalism."[65] John Mitchel reported in his *Jail Journal* that he and Meagher "talked much, however, of the Van Diemen's election, and of the Australasian League wherein I find Meagher takes considerable interest."[66] He wrote that "Meagher, also, has not been idle in this good cause; nor is his influence small at Ross and Campbell town."[67] After the anti-transportationists won the election in 1851, Jenny Mitchel wrote: "Some months past there has been a good deal of electioneering excitement in this island. It is the first time they have got an elective legislation. The government party had been beaten almost everywhere. There is a large majority of anti-transportationists returned."[68] For his part, Mitchel reported that "we both [Mitchel and Meagher] sympathize very heartily with the effort of the decent colonists to throw off the curse and shame of convictism—not that the change, indeed, would at all affect us, Irish exiles."[69] The language regarding shame and masculinity that the Young Irelanders had employed in Ireland bore a resemblance to the common argument in Australia that transportation was fundamentally emasculating. The vicar-general of New South Wales, William Bernard Ullathorne, wrote that "sixty thousand souls are festering in bondage. The iron which cankers their heel, corrodes their heart; the scourge which drinks the blood of their flesh, devours the spirit of their manhood."[70] Anti-transportation activists in Van Diemen's Land often linked such arguments to others that sought to portray the convicts as sexual deviants who were a "polluting, demoralising, and profoundly de-civilising force."[71] Others, like John Frost, a Chartist who had been transported to the island, saw transportation itself as the cause of the evil. In a harrowing critique of the convict system, he alluded to rape and sodomy, claiming that it was "almost impossible for a good looking youth to be sent to these places without falling victim to this hellish system, for if other means fail, he will be forced."[72] This is particularly striking when juxtaposed against "a discourse of the virtuous free settler" that Australian settlers had cultivated.[73] These specific arguments regarding what were considered proper gender roles and sexual behaviors all reinforced the position that not only was transportation immoral in and of itself but also that it made living a morally upright life in Australia impossible.

As well as providing an anti-government (which was, effectively, anti-British and anti-imperial) issue around which to rally, attaching themselves to the anti-transportation campaign provided the Young Irelanders with a local constituency, which they would not have found among the colonial administration in Hobart. For instance, in 1852 Mitchel noted that "O'Doherty is still in charge of a hospital in Hobart town as house Surgeon, & is rather pleasantly situated there [but] he has however no 'society' whatever. The people of Hobart town, that is the official people & their families, & the wealthy merchants, whose ambition is to go to Government House, all of course keep very shy of us."[74] On the other hand, there were clearly members of Van Diemonian society eager to be associated with the Irish convicts. This is confirmed by the presence of events like a "public meeting" held in West Maitland "for the purpose of adopting a petition to the Queen for the pardon of William Smith O'Brien, John Mitchel, Patrick O'Donohoe, Thomas F. Meagher, John Martin, Kevin Izod O'Doherty, and Terrence Bellew McManus."[75] In simultaneously engaging with local politics and keeping alive their own political campaigns as Irish nationalists, the Young Irelanders in Van Diemen's Land established a pattern that would continue throughout their careers abroad.

However, as was also the case with their views about economic policy in Ireland, as a group the Young Irelanders were far from ideologically homogenous, and even on the issue of transportation they were not unanimous, despite the fact that they themselves were its victims. Writing about his time in Van Diemen's Land, O'Brien used the gendered rhetoric regularly employed by Young Ireland to describe the role of the state, stating that "transportation is the most advantageous kind of secondary punishment, provided it be carried on without inflicting an injury upon communities, whose social welfare a paternal Government is bound to protect."[76] Thus, he argued, while transportation had been beneficial for the colonization of Australia, it would have been better suited to "an uninhabited group of islands, such as the Falkland Islands" than to Van Diemen's Land, which was both "a country thickly peopled with aboriginal inhabitants" and "a rising colony."[77] Further along the spectrum was John Donnellan Balfe, who had been a government spy in the leadership of the Irish Confederation and in 1850 moved by choice to Van Diemen's Land, where he took up a government position with responsibility for managing convicts.[78] He did not have the same direct experience of the convict ships as Mitchel, Meagher and the others. Consequently, he angered the Young Irelanders in Van Diemen's Land and in Ireland, most of whom opposed transportation—or, at the very least, did not want to see anyone with any links to Young Ireland, however discreditable, being associated with its administration.[79]

The other key Young Irelander whose position on transportation gives us a sense of the ways in which the movement's politics adapted to local circumstances was Patrick O'Donohoe. Initially, O'Donohoe objected to the argument that ordinary convicts were inherently immoral. Indeed, the newspaper was targeted at a working-class and convict readership.[80] On 9 February he wrote that that the anti-transportationists were "branding the largest section of them [people who had been transported] as contaminated, or unworthy to enjoy the very privileges, which they solicit their aid in obtaining."[81] This had followed an article in the previous issue in which O'Donohoe argued that "hell often does make its appearance upon earth. Glimpses of its horrors, neither few nor far between, may be seen in the back-slums of the city of London, and in the hells of the West-end, in the Faubourgs of Paris, on the Prada of Madrid."[82] For O'Donohoe, crime had a societal cause, and, as such, it was unfair and immoral to regard convicts as irredeemable. However, as the 1850s progressed, O'Donohoe came to oppose transportation, with his reasoning grounded in Young Ireland's understanding of rights. He wrote that the "British government, nor any other government, cannot transport its moral contamination here without breaking down that barrier of security which, in every part of the civilized world, is acknowledged and respected and which is understood to be 'The Right of Nations.'"[83] In the case of Van Diemen's Land, O'Donohoe was essentially forced to choose between his conviction that the colonists could choose their own form of government—and in so doing ban transportation—and his belief that convicts could be redeemed by removing them from the society that caused them to commit crime. Ultimately, O'Donohoe decided to privilege the right of the incipient Van Diemonian community to refuse to take responsibility for Britain's "moral contamination" (using a phrase that ascribed blame for the immorality of the convicts to Britain) over his belief that convicts could be entitled to liberty in Van Diemen's Land.

Whether or not they were in favor of transportation, many of the Young Irelanders decided that they would not be bound by its conditions. Both McManus and Meagher escaped in early January 1852, McManus to San Francisco aboard the *Elizabeth Thompson*, having left Van Diemen's Land before the local authorities could challenge a court ruling that declared the revocation of his ticket of leave illegal.[84] Meagher wrote to the local magistrate to surrender his ticket and then slipped onto the ship, arriving four months later in New York City.[85] Both were met with heroes' welcomes. In Meagher's case, however, a controversy arose among other Young Irelanders about his actions in the days leading up to his escape, because he had surrendered his ticket of leave by post, thereby passing up an opportunity for heroic resistance. Jenny Mitchel wrote: "We do not like the way the thing was done. If he had awaited the constables in his house, allowed them to arrest him, then overpowered them and escaped, not a word could have been said, as now there is, and this would have been easily done, for those who are qualified to know, think the constables would not have dared to resist."[86] If the reality was less than valiant, there was no reason why the story could not be a tale of derring-do. Accordingly, the *Launceston Examiner* published a report (republished in various Australian newspapers) on the "naked truth" of Meagher's escape St. Valentine's Day 1852,[87] in which Meagher got close enough to the chief district constable to yell, "You have come to arrest me. I am here. I am O'Meagher [*sic*]. Catch me if you can."[88] Meagher had not been pursued, the paper claimed, because his supporters far outnumbered the chief constable's force, which consisted of only one other man, and that bloodshed would have ensued had there been a confrontation.[89] *The Nation* also reported on Meagher's escape, focusing on another constable who accompanied the chief constable, "a ruffian just emancipated from the convict gangs."[90] Although this was a relatively common police practice at the time, it again shows the distinction being made between (immoral) criminal convicts and (moral) political exiles.[91] At the core of these accounts, however, was the question of honor—one of the principles in terms of which the Young Irelanders wrote about their escapes and those of their comrades. Even where it was disputed, Meagher's escape from Van Diemen's Land would become part of the self-mythologization of Young Ireland.[92]

Other Young Irelanders escaped after McManus and Meagher. Patrick O'Donohoe succeeded in escaping in December 1852, first to Melbourne on board the *Yarra Yarra*, where he was hidden by an Irish sympathizer, John O'Shanassy (who ran a drapery and would later become premier of Victoria). From there he was sent to Sydney, where he was smuggled aboard the *Oberon* and traveled to San Francisco.[93] O'Donohoe argued that his treatment by the governor, who had revoked his ticket of leave a number of times, violated the original terms of his parole: "I stood before God and man absolved from the moral and honourable responsibility originally implied and understood by the 'parole' entered into by myself and the other state prisoners."[94] However, the other Young Irelanders were unlikely to have seen it this way, especially given their reaction to the details of Meagher's escape.[95] The last of the Young Irelanders to escape was John Mitchel, who fled to the United States in 1853. Mitchel was aided by Patrick Smyth, who had come to Van Diemen's Land intending to spring a Young Irelander free and take him to the United States; Mitchel agreed to make an attempt. In line with his pronouncements on the honor of Meagher's escape, Mitchel went to the local magistrate in person, along with Smyth, to hand in his ticket of leave. Both were armed at the time, which may have influenced the magistrate's decision not to give chase until they had left.[96] Mitchel escaped on a horse that some accounts suggest he had bought from the magistrate immediately prior to the escape.[97] In giving the magistrate the opportunity to arrest him, Mitchel placed the importance of escaping *honorably* above that of escaping *successfully*; again, the story of the escape was as important as the fact of escaping.

Moreover, as we will come to see in the next chapter, for a group who relied upon their own status as heroes for social capital, honor and a good story were important.

Responsible Government

The Young Irelanders' engagement with colonial politics in Van Diemen's Land went beyond the campaign against transportation. Some became involved in the campaign for responsible government, as the colony aspired to become a self-regulating political unit, not simply a conveniently remote appendage of Britain. This was partly related to anti-transportation, a policy that—as we have seen—was favored by a majority of the settlers in Van Diemen's Land, but opposed by the imperial government in London. It was in this wider context that responsible government—and, with it, the right to make decisions about issues such as transportation—became a key issue in the colony. In 1853, William Smith O'Brien took it upon himself to propose a new constitution to be used when the colony had achieved self-government.[98] Although it had no official status, it was published in the *Launceston Examiner*, whose editor was particularly complementary toward O'Brien's proposals. Most of the document is comprised of descriptions of the way the government would be structured, the role of the judiciary, and other matters concerning governmental functioning.

The conclusion of O'Brien's proposed constitution for Van Diemen's Land contains an important prefiguration of a phase of development of the Southern Hemisphere colonies beyond mere self-government. O'Brien offered suggestions that could be activated "in case the other colonies of Australia should be disposed to form a confederation."[99] O'Brien saw the Federation of Australia as a logical extension of responsible government and argued that, if the individual Australian colonies could be granted responsible government, it followed that by joining together they could create a stronger state and nation. At the time, the more immediate issue of transportation blocked any such action, as the Colonial Office feared that the Australian colonies working together might end transportation. In an 1851 letter, colonial secretary Earl Grey wrote to William Denison: "What I am more alarmed about is the probable success of the efforts which seem to be making to unite all the Australian

colonies in common opposition to the system of transportation."[100] Grey
also expressed his reasoning behind his opposition to the Federation of
the Australian colonies: "If as it appears all the most respectable colonists
and the Bishops join in this it is plain that an affect will be produced on
public opinion here which will render it quite impossible that transportation should be continued."[101] Whereas Grey's concern focused on the
specific issue of transportation, O'Brien (and, after him, Duffy, who took
up the cause in the 1860s) viewed the problem not in relation to any specific matter, but in terms of who had the right to make decisions—any
decision—regarding the lives of those living in Australia. Like O'Brien,
Duffy saw from an early stage that the Federation would not only give
Australians critical mass to adopt a position that differed London's; the
process of uniting politically would also create a national consciousness
fundamentally different from the understanding of citizenship held by a
resident in a colony run by unelected administrators.

As O'Brien pointed out, there were strong practical reasons behind
the suggestion that the Australian provinces could create a federal state.
In this line of reasoning, O'Brien argued that the proposed government could regulate a number of matters important to the people who
lived in Australia: "Intercolonial tariffs, postage, electric telegraph,
light houses and beacons, a penal settlement, extradition of criminals,
copyright and patent for inventions, professional qualification, a mint,
bankruptcy and to laws for more easy recovery of debt due in one colony by persons residing in another, naturalisation, minimum price of
public land, defence against a common foe. Any other matter which
can affect the common interest of the colonies may be entertained by
such confederation."[102] Supporters of federation in Australia would
make this argument for years to come: that if the settler colonies were
to become increasingly more advanced, they would also face challenges
that were better handled by a larger state.

However, before any real discussion of federation in Australia could
commence, the more pressing issue in Van Diemen's Land was responsible government, which was granted on 1 January 1856. Consequently,
Van Diemen's Land became Tasmania.[103] Yet with responsible government came questions as to how Tasmania should be governed. Having already proposed a constitution for the settlement before it became
self-governing, O'Brien waded into the debate. By this point he had

been pardoned and had returned to Ireland, where he wrote his *Principles of Government, or Meditations in Exile*. As the title suggests, these were informed by his time in Van Diemen's Land, elevated to universal principles, particularly with respect to the extent to which governments are entitled to restrict individual freedoms in furtherance of the public good. He wrote that, "being entirely cut off from the opportunities of research into matters pertaining to the nationality of Ireland, I was compelled by necessity to generalize my ideas, and to write as a citizen of the world, rather than as an Irish patriot."[104] At the core of the text is an argument for the existence of qualified universal basic human rights. "Among the fundamental principles which ought to govern legislation," he stated, "we may specifically notice the following:—*natural rights may be invaded or circumscribed to no greater extent than 'the welfare of society imperatively requires.'*"[105] He put forward the view that "natural liberty is the right which each man possesses to say and do what he pleases."[106] However, he then asked if "social or civil liberty," which "is the right to say and do everything that is not injurious to others," could be a legitimate restriction on natural liberty.[107] He answered by taking the position that "every restriction which unnecessarily interferes with this right is an infringement of social liberty."[108]

In what followed, O'Brien's line of thinking implies that he saw his work having application in the practical work of state formation, by suggesting how these rights must be respected in relation to taxation, freedom of movement, and freedom of the press. In each case, O'Brien argued that, while limited restrictions were necessary for the general good of society, the government should not interfere with natural rights, nor tax too heavily, and that there were intrinsic "natural rights of man" that any government, imperial or local, should not violate.[109] Nonetheless, O'Brien brought a distinct perspective to his writings that clearly reflected Young Ireland's political thought. He wrote that "if a nation voluntarily prefers servitude to freedom—in other words, if the individuals of whom it is composed shrink from the task of preforming faithfully and honourably the functions and duties which are incidental to the exercise of self-government," then they did not deserve liberty.[110] This idea that liberty and its "institutions . . . can be upheld only by the unceasing action of public spirit" was one of the Young Irelanders' key creeds.[111] It had inspired their rebellion in 1848 and would be central to their concept of citizenship across the world, even if it would seldom be articulated with this degree of universalist abstraction. Moreover, it was key to "Victorian liberalism," which Eugenio Biagini has argued "was both individualist *and* republican at one and the same time"—meaning that participatory citizenship was essential to securing liberal conceptions of individual rights.[112]

When we read O'Brien's *Principles of Government* carefully (or examine his actions and writings in other contexts, such as his attitude to transportation), we find that he did not oppose colonialism on principle. Indeed, he contended that "there is no more legitimate mode of extending the power and influence of a country, or of providing employment and subsistence for its redundant population, than the establishment of colonies."[113] He saw colonization as an "important branch of social policy" through which governments could improve the lives of their people.[114] Nevertheless, he asserted that "the prior claims, the 'vested' rights of the aboriginal population ought to be distinctly recognized, and carefully maintained, as paramount to those of the intruding population."[115] As Ann Curthoys and Jessie Mitchell have shown, his application of these ideas to the aboriginal population was particularly progressive for the 1850s.[116] Not only did O'Brien argue that the aboriginal population were entitled to rights, which at the time was not a given; he also stated that they "may justly claim the protection of the metropolitan government against the aggression of its colonists."[117] This, he said, was because, "however ardently we may advocate the principle of self-government, we cannot object to the exercise of an over-ruling authority, when that authority is applied to protect the fundamental rights of mankind."[118]

The response of the press in Tasmania to O'Brien's *Principles of Government, or Meditations in Exile* is of particular interest. Quoting it directly, the *Launceston Examiner* wrote that they hoped the pass system for convicts would be dismantled "so that here, as well as elsewhere, 'national rights' may be 'invaded [infringed upon] or circumscribed' to no greater extent than 'the welfare of society imperatively requires.'"[119] That the newspaper considered rights vested in the nation, whether that be Tasmania or a yet-to-be Australia, was significant. It suggests that the Young Irelanders' understanding of the importance of the nation, which had been developed in Ireland and saw the nation as the guarantor of liberty, had found an audience in Australia. It is local reactions like this that allow scholars to claim that "O'Brien would play an important part in the shaping of Australia's emerging sense of itself."[120]

In spite of their engagement with the political development of Van Diemen's Land, most of the most prominent Young Irelanders had already left the colony by the time it became Tasmania in 1856. After he was granted a conditional pardon in 1854, Kevin Izod O'Doherty moved to Paris. Upon receipt of an unconditional pardon in 1856, he returned to Ireland. John Martin, who, like O'Doherty, had been involved with time *Irish Felon*, also received a conditional pardon in 1854 and likewise moved to Paris. He, too, returned to Ireland following his receipt of an unconditional pardon 1856. William Smith O'Brien, who was allowed to leave in 1854 on the condition that he did not return to Ireland, moved to Brussels and was granted an unconditional pardon in 1856, which allowed him to return to Ireland.[121] All of the less senior Young Irelanders who had been sentenced for the attack on Cappoquin police barracks received pardons after 1854, largely because of the intervention of John Martin, who campaigned on their behalf.[122]

Conclusion

The experiences of the Young Ireland generation in Van Diemen's Land were essential to their formation as a group with international influence. The transnational campaign to secure their release played an important role in the creation of the networks that would produce a transnational Irish nationalism. Moreover, the Young Irelanders' engagement with Irish politics from abroad can be seen as the beginning of what would amount to a century of Irish political participation from abroad. At the same time, their engagement with politics in Van Diemen's Land—and in Australia more broadly—and their attempts to ensure that "all the religious and moral virtues should be encouraged and cultivated" in the emerging state was important to the later development of an Australian nation, as well as to their colleagues' future involvement in state formation in Canada and the United States.[123] Their focus on ideas of honor, morality, the gendering of imperialism, and, ultimately, a concept of qualified liberty can be seen both as a continuation of how they understood politics in Ireland, and as an indication of how they would engage in politics in other parts of the world.

3

The United States of America, 1848–1861

In Boston on St. Patrick's Day, 1851, Thomas D'Arcy McGee wrote, "Whether we may wish it or not, one half of Ireland is here."[1] While it was a slight exaggeration to say that half of Ireland was in the United States, Irish migration there was substantial. Between 1846 and 1855, 1.5 million Irish people emigrated to the country, leaving approximately 5.7 million people in Ireland.[2] Indeed, by 1860, one in five Irish-born people in the world lived in the United States, and in New York City—the center of the Irish American world at the time—25 percent of the population had been born in Ireland.[3] For most Irish migrants, America offered plentiful employment, a relatively cheap crossing, and an escape from Ireland's economic and social devastation. For the Young Irelanders, it held an additional attraction: the ideological pull of a nation that they associated with democratic ideals. "I foresee that America will be the visible providence of the world," Thomas Francis Meagher told the *New York Times* in 1852, "and that whilst she encourages the weak, the struggling and the oppressed, she will augment her own power of doing good by winning the confidence and love of every race. Thus will be accomplished the freedom of the world."[4] In a similar vein, John Mitchel called for an alliance between the "votaries" of democracy in Europe and American democracy.[5] Thomas D'Arcy McGee, who embraced this idea, wrote that Americans, "being themselves free, nothing is left for them so glorious to do as to impart their freedom to others."[6]

A close look at the Young Ireland generation is central to a necessary recasting of our understanding of Irish people's engagement with American political thought. It does so by way examining three key clusters of ideas that were central to American political thought in the 1850s: nativism, manifest destiny, and the cultural nationalism associated with the Young America movement and the ways in which Ireland interacted with those ideas. While all three interacted in multiple, complex ways, it is useful to first distinguish between them and to sketch the outlines of their interconnections.

Perhaps the most threatening political idea, from a Young Ireland generation perspective, was nativism, which arose in the mid-1840s in response to rising levels of immigration to the United States from Europe (particularly by Catholics, including Irish Catholics).[7] It held that a distinctively American notion of liberty going back to the Revolution of 1776 had an Anglo-Saxon, Protestant foundation, and, consequently, any extension of Catholic political influence was in danger of eroding a fundamental quality of American political culture.[8] The sources of nativism were complex. The roots of American religious prejudice went back several generations to multiple European religious conflicts; the deep-seated fears on which they based were fueled in the 1840s and 1850s by the visible increase in Irish immigration and the subsequent economic downturn of the 1850s feeding competition for resources. Ultimately, this volatile combination of fear and ideology drove the campaigns of the Know-Nothing (or American) Party, founded in 1854, and their principal newspaper, the *Native American*.

If nativism was primarily reactionary, a concept of America battening down the hatches against growth through new migration, the second important political idea circulating in the America in which the Young Irelanders arrived was expansive and oriented toward the future: that of manifest destiny, which held that American democracy was divinely ordained to spread across North America. As a concept, it was, as Stephen Hahn notes, "deeply laid in the political culture and embraced virtually across the political spectrum."[9] Taken to its logical conclusions, it also held that American liberty should spread across the world. However, manifest destiny was not always distinct from nativism, and there existed a strongly anti-Catholic version of the doctrine: that Anglo-Saxon, Protestant, Americans alone were destined to civilize the North American continent.[10] This existed in parallel to a second, more extensive, understanding of manifest destiny, in which the notion of what constituted a uniquely American people was understood in more generous terms that could and did encompass Irish Catholics.[11] It was this conception of manifest destiny that the Young Irelanders embraced.

Underpinning the political culture of the United States in the 1840s and 1850s was a third element: a new awareness of American cultural nationalism, which found expression in the movement that became known as Young America. Although not a single idea, Young America was nonetheless a profoundly influential political and cultural force, encompassing Democratic politicians, writers, and painters, whose ambition (and lack of specificity) can be measured by the words of John O'Sullivan, editor of the principal Young American journal, the *Democratic Review*: "All history is to be re-written; political science and the whole scope of all moral truth have to be considered and illustrated in the light of the democratic principle."[12] O'Sullivan, a Catholic and the son of an Irish immigrant, is widely credited with popularizing the term "manifest destiny" in 1845.[13] Partly because of O'Sullivan's influence (and that of a number of other Irish figures), Young America opposed nativist claims that America was narrowly Anglo-Saxon and Protestant in character; views expressed in the *Democratic Review* were often virulently Anglo-phobic. It was thus more than the name that attracted the Young Ireland generation to Young America. For figures such as O'Sullivan (and, indeed, Meagher), Young America's expansive vision of American democracy, particularly when defined in opposition to the British political system, offered a means for Irish people to overcome nativist anti-Catholic prejudices.

It was into this volatile and formative US political culture that the Young Irelanders arrived. Here, as in Australia (and later Canada), they would very quickly become immersed in the political debates of the country in which they made their homes. This makes it all the more surprising that the place of the Young Irelanders in the development of American political thought in the mid-nineteenth century has rarely been considered.[14] When the movement is in fact mentioned by scholars of US history, such as Yonatan Eyal and Edward Widmer, it is often briefly and in passing, frequently in the context of other Young European movements.[15] While Irish immigrant contributions to and engagement with American political culture is more commonly considered with regard to powerful state and municipal networks like Tammany Hall in New York than with national politics in nineteenth century America, the Young Irelanders were different in this regard. It was in the Federal and Confederate governments that they saw political power vested, as opposed to the powerful state and municipal governments. This makes sense, given that in Ireland they had seen the nation as essential to the power of the state; however, in the nineteenth-century United States, explicit advocacy for national government was an unusual position. Furthermore, for scholars of the Irish in America, the integration of the Irish into American political culture is usually dated to the Civil War in the 1860s, or even later.[16] We can push this development back at least a generation, to the time when the Young Irelanders arrived in the United States after the failure of the rebellion of 1848.

Young Ireland in the United States

The route to the United States taken by the Young Irelanders following the failure of the 1848 revolt was not direct, and not always entirely voluntary either. Richard O'Gorman, John O'Donnell, Daniel Doyle, P. J. Smyth, and John Blake Dillon all fled to New York.[17] The arrival in the United States of Thomas Francis Meagher, Terrence Bellew McManus, Patrick O'Donohoe, and John Mitchel, all of whom had escaped from Van Diemen's Land, were significant public events. Meagher and McManus arrived in San Francisco to a rapturous reception, feted by local politicians and newspapers, as did (later, and separately) Patrick O'Donohoe and John Mitchel.[18] To some extent, the celebrity status of the Young Irelanders can be attributed to the extensive US press coverage of their activities in Van Diemen's Land and their subsequent escapes.[19] It is possible to find reports on Young Irelanders in exile not only in newspapers based in cities with large Irish populations like New York, Boston, and Chicago but also in newspapers with a more national reach like Washington, DC–based *The Republic*, as well as far more local publications, such as the *Miners' Express* in Dubuque, Iowa.[20] In October 1853, the *Chicago Tribune* triumphantly reported the escape of John Mitchel and John Martin from the colony, declaring "the brave compatriots of Thomas Francis Meagher, in the unfortunate revolutionary movement in Ireland, and his associates in exile, have made their escape from Australia"—*albeit* erroneously in Martin's case, given that he actually remained in Van Diemen's Land until he was conditionally pardoned in 1854.[21] One correspondent in Lynchburg, Tennessee, wrote home to Ireland that "another of the Irish exiles have arrived in New York and is producing great excitement among the people here."[22]

The celebrations that typically met the Young Ireland leaders when they landed in the United States were usually organized either by local Irish associations or by important political figures. For instance, John F. Crampton, Britain's minister to the United States, reported that John Mitchel had been "received by the Governor of the State [of California] at a banquet at which what they call the 'exercises' of the evening were exclusively devoted to the abuse of Her Majesty's Government."[23] This was indicative of a strong tradition of Anglophobia in the United States, where memories of the War of 1812 and the American Revolution lingered. An argument could be made that the reason for the warm and vocal welcome extended to the former Young Irelanders was because in America "Irish votes were valuable and worth courting" by both Whigs and Democrats, whose politicians attended and organized these events.[24] However, it should be noted that in spite of the Young Irelanders having been involved in a rebellion in Ireland, they were not seen as subversives who would threaten the country (although Mitchel would in fact rebel against it), partly because their rebellion against England made it, for some, a case of "My enemy's enemy is my friend." It has been argued that, in California, at least "the official view was to identify with the cause of Irish freedom."[25]

In any case, after the Young Irelanders arrived in the United States, the vast majority of them settled in New York City, at least initially. For a period in the early 1850s, Thomas Francis Meagher, John Mitchel, Thomas D'Arcy McGee, Richard O'Gorman, Michael Doheny, P. J. Smyth, Patrick O'Donoghue, John O'Mahony, Thomas Antisell, and John Blake Dillon were all living there. Mitchel in his *Jail Journal* described it as "a constellation of cities—a ganglion of human life."[26] The concentration of so many Young Irelanders in New York and their ability to communicate with Ireland made that city an important part of the Irish public sphere. For instance, John Mitchel's influential *Jail Journal*, was first published in serialized form in 1854 in the *Citizen*, a newspaper that Mitchel founded in New York. It was only later in the same year that it was published in a single volume in Dublin, where it quickly became one of the "central works in the Irish nationalist canon."[27] That a work first published by an Irish writer in New York became central to political thought in Ireland tells us that the Irish public sphere was expanding, facilitated by technologies like steam-powered print, cheap paper, and oceangoing steam travel as much as by emigration, voluntary or otherwise.

Marshall McLuhan has argued that "the personal and social consequences of any medium—that is, of any extension of ourselves—result from the new scale that is introduced into our affairs by each extension of ourselves, or by any new technology," rather than as a result of the information that is communicated by the new technology.[28] Though he has been criticized on the grounds of "technological determinism" by Brian Winston and others for minimizing the role of human agency in historical processes,[29] McLuhan offers a powerful explanation as to how communications technology can impact society.[30] That these technologies brought a "new scale" into what we might call the "concept of the nation" was one of the significant features of the Young Ireland generation and their continuing impact after the rebellion of 1848. In the late 1840s and early 1850s, there were few better places to bring this into being than New York, already a nexus point, both for print and communications culture in the United States and for a transatlantic world undergoing a technological transformation as a result of steam travel and the undersea telegraph.

The presence of a number of educated Young Irelanders in New York City created a network that increased their influence in Irish American society. For instance, O'Gorman became a prominent lawyer and then a jurist and went into practice with another Young Irelander, John Blake Dillon, which made them part of the "two per cent of professional people among the Irish in New York" at the time.[31] Joining them in that 2 percent from 1848 to 1854 was Thomas Antisell, a doctor who would later move to California.[32] This concentration of Young Irelanders contributed to a sense that New York was a key place from which Ireland's destiny would be shaped. Thus, in January 1854, Mitchel wrote that "mankind is once more becoming charged with the electricity of Revolution, and one of the poles of that battery we believe to be situated somewhere in, or about New York."[33] Mitchel's choice of metaphor was characteristic of a generation acutely aware of the importance played by new technology in their politics, and to the reasoning behind why it would be possible for a group of Irish people in New York to instigate rebellion in Ireland. This sense of themselves as the vanguard of the coming revolution was compounded by the presence of other

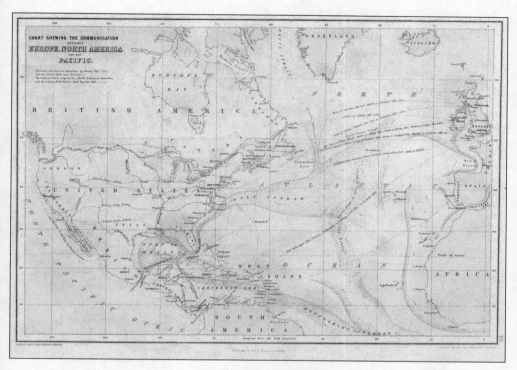

Figure 3.1. John Bartholomew, *Chart Shewing* [sic] *the Communication between Europe, North America, and the Pacific.* Edinburgh: A. & C. Black, 1856. Courtesy David Rumsey Map Collection, David Rumsey Map Center, Stanford Libraries.

European revolutionaries in New York, like the Hungarian Louis Kossuth, who "captured American attention like no foreigner had since the Marquis de Lafayette."[34] Although Kossuth's popularity would wane, his initial exile to the United States was important for the Young Irelanders. Mitchel would laud him as "a great genius and hero," and his presence in the city was clearly central to his conviction that a revolution in Ireland could be effected from New York.[35]

The Young Irelanders' ability to forge networks of influence almost as soon as they arrived in New York was in no small part due to their celebrity. When Mitchel came to New York in 1853, a lavish celebratory banquet was held, attended by 600 guests, followed by a reception at the Broadway Theatre—the largest theater in New York at the time—with 1800 attendees.[36] The report on the banquet in the *New York Daily*

Times was almost two pages long, listing the luminaries in attendance, including Judge Thomas Emmet, a very prominent New Yorker who was the son of United Irishman Thomas Emmet and a nephew of Robert Emmet; Ambrose Kingsland, the former mayor of New York City; and Horace Greeley, a wealthy Irish American newspaper publisher whose *New-York Tribune* has been called by Adam-Max Tuchinsky "the most important newspaper" of the time.[37] Also attending were Thomas Francis Meagher and other former Young Irelanders, including P. J. Smyth, Richard O'Gorman, John Blake Dillon, and Michael Doheny. Charles O'Conor, the US district attorney, presided over the evening. In his speech, O'Conor spoke of how "parties—representing the great City of New York," from all sides of the political and religious divides in the city, "have assembled this evening in conformity with the principles upon which our government is founded, and which our people delight to honour."[38]

O'Conor's address shows us the insertion of the Young Irelanders in the ongoing American debates over the nature of American democracy. O'Conor told his audience that there was a direct connection between the American Revolution of 1776, the United Irish Rebellion of 1798, and the Young Ireland Rebellion of 1848. He remarked that "the chain of union between lovers of liberty throughout the world" bound Young Ireland to "the fathers of this Republic."[39] In placing the last of the three rebellions in the same lineage as the American Revolution, O'Conor and others played an essential role in connecting Young Ireland with notions of American liberty. The discussion of this influence of the American Revolution on the United Irishmen and Irish republicanism, which is grounded in historical reality, has been commented upon in recent years by scholars such as Johnathan Israel and Vincent Morley.[40] What O'Conor did in 1853, however, was to ensure that the connection was not only evident but generally accepted by the New York media and the reading public. Its effect for the Young Irelanders was to place them at the heart of an idea of American democracy.

Behind the toasts and the speeches, the receptions accorded to the Young Irelanders must be seen in the context of a general anxiety circulating in the United States in the late 1840s and early 1850s in which debates about slavery and rising levels of immigration were creating a sense that the American republic was under threat.[41] One response was to look back to the American Revolution of 1776 as a mythologized moment of unitary origin, leading one historian of the period to call the idea of the revolution "the strongest cultural tie" in the United States at the time.[42] Earlier, in 1834, George Bancroft (who was linked to the Young Americans) had published his extensive *History of the United States, from the Discovery of the American Continent*, in which he told his readers that "the coming period will show why we are a united people."[43] A few years later, in 1837, another Young American, the poet Ralph Waldo Emerson, wrote the essay "Concord Hymn," in which he memorably characterized the revolution as having "fired the shot heard round the world."[44] When Henry Longfellow's poem "Paul Revere's Ride" was published in 1860, it added yet another powerful element to the American origin myth.[45] It is possible, however, to read works such as these not simply as celebratory, but as anxious responses to a sense that the idea of American democracy was being lost at a time when the American Revolution was being claimed both by those who were pro-slavery and those who were antislavery.[46]

It was in this heated political environment that the Young Irelanders landed in the years after 1848, and the debates outlined above form part of the explanation of what inspired six hundred New Yorkers to attend a dinner in Mitchel's honor. The presence of Mitchel and the other Young Irelanders in the United States served as a tangible proof that America was still the home of the liberty and democratic ideals for which the revolution had been fought. A similar story was told in Britain, where the presence of Italian exiles like Mazzini stood as proof to the British public of the spread of British ideas of liberty across Europe.[47] In the United States, Mitchel was a living, breathing revolutionary hero. This in turn fed a sense of American exceptionalism, which centered on the idea that Americans were uniquely situated to combine democracy and law to create from a revolution a successful republic and were thus obliged to propagate this formula across the world.[48] Indeed, O'Conor was unambiguous on this point, telling his listeners that Mitchel had escaped "from the stranglehold of the tyrant to the threshold of American liberty."[49] What is more, such a view had traction outside of the Irish community in the United States at the time. For instance, William H. Seward, the former governor of New York and in 1853 a US senator who as secretary of state in the late 1860s would be at the center of diplomatic wrangling about British jurisdiction over Irish American Fenians, described Mitchel as "a fugitive from the penal laws enacted by the British Parliament, for the enslaving of his native land."[50]

All of this was enabled by the fact that, even before 1848, the United States loomed large in the imagination of the Young Irelanders, and stories about the country in *The Nation* were almost overwhelmingly positive. Ann Andrews has argued that these were some of the most common articles in *The Nation*.[51] For instance, in 1847 the newspaper printed a story about General Joseph Reed, the president of the Supreme Executive Council of Pennsylvania and delegate to the Continental Congress, refusing a bribe of ten thousand guineas from the British under the title "Lessons for the People," pointing up the incident as an example of "patriotic integrity."[52] The Young Irelanders were also acutely conscious that their own ideological forebearers, the United Irishmen, had drawn some of their strongest inspiration from the American Revolution.[53] For all of these reasons, the American and the Young Ireland revolutions became mutually reinforcing mythologies. America inspired Irish nationalism, and, in turn, the Irish revolutionaries of 1848 reinforced the idea that the American Revolution was alive and well.

Indeed, the only volume in the Library of Ireland not to deal with an Irish topic was Michael Doheny's *History of the American Revolution*.[54] It was written for the same reasons as the other texts in the library: to promote the idea of freedom in Ireland. As Doheny told his readers, "My labour, such as it was, had, above all things, for its object the advancement of my countrymen's information, feelings, hopes, courage, and prospects."[55] Here, as elsewhere, Young Ireland's understanding of history is explicitly instrumental (see chapter 1). In this case, however, it meant that as the myth of the American Revolution was being shaped in the United States, the Young Irelanders were participating in that process, *albeit* from the other side of the Atlantic. What is also significant in the present context is that Doheny chose not to focus solely on Irish participation in the American Revolution. "My impartiality may appear questionable," he wrote, "if I selected them [Irish people] as leading characters in the history of a great people, of whom they formed but a proportionate part."[56] Instead, by resisting the temptation to single out the Irish role in the revolution, Doheny makes a stronger argument: regardless of any specifically Irish involvement, he effectively claims the entire American Revolution for his own revolutionary movement in Ireland, in which both moments—America in 1776 and (aspirationally) Ireland in the 1840s—become part of a longer history of British imperial rule being replaced by national governments. As Doheny's *History* demonstrates, the Young Irelanders were equipped with a narrative that made a place for them in American history well before they ever set foot on American soil.

Thomas D'Arcy McGee

Some of the Young Irelanders who moved to the United States after 1848 had even more tangible links to the country. Among the most prominent was Thomas D'Arcy McGee, who between 1842 and 1845 had lived in Boston, where he had been a relatively successful journalist and popular lecturer among the Irish American community and had played a key role in rallying American support for Repeal.[57] It was largely as a consequence of his reputation in America that, when McGee returned to Ireland in 1845, he was able to begin work almost immediately with the *Freeman's Journal* and rapidly rise to prominence within Young Ireland.

Following his second, forcible, emigration to the United States, McGee set about reestablishing himself in journalism. He first moved to New York, where he founded a newspaper called *The Nation*—a title clearly evoking its Irish counterpart—that was marketed as "a weekly newspaper devoted to Ireland and her Emigrants."[58] In it, McGee argued that Irish emigrants in the United States could "best assist Ireland out of slavery and misery."[59] The newspaper promoted the view that "the liberation of Ireland is the Labour of our Race" and sought "by impregnating the Irish mind with large and heroic views of duty" to encourage Irish Americans to work for an Irish Republic.[60] McGee's notion that Irish America could join with the Irish in Ireland to inspire a rebellion in Ireland would prove short lived. Charles Gavan Duffy, the Young Irelander for whom McGee had the most respect and about whom he wrote a hagiographic memoir, intervened and pointed out the flaws in McGee's plan.[61] In a letter Duffy told him that "the notion of turning Ireland into a Republic by force of pre-paid letters is mere midsummer madness," because "the sick and poverty-stricken people" needed "comfort and confidence" rather than incitement to rebellion.[62] McGee listened to him, and in 1849 he wrote in *The Nation* that "the great fact in the present condition of Ireland is the new era made by the famine."[63] Over time, this interrogation of the possibilities of turning Ireland into a republic by use of force would take him on a very different political trajectory to that of colleagues, such as Meagher or Mitchel, and that would be much more conciliatory to Britain and to British ideas of democracy. Through 1849 and into the early 1850s, however, McGee was still very much the Young Ireland revolutionary in exile, and in the summer of 1850 a group of prominent Irish Americans induced him to move back to Boston and publish there a new newspaper for the Irish community, the *Boston Daily Times*. In this paper he reported extensively on Irish, Scottish, and German news and penned numerous profiles of leading British and Irish radicals and sought "to counter the prejudices of British newspapers with real facts."[64]

While in Boston, McGee also wrote his *History of the Irish Settlers in North America, from the Earliest Period to the Census of 1850*, which was published on St. Patrick's Day 1851.[65] One might be led—reasonably enough—to assume it to be a survey of Irish immigrant experiences in North America; in fact, the book's real focus is the American Revolution and its causes and consequences. Unlike Doheny's *History*, which was written for an Irish readership and claimed a kinship between the activities of Young Ireland and the American Revolution by association, McGee placed Irish people at the heart of most of American history. In placing the Irish in a narrative of American history, a central problem for McGee was that most of the early Irish settlers had been Ulster Protestants. He used various strategies to overcome this inconvenient fact, sometimes praising them as "Celtic stock,"[66] or, when telling his readers that Andrew Jackson, the American president of Ulster origin, was "of Irish parents," he neglected to mention their religious background as Presbyterians from Antrim.[67] By contrast, when introducing his readers to Edward Kavanagh, a state senator, an acting governor of Maine, and a strong Jackson supporter, McGee took care to mention Jackson's "strong Irish and Catholic tendencies."[68] Mc-

Gee's presentation of the Irish in America was thus implicitly sectarian and relied upon an attempt to claim as Catholic (or, at least, obscure the Protestantism of) many of the Irish at the forefront of establishing American democracy.

The problem of religion aside, for McGee the process of state-building following the Revolutionary War was a project to which the Irish could legitimately lay claim: "Nearly all the colonial charters were expanded into constitutions, or substituted by more liberal instruments, and in all such changes the Irish race had hand and part."[69] In tone, this passage is characteristic of the entire volume, in which it emerges that "the Irish had colonised, sowed, and reaped, fought, spoke, and legislated in the New World"; that they had been instrumental in the establishment of the US Navy; and that they were responsible for the spread of the Catholic Church in North America, whose "plantation in America [was] the greatest labour of the Irish Hercules."[70] Looking forward, the book argued that the colonization of new territories in the American West offered an opportunity "to win respect for a fallen race," as they were spaces in which the Irish could thrive and where few "obstacles exist to the successful establishment" of Irish emigrant communities.[71] What makes McGee's history more than mere ethnic boosterism is the underlying narrative that colonization had an essential role to play in providing Irish people with space to reclaim their national honor. In McGee's account, with Ireland devastated by the Famine, the only option open to the Irish was to transform themselves from the colonized into colonizers, even if this meant ignoring those who would in turn be displaced by Irish colonization: the Native Americans of the American West. In the context of the current argument, what stands out as particularly relevant here is that, in the process of writing the Irish into the American historical narrative, we see McGee acceding to the logic of colonization.

The *Boston Daily Times* gave way to a newspaper significantly called the *American Celt and Adopted Citizen*, in whose pages we can track the change taking place in McGee's viewpoint. Whereas in Ireland he had been a liberal republican who sought the establishment of secular schools as a means of countering sectarianism, by 1851 McGee had come to see the world as a contest between Catholicism and Protestantism.

His embrace of this narrative of conflict came about in part through his embrace of the ideas of the Catalonian priest Jaime Luciano Balmez. In his *Protestantism and Catholicity Compared in their Effects on the Civilisation of Europe*, which first appeared in an English translation in Baltimore in 1851, Balmez argued that Catholicism had spread order and knowledge throughout Europe, replacing chaos and ignorance. The social order brought by Catholicism was broken by Protestantism, which privileged "private judgement for public and lawful authority.[72] Indeed, as David Wilson has pointed out, McGee's writings on religion for about three years after 1851 are virtually indistinguishable from Balmez's.[73] Of particular relevance here is an article of May 1851, from *American Celt* purporting to put on record "the deliberate opinions of Thomas D'Arcy McGee,"[74] which stated: "Our Protestant friends know that we have ever maintained with them, that Protestantism was no religion; that it had no apostolicity, no unity, no authority."[75] The idea that Protestantism could not even claim to be a religion was clearly sectarian, but nonetheless widely shared within some strands of Catholic culture.[76] Yet saying so left McGee in an awkward position, as many of the Young Ireland colleagues whom he had regularly celebrated were Protestants. At one point he tried to explain his way out of the contradiction, writing that "Protestantism had nothing to do with it. They [Forty-eighters] were patriots in spite of it."[77]

While McGee's rapid turn toward sectarianism in the early 1850s may seem unusual, it can be understood within the combined context of American politics and society in the 1850s and British policy in Ireland, which led him—at least for a time—to embrace an increasingly ultramontane Catholicism, even when this meant offending constituencies whom some of his Young Ireland colleagues were able to court. "I established a journal on reaching America," Michael Doheny would later quote him as saying, "and whereas my spine is not made of whalebone nor my conscience of indiarubber, I spoke the truth as I knew it in all things freely—thereby offending diverse parties. This, I believe, could not be helped."[78] It is also worth noting that, in this regard, McGee was not an outlier among Irish Catholics in the United States; in many ways, his embrace of ultramontanism represented the general direction of Irish Catholicism, which Colin Barr has described as "Hiberno-Romanism" and "was itself a subset of a wider neo-ultramontanism that swept the Catholic Church in the nineteenth century."[79] In fact, McGee ultimately had to leave Boston because, as the *American Celt* became increasingly more ultramontane, it entered into direct competition with the established *Boston Pilot*, to which he had contributed in the early 1840s; there were simply not enough readers to support them both. At the behest of the Catholic bishop of Buffalo, John Timon, he then moved to Buffalo, New York, which was booming at the time, and where the absence of ultramontane competition ensured his newspaper's continued success.[80]

In part, the retreat into ever-greater orthodoxy by American Catholics—particularly Irish Catholics, including McGee—was in response to nativism. Nativist politics centered around New York and Philadelphia,[81] both of which had large Irish populations, and, while mostly peaceful, it caused occasional outbreaks of violence.[82] Nativism was initially politically organized as the (to modern eyes ironically named) Native American Party and renamed the American Party; they were most commonly known, however, as the Know-Nothings.[83] Know-Nothings premised their critique of Catholicism on the claim that Catholic loyalty to the Pope and the Church made them incapable of participating in American democracy.[84] It should be noted that such logic was far from unique to the United States in the 1850s.[85]

For the Irish in the United States, this situation was particularly acute after the Famine, because it was increasingly assumed that "most Irish migrants had been paupers at home," which fueled prejudices against Irish Catholic migrants of all classes.[86] An overall slowdown in the US economy, beginning in 1854, exacerbated these prejudices; by December 1854, for instance, less than one-fifth of building workers in New York were employed in their trade.[87] Nativism would become a less potent political force after peaking in 1855, when emigration to the United States dropped sharply.[88] Many nativists in the latter half of the 1850s transferred to the Republican Party, even though it "made no concessions to them in their platform."[89] Nevertheless, in spite of the short period in which nativists wielded significant political power, the experiences of the late 1840s and early 1850s created a lasting sense of grievance against them among the Catholic Irish American community.

It is against the background of nativism and the global Catholic move toward ultramontanism that we must read McGee's experiences in the United States. The discrimination faced by Irish Catholics forced McGee to revisit his *A History of the Irish Settlers in North America, from the Earliest Period to the Census of 1850*. In an appendix that he wrote in May 1852 and added to all later editions, his celebratory tone changed, as he became increasingly alarmed that the pressures of discrimination and the allure of assimilation was diminishing what he saw as the defining characteristic of the Irish—their religion. "The first Irish generation in America can be traced very easily from the side of the emigrant ship to the interior," he wrote. "They can be told by their faces, habits, speech, and old religion; for wherever they are, the cross is the sign under which they conquer. But their children, born twenty and thirty years ago, in this land, where are they? If we look for them in our churches, we do not find them."[90] It was this combination of forces that led McGee to begin to think that the best way for Irish Catholics to counter the effects of bigotry and assimilation in the United States and continue to "conquer under the sign of the cross" was to move to an area in which Irish Catholics could be in a majority. One option was to create an Irish colony in the American West. The other option was Canada.

In Canada, the presence of a large French-speaking Catholic population had many of the accommodations for Catholics, such as separate schools and political organizations, that McGee thought would arrest the decline of Catholicism among the Irish community in the United States. In actual fact, there were considerable tensions between Irish and Francophone Catholics in Canada (to be explored in chapter 5), but these did not seem to concern McGee, at least not initially. There was one major problem, however: Canada was part of the British Empire. It is indicative of McGee's priorities that he was willing to overlook this detail. Announcing that "the British flag does indeed fly there, but it casts no shadow," he emigrated to Canada in the spring of 1857, citing discrimination against Irish Catholics in the United States as one of the main factors behind his decision to leave.[91] In 1866, McGee would argue in a pamphlet published in Montréal that Fenianism had arisen in the United States out of a disillusionment with the country comparable to his own, because "the active spirits are conscious that, being Irish, they have no hopeful public career in the land of the 'Know-Nothings.'"[92]

Thomas Francis Meagher and Young America

The experiences of former Young Irelanders in America were not as bleak or as uniform as a simple reading of McGee's pamphlet would suggest, and in some ways those Irish immigrants with connections and some reputation—such as the exiled Young Ireland leaders—could exercise their social capital to establish themselves in political life as both Irish and American. One such Young Irelander was Thomas Francis Meagher. Although in many ways exceptional, he can be studied as an illustration of how some Irish Catholics climbed the ladder of American respectability and political influence. Meagher engaged in a particularly effective campaign of "self-fashioning," in the sense of the term coined originally by Stephen Greenblatt in reference to sixteenth-century England.[93] Through the American press and at public meetings, Meagher interwove his story with that of other Irish migrants to the United States during the 1850s and 1860s among whom he quickly established himself as a potential leader.

Meagher's escape from Van Diemen's Land in 1852 was widely reported and almost universally praised across the United States. One of the most commonly republished articles about him came from the *New York Herald*, which described his escape "from his own lips."[94] This allowed Meagher to shape the story of his getaway, to take control of a narrative that contained the potentially embarrassing implication that he might not have lived up to the ideal of the heroic rebel when he turned in his ticket of leave by post (rather than, say, staring down the constables with pistols drawn). Nonetheless, it was clear by implication that American readers knew of the controversy he had left behind him. The *Burlington Free Press*, for instance, republished a story that first appeared in the *Launceston Examiner* in Van Diemen's Land that was at pains to stress that "when the details are given it will be seen that O'Meagher [*sic*] did not compromise his parole"; the allegations, the paper assured Vermont readers, "have no imputation on the personal honour of the 'Irish rebel.'"[95] For the most part, however, the American press was content to overlook Meagher's use of the post office to effect his escape and instead embraced him as a new military hero, with an emphasis on his masculine qualities. In June 1852, the *Baton-Rouge Gazette*, for instance, told its readers that the *New York Daily Times* "says that Mr. Meagher is a gentleman of marked ability—great frankness and manliness of character, and of easy, quiet, and polished manner."[96] That same month, the *Weekly National Intelligencer* in Washington, DC, declared that Meagher delivered his speeches "in a truly eloquent and manly strain."[97] In 1853, New York's *Illustrated News* wrote of Meagher's "florid complexion and manly bearing."[98] This portrayal of Meagher as an honorable man of action can be seen as a continuation of the argument made by Young Ireland in Ireland in the 1840s that sought to counter the portrayal of Irishmen as subservient (and therefore emasculated) figures who could not participate in self-government—except, in this case, it was directed against the image, portrayed by Know-Nothing politicians, of impoverished Irish immigrants.

Once in the United States, Meagher embarked upon a speaking tour, which was also widely covered in American newspapers. The *New York Times* reported in 1853 that "Thomas Francis Meagher, the Irish patriot and orator, lectured . . . upon the subject of 'Irish politics in 1848'" in New Haven, Connecticut.[99] Early in his time in the United States, Meagher often returned to subjects upon which he had lectured in Ireland, particularly where these dovetailed with American political concerns. One letter to the *Portsmouth Inquirer* argued (erroneously) that Meagher's speeches about protectionism in Ireland had sought free trade for Ireland rather than tariffs on English manufactures, but nevertheless praised a speech that they had—perhaps willfully—misunderstood.[100] The *New York Daily Times* described Meagher as a man "who has given . . . unquestionable proofs of his devotion to the welfare of his country."[101] He won similar plaudits in Louisville, Kentucky, where his speech was described as containing "delicate yet graphic touches, such fervour, such fire."[102] In New Orleans, "at the particular request of the citizens Mr. Meagher delivered a lecture on Monday night, on the political affairs of Ireland in 1848."[103] Moreover, the increasing connectedness of the American press, assisted by the telegraph, meant that a speech given on one side of the continent could be reported on the other—as did, for instance, the *Weekly Pacer Herald* of Auburn, California, on a speech Meagher delivered in Boston in August 1853.[104]

We can understand Meagher's speeches and their reporting as part of a process of what Tom Wright has recently called "cultivating an

Irish American counterpublic and group identity": an alternative public sphere that operated outside of, and challenged the cultural norms of, the dominant "Anglo-American commons" that had previously dominated speech-making and cultural production in the United States.[105] They did so by "promoting a distinct brand of international solidarity based on the progress of global republican ideals, and a cultural worldview that turned away from the hierarchies and symbolism of Britain."[106] In an environment in which the public sphere was increasingly moving away from British influences, Meagher, whose arguments seemed inspired by American conceptions of democracy, managed to make his message—and himself—relevant to a broader audience who sought to move American culture and politics toward a distinctly American cultural and political sphere. In effect, Meagher helped to create a new geography of political ideas, in which Ireland and the United States were contiguous republics (or, in Ireland's case, an aspiring republic). Moreover, the extent to which his speeches were reported on by newspapers outside of the cities in which they were made suggests that Meagher himself, rather than the meetings, provided the primary point of interest. While his speaking tour helped to establish his reputation as a leader among Irish Americans, that reputation ultimately rested on the cultural capital he had generated through his actions in Ireland in the 1840s.

No less than Mitchel's or McGee's, Meagher's reception in the United States was defined by ongoing political debates within the country. Nativism provided one such context, but so, too, did the Young America movement, in a way that particularly suited the image Meagher sought to project. Young America drew inspiration from a number of European movements of the same name; at the same time, following through on the nationalist logic of those movements led this faction within the Democratic Party to seek to define a specifically American ideology that was forward looking and future oriented.[107] At one level, this might seem paradoxical—following a European model to create something distinctly American—but it had a logic. It was in their orientation toward the future that the Young Americans saw themselves make an ideological break with Europe. In a speech at New York University on 30 June 1845, the influential writer and editor Cornelius Matthews proclaimed: "Whatever that past generation of statesmen, law-givers and writers was capable of, we know. What they attained, what they failed to attain, we also know. Our duty and our destiny is another from theirs. Liking not at all its borrowed sound, we are yet (there is no better way to name it), the Young America of the people: a new generation; and it is for us now to inquire, what we may have it in our power to accomplish, and on what objects the world may reasonably ask that we should fix our regards."[108]

What connected Young Ireland and Young America was the self-consciousness with which they spoke for a new generation who believed themselves destined to create a new culture and politics. This would have been as familiar to those who had read Young Ireland's "Prospectus of the Nation"[109] as it would have been to those who attended Ralph Waldo Emerson's influential lecture in Boston in February 1844 where he used the term "Young America" for the first time.[110] Emerson told his listeners: "It is remarkable, that our people have their intellectual culture from one country, and their duties from another. This false state of things is newly in a way to be corrected."[111] Again, anyone paying attention to events in Ireland that year would have heard something very similar. In their turn, the Young Irelanders in America picked up this rhetoric, with McGee arguing in his *History of the Irish Settlers in North America* that "it is not worthy of this great nation to take its political philosophy second-hand from any nation."[112] In believing that America needed to develop its own intellectual culture, distinct from European culture (in particular English culture) and that this would educate the American public, Emerson and other Young Americans were as much cultural nationalists as their Irish contemporaries were. Accordingly, in addition to Emerson, they counted among their numbers authors like William Cullen Bryant, George Bancroft, Herman Melville, and Nathaniel Hawthorne, all of whom sought to create a uniquely American literature.[113] As well as attracting an impressive array of writers, Democratic politicians who associated themselves with the Young America movement managed to climb to the top of the American political ladder. These included James K. Polk, who was US president from 1845 to 1849, followed four years later by Franklin Pierce, who was president from 1853 to 1857. They shared with their literary colleagues a rejection of "European" (often a synonym for "English") cultural and political models in favor of American models; as such, the Young American movement produced fertile soil for a Young Irelander abroad such as Thomas Francis Meagher.

Soon after his arrival in the United States, Meagher wrote an article for the *United States Magazine and Democratic Review*, one of the principal exponents of Young Americanism, which had been founded by an Irishman, John O'Sullivan, who edited the magazine until 1846. Like *The Nation* in Ireland, the *Review* had both cultural and political goals and to this end published a combination of literature and writing about politics, both of which were essential in shaping Young America's view of the world.[114] In an article that offered American readers a view of the Young Ireland perspective via an account of his own escape from Van Diemen's Land, Meagher wrote that "the English aristocracy are memorable jailors."[115] He went on to make the statement that the English people are "more degraded, and more indifferent to liberty than any other in Europe."[116] This criticism of the British state and of English "liberty" was, of course, a message to which Young America was very receptive. Meagher continued by arguing that the ultimate goal of the Young Irelanders, who "have most anxiously and nobly endeavoured to break down this British embargo upon a nation's life," was "to throw open Europe to the world through Ireland."[117] At a stroke, Meagher connected the Irish cause to a wider, global liberation movement, of which Young America considered itself the vanguard. In doing so, he added to a historical narrative that included Doheny's *History of the American Revolution* and would be developed in McGee's *History of the Irish Settlers* and that integrated Irish and American history into the same tale of liberation. At the same time, he tapped into one of the most potent of the Young Americans' ideas: manifest destiny.

Manifest Destiny

It was the *Democratic Review*, a periodical founded by an Irishman for which Meagher wrote, that generated a phrase in the American political vocabulary that would reverberate in our own times. The term "manifest destiny"—a concept later given particular political force by President Polk—was probably coined by the paper's founder, John O'Sullivan, who wrote in 1845: "Our manifest destiny to overspread the continent allotted by Providence for the free development of our yearly multiplying millions."[118] This idea became central to the way Americans understood settler colonialism in the American West. Manifest destiny was rooted not only in the geographical possibility of American expansion westward but also in the powerful notion that American expansion was "a divine agent in the historical redemption of humanity," which thus obligated America to civilize and democratize the world.[119] At its core was an inherently racist idea that the existing population of Native Americans in the American West was either irrelevant, or else needed to be civilized. Notwithstanding, the idea became popular across the political spectrum, and, in the context of the 1840s, the Young American's conception of democracy was broad based and radical, even if also selective and exclusive of African Americans and Native Americans.[120] Moreover, while O'Sullivan and the term's main proponents were Democrats, Whigs like Horace Greeley (who had sponsored Meagher's newspaper enterprise) adopted a similar approach to American expansion.[121] Greeley was famous for popularizing the slogan "Go West, young man, go West and grow up with the country."[122] The widespread popularity of—and agreement on—the ideas behind American expansion meant that Irish people in the United States could adopt and adapt those ideas for their own purposes, aided by the perception of Irish nationalists as akin to American nationalists in their shared rejection of what both saw as British constraints on liberty. Meagher and the Young Irelanders could thus work with both key Democrats and key Whigs (many of whom later became Republicans as American political parties took their modern forms); indeed, some former Young Irelanders, including Meagher, would switch their allegiance to the Republican Party at the beginning of the Civil War.

It was the key word "liberty" that justified expansion for believers in the doctrine of manifest destiny. For instance, O'Sullivan would celebrate "the right of our manifest destiny to overspread and to possess the whole of the continent which Providence has given us for the development of the great experiment of liberty and federated self-government entrusted to us."[123] Meagher can also be seen reflecting this idea in a speech in New York to the Common Council of Brooklyn in June 1852, when he told his audience that "I foresee that America will be the visible providence of the world, and that whilst she encourages the weak, the struggling and the oppressed, she will augment her own power of doing good by winning the confidence and love of every race. Thus will be accomplished the freedom of the world."[124] This was a consistent line of argument for Meagher. For instance, on 26 May 1853, the *New York Daily Times* reported on a speech for "the Benefit of the New-York Volunteers, at Metropolitan Hall."[125] In it Meagher told his audience:

> May that flag never fail to find less eager champions than you have been, to shield it from disgrace, and bear it like a charmed robe, unhurt through the flames of war. May that flag never lose one star; but as the Old Thirteen have multiplied in time, may others no less brilliant be added thereto; and may the constellation, which first shone out through the tempest and the lightnings, and has now become fixed in the blue expanse of peace, on every sea be seen; and may the nations journeying, like the kings of old, to a nobler worship, be led to a new faith and destiny by the light it gives![126]

Meagher's forceful embrace of the concept of manifest destiny included not only Oregon and Utah but also Ireland as a site for "the historical redemption of mankind" in the irresistible march of "a new faith and destiny."[127]

As much as Meagher would like to align Young Ireland and Young America, certain differences could not be overlooked. For instance, unlike the Young Irelanders, the Young Americans did not have the same access to narratives of past glories other than those relating to the moment of revolution in 1776. Instead, Young America argued that the future was central to how they understood the place of the United States in world history. O'Sullivan wrote that the "the expansive future is our arena, and for our history. We are entering on its untrodden space."[128] Part of O'Sullivan's forward-looking view can be explained in terms of the relatively short history of European settlements in North America; indeed, the longer history of the western part of the continent properly belonged to the Native Americans, the very people who would be dispossessed by westward expansion. This left less scope to mythologize the distant past in the same way that Young Ireland had done in Ireland. A forward-looking nationalism, on the other hand, justified the processes of settler colonialism at the center of the idea of manifest destiny. This combination had an enduring effect on the Young Ireland generation, reorienting their sense of political narrative. For instance, in a collection of annotated newspaper clippings from around the world that he kept throughout much of his life, Charles Gavan Duffy noted at a point in the 1860s: "Every American looks as if his eyes were gazing into the far West and the far future."[129] The idea that Americans looked toward the future was especially appealing for the Young Ireland generation, for whom the writing of history had always been instrumental, more concerned with creating a future than with preserving what they saw as the vestiges of a culture largely occluded by colonization. Encountering a country in which it could be made to appear that there was no history so overwhelming that it required rewriting must have seemed like an entirely new kind of freedom.

Race played a fundamental role in justifying manifest destiny. At its core was the idea that the Caucasian race was destined to bring democracy and liberty to the American continent.[130] However, as previously discussed, Americans were divided as to whether this predestinate people was confined to Anglo-Saxon Protestants; the intellectual basis for manifest destiny and Young Americanism included groups like the National Reform Association, which advocated for broad land distribution as key to the health of American democracy (as Duffy would argue for Australia).[131] Manifest destiny, therefore, clearly had scope to be a more inclusive ideology. Understandably, the Young Irelanders took a wide view as to who and what it included. One implication of this wider interpretation was that it allowed for a significantly more geographically expansive understanding of America's destiny, and the Young Ireland generation were some of the first to argue for its transatlantic nature. If American democracy and liberty were not the unique characteristics of the Anglo-Saxon race, this made possible the admission of the Republic of Texas to the Union (strongly supported by O'Sullivan), or even the annexation of Mexico. Nativist supporters of the Anglo-Saxon Protestant conception of manifest destiny would view these prospects with alarm, fearful of the effects of an "influx of dark-skinned Catholics" on the Union.[132] Likewise, for the adherents of a manifest destiny based on Anglo-Saxon superiority, Native Americans could never embrace American ideals of liberty and democracy; thus, American expansion required a policy of "Indian removal," a form of ethnic cleansing in which indigenous people were either forcibly removed from their land or massacred.[133] By contrast, for O'Sullivan or Meagher, in order to make a place for Irish Catholics in America, it was necessary to have an understanding of manifest destiny that at least allowed for the possibility that, by embracing American ideals of liberty and democracy, anyone could become American.

In choosing to align themselves with Young America and, in particular, O'Sullivan's interpretation of both Young America and manifest destiny, the Young Ireland generation made a conscious ideological choice that is consequential for our understanding of their political thought in Ireland. O'Sullivan, a liberal, saw liberalism as the ideological force that connected Young America with its European counterparts, including Young Ireland.[134] It is worth considering why the majority of the Young Ireland generation aligned themselves closely with American liberalism, when the United States also had strong republican and democratic traditions with which they could also have aligned themselves. Given their reticence with regard to democracy in Ireland, it is easy to see why it was unlikely that they would have fully embraced universal democracy along American lines. However, given the common association between Young Ireland and republicanism, it is curious that when placed in an environment in which a whole-hearted embrace of republicanism was possible, most of them (Mitchel was a particularly notable exception) instead choose liberalism. That they made such a choice in the United States, where they had the freedom to choose, shows the extent to which liberalism was at the core of their politics in Ireland.

It was in such an environment that for Meagher the concept of manifest destiny became more than simply rhetoric or even an idea, leading to his participation in a number of colonial schemes. In particular, he became involved with the wealthy Philadelphian shipbuilder Ambrose W. Thompson, who was the instigator of a scheme of informal imperialism in Central America, a plan to build a railway across Chiriquí in modern-day Panama to connect the Pacific and Atlantic Oceans. The plan attracted more official support when Thompson convinced Abraham Lincoln, then president of the United States, that freed slaves could be offered land there. Indeed, Meagher, in an 1859 letter to John F. Boyle—a friend of Lincoln's successor Andrew Johnson[135]—portrayed the scheme as an "opportunity offered by the White House."[136] By April 1862 Congress had appropriated money "to aid in the colonization and settlement of . . . free persons of African descent" in Central America.[137] As Thompson's agent, Meagher stood at the center of the attempted colonization. In 1859, the foreign minister of Costa Rica, Jesús Jiménez Zamora, wrote to Thompson to assure him that "Mr. Thomas Francis Meagher has placed in the hands of the Provincial President, your request directed to this Government, from . . . the 5th Sept."[138] Jiménez Zamora continued by telling Thompson that "verbal explanations have been made to Mr. Meagher" to "conclude with the constitutional Government the contract for Rail Road and colonization."[139] Although the scheme never came to pass, Meagher's involvement in it was consistent with his ideological affinity with Young Americanism. Meagher defended American colonialism in Central America by arguing that it was emancipatory. Speaking of William Walker's ill-fated colonization of Nicaragua, he contended that its intent was "to free the people, not to enslave them, and in his analysis Meagher firmly connected manifest destiny with notions of liberal imperialism.[140] When Meagher wrote about his experience in Chiriquí for *Harper's Magazine*, he described "the energy, quick intelligence, nerve and enterprise of Mr. Ambrose Thompson, Jun.—a young and successful representative of that spirit of practical and enlightened adventure which so strongly marks the American character and is destined to achieve for the American people so vast a measure of prosperity and national power."[141] The article did not just link Meagher's involvement with the Costa Rican scheme with the ideology of manifest destiny; he spoke, as always, as a Young Irelander. This in turn allowed Meagher to build a reputation as an effective colonist and a committed American, implicitly aligning these identities with Young Ireland.

Indeed, Meagher used his involvement in the Costa Rican scheme to further bolster his reputation by enhancing a heroic reputation that rested on his activities as a patriotic rebel in Ireland. It also helped that Meagher projected a particularly masculine self-image, as Amy Greenburg has detailed.[142] He published his account of his involvement in the Costa Rican scheme with an eye on a popular audience, presented so as to construct for its author "magisterial status," placing his exploits squarely within the genre of mid-nineteenth-century accounts of masculine adventuring in the imperial cause.[143] What are likely to have been his most widely read writings were published in *Harper's Magazine* in 1860, in which he depicted himself and his comrades as intrepid explorers hacking their way through exotic landscapes "with verdure so vivid and exuberant at their feet—with streams, so vitalizing and refreshing, breaking the paths their swords laid open."[144] Meagher's efforts to craft through writing an identity for himself in the United States can be considered an attempt at self-fashioning, although, in Meagher's case, with reference to masculine American ideals.[145] None of this was accidental; Meagher's contributions to *Harper's Magazine* were part of what can be seen as a conscious plan—along with what he described as "my visits to different parts of the Union" and "my well-known identification with American principles"—to make himself known to the wider American public.[146]

Mitchel, Meagher, and *The Citizen*

On 7 January 1854 the first issue of *The Citizen* newspaper was published in New York City, edited by John Mitchel, who was "assisted by Thomas Francis Meagher."[147] It was here that John Mitchel first published in serial form his hugely influential *Jail Journal.* According to contemporary US accounts, the paper was successful, with California's *Columbia Gazette* reporting in 1854 that "*The Citizen*, which was started with funds contributed by Meagher, has nearly paid for itself, and makes Mitchel well off."[148] The paper's name was no coincidence. *The Citizen* used its influence to advance an understanding of American citizenship that allowed the Irish to remain part of an increasingly global Irish nationalist community.

The front page of *The Citizen*'s first issue strongly reflected a concept of the place of the Irish in America that relied on ideas of manifest destiny. In its manifesto, *The Citizen* opined that "the movement of all the Western and Southern nations of Europe is towards Republicanism."[149] In a passage worth quoting at length, Mitchel argued that Irish people would be central to this expansion of Republicanism and democracy to Europe:

> Intending, themselves, to be true and loyal American citizens, they will recommend no course of policy which would isolate the Irish or other European refugees from the common action of this great Republic. They will inculcate, and with all their power assist, a careful, loving study of those wise

and just institutions under which, here in America, they have found both a refuge from their enemies, and a school and example of the grand doctrine they mean to enforce. To become in good faith citizens and armed soldiers of America, is to enlist under the banner of Universal Democracy.[150]

Moreover, the article continued by arguing that Mitchel and Meagher "will bear for ever in remembrance the heavy debt of gratitude which expatriated Irishmen owe to America, for her powerful protection and her ready sympathy; and will piously watch and prepare for an occasion to discharge that sacred debt."[151] Irish people could discharge this sacred debt by bringing democracy to Ireland, a process in which *The Citizen* saw itself as playing a part.

There was, however, a contradiction in the former Young Irelanders' embrace of manifest destiny. In promoting westward expansion (or, indeed, settlement in Costa Rica), Mitchel and Meagher were effectively encouraging imperialism, against which they had railed in Ireland. This was highlighted by another line in *The Citizen*'s manifesto that is typical of Mitchel's writing about England more generally. Referring to the "hypocritical British pretence to 'liberalism' made by the British government," Mitchel asserted that although Britain claimed it was spreading civilization and liberalism around the world, this was actually mere rhetoric and a mask for English power.[152] While Michel and Meagher's brand of anti-Englishness had broad appeal in the United States, particularly among the Young Americans, the argument that liberal ideals were simply a cloak for imperial conquest had the potential of backfiring: it could equally be applied to American claims about their own mission to spread democracy to new territories. However, they thought this a risk worth taking, for the embrace of American manifest destiny allowed them to make the argument that democracy would be carried to Ireland from America.

The Citizen thus claimed that it sought to unite Irish people with "votaries of Democracy militant in Europe, and of Democracy victorious in America" and to "help them in striking this alliance."[153] This transnational coalition may have been new, but *The Citizen* borrowed a number of key techniques from *The Nation* in making its claims. It had, for instance, a strong educational element, most explicitly instructional in the form of extracts from lectures by the former Young

Irelanders themselves, such as Mitchel's speech "The Position and Duties of European Refugees" from 1854.[154] In it, Mitchel outlined the duty that he believed "lies upon all naturalized citizens" of the United States to prove their loyalty in order to obtain citizenship.[155] "Citizenship (of what Commonwealth so ever it be) is a clear and precise idea," he contended.[156] "The Citizen, as a Citizen, belongs absolutely and exclusively to the State—that is to say, to the community which protects him, which gives him civic privileges, rights, and power, which guarantees to him the secure exercise of them by its laws, which guards the sacredness of home, and the quiet enjoyment of the fruits of his industry; that community has a clear title to his sole and undivided allegiance."[157] This understanding of citizenship reflected the oath taken by naturalizing citizens, as Meagher had on 9 October 1852, stating that "I, Thomas Francis Meagher, do declare, upon oath, that is, *bona fide*, my intention to become a citizen of the United States, and to renounce forever any allegiance to any foreign prince, potentate, or sovereignty, and particularly to the Queen of Great Britain and Ireland to whom I am now subject."[158] This conception of citizenship countered nativist fears that immigrants might harbor competing loyalties. The Irish—particularly those like Meagher who were both Catholic and had been convicted of treason felony against the crown—focused their concern on their religion, with many nativists arguing that "these Irish are not fit for Republicanism" because of their Catholicism.[159] While not Catholic himself, Mitchel contested such views forcefully: "That conclusion I take the liberty of calling stark nonsense. . . . Republicanism is not so sensitive a thing."[160] Instead, Mitchel proposed that "we act in the affairs of our native country, and interest ourselves in her movements and her destinies precisely so far as a native-born citizen may properly do, as an American. and no farther. There is the simple rule."[161] From this line of argument, something very influential followed: for Irish people to become American, they had to prove their loyalty to the United States. If—as Meagher and Mitchel contended—Irish people in the United States could both retain an obligation toward advancing Irish independence and swear their loyalty to America, then the struggle for Irish independence was, by a stroke of associative logic, transformed into an American struggle.[162]

Conclusion

Returning to the lines that opened this chapter, the thread that binds together the story of the Young Irelanders in the United States is encapsulated in Meagher's forecast that "America will be the visible providence of the world," which would bring about "the freedom of the world."[163] In embracing both an American republican understanding of freedom and a belief—grounded in manifest destiny—that the United States was preordained to propagate it across the world, the Young Irelanders carved out a place for themselves in the United States by making Ireland part of that destiny. They argued and convinced influential Americans that their actions in Ireland during the 1840s were part of the same cause of expanding American democracy and freedom that was colonizing the western states. In doing so, the Irish exiles created a space in which Irish people could assert their Irish identity while at the same time affirming their claim to American nationality. As the United States moved toward Civil War in the opening years of the 1860s, many Irish people in America would seize the opportunity to prove their loyalty to the United States in more tangible form by joining the Union Army, acting on the belief that, in so doing, they were also fighting for Ireland. Even those Irish people who joined the Confederate Army (which they did in smaller numbers) fought for an idea of America. In both cases, the Young Irelanders in the late 1840s and 1850s helped to lay the intellectual, cultural, and political groundwork that would place Irish people at the center of the American national story during the war. At the same time, the American Civil War would push the tensions and contradictions that existed within Young Ireland well beyond the point of breaking.

On 21 September 1865, in a letter to secretary of state William H. Seward, the Fenian Brotherhood in Chicago wrote: "During the recent war for the preservation of the Union in America, and the preservation of liberty in the world, our organisation has given the best blood of our race, to the man, and in all its actions has pledged itself to the Union willing to live or die with American independence."[1] To many Irish people in the United States, not least the Brotherhood, the outbreak of the Civil War provided them with an opportunity to claim their place as US citizens.[2] The idea prevalent among Irish Americans that citizenship—and the democratic rights it entailed—were earned rather than inalienable had its roots in the ideas of Young Ireland in Ireland in the 1840s. As such, we must consider the previously unexplored origins of the Young Ireland conception of citizenship, and its development among the Irish in the United States in a period during which the understanding of US citizenship and nationality came under pressure from other quarters.

The inescapable event in this regard was the American Civil War, to which the Irish American response was complex. Most Irish people living in the United States lived in the Union States; however, there were Irish people—and members of the Young Ireland generation—fighting on both sides.[3] For many, the key issue came into focus with Abraham Lincoln's announcement in January of 1863 that "all persons held as slaves within any State or designated part of a State, the people whereof shall then be in rebellion against the United States, shall be then, thenceforward, and forever free."[4] For many Irish Americans, what they had seen as a more complex debate increasingly narrowed to a clash over abolition, an issue on which many were far more ambivalent than on defense of the union. This sense of ambivalence—and even outright hostility—was heightened by the announcement of a draft in May, 1863, which led to riots, some degenerating into race riots. The introduction of a draft on 3 May 1863 proved particularly galling for many working-class Irish people who understood "conscription as one of a train of wartime Republican assaults on their livelihood and culture."[5] Irish opposition to the draft was expressed most violently in a series of New York City draft riots on 11–16 July 1863, which "exhibited a virulent racism" extreme even by the standards of the American North, riven by conflicts over slavery.[6] While the protests may have started out as an objection to the draft, they quickly turned into race riots. Many poor and working-class Irish directed their anger at Black New Yorkers instead of at the Republicans who had imposed the draft.

There were a number of complex causes for these events, but many Irish people seemed concerned that "emancipation would bring north hordes of low-wage black freedmen to compete for employment."[7] They viewed this through the lens of a political and "religious culture contemptuous of the Republicans and their black 'contrabands.'"[8] The rioters attacked and burned two Protestant churches, the homes of many Black people and abolitionists, and the Colored Orphans Asylum, buildings all "symbolic of black political, economic, and social power."[9] Over the course of five days, eleven Black men were lynched. The consequences of the draft riots would be felt long after they were subdued by Union soldiers. Many Black people left Manhattan and moved to other New York neighborhoods. The violence became evidence to many Americans of the disloyalty of Irish people more broadly.[10]

At the same time, by the 1860s, the composition of the Irish community in the United States was complex, and it would be a mistake to characterize the draft riots as reflecting the feelings of all poor and working-class Irish about the draft in particular and the Civil War in general. The official response to the draft riots involved large numbers of Irish policemen, and the Sixty-Ninth Irish Regiment played a key role in quelling the riots.[11] Moreover, outside of New York City, "Irishmen in Connecticut and Wisconsin remained steadfast in their support of the war."[12] These people were more upwardly mobile than the Irish in New York, and they lived in areas where the Irish were in a smaller minority.[13] Furthermore, among those Irish who held prominent positions in society and who did not fear competition from lower-paid Black labor, a number of important figures remained strongly committed to the Union throughout the war. One of the men who had been most vociferous in encouraging the Emancipation Proclamation was Horace Greeley, who wrote his influential "Prayer for Twenty Millions" in the *New York Tribune*, of which he was an editor. He argued that "every hour of deference to Slavery is an hour of added and deepened peril to the Union."[14] Just days before the draft riots, Greeley wrote to the Irish American Catholic archbishop of New York, John Hughes, asking him whether his "great influence" had been "steadily exerted in stern resistance" to the "un-Christian, inhuman spirit of negro hate."[15] Hughes, like many other members of the Irish American elites, held an ambiguous position on slavery, maintaining the "position that un-planned emancipation would counteract American constitutional pre-rogatives."[16] However, as a leading Irish Catholic, one of Hughes's top concerns was the integration of Irish people into American society, and he saw the Union and the Republic—and Irish professions of loyalty to both—as essential to achieving this aim.[17] This inclined him to throw his support fully behind the Union cause, even in the face of strong Irish Catholic opposition to the war. In short, when we focus on the Young Ireland generation's response to the war, we need to keep in mind the context in which they lived, in terms of an Irish American community whose reactions differed depending on geography as well as class.[18]

The 1860s in the United States has been described by Eric Foner as the decade of a "second founding," which "took place in response to rapidly changing political and social imperatives at a moment when definitions of citizenship, rights, and sovereignty were in flux."[19] The Young Ireland generation took an active role in this process of redefini-tion, capitalizing on the reputation they had built in the United States in the 1850s in order to function as leaders who could mediate between the Irish community and American political elites in a volatile political environment in the years leading up to and during the Civil War. If the Manhattan draft riots seemed to be shaping a narrative of the place of the Irish in American political culture, members of the Young Irelanders would be instrumental in shaping a counternarrative, in which service in the Union Army could be used as a means of claiming a national-ity that was simultaneously, and without contradiction, American and Irish. Building on service in the Union Army and relying on a collective desire to forget the ugly racial tensions of the draft riots, in the period immediately following the Civil War the Fenian Brotherhood sought to cast participation in militant Irish nationalism—and its stated aim of bringing about an American-style democratic republic in Ireland—as an expression of fealty to American ideals. Complicating this dynamic, however, was the nature of the Civil War itself, which, at its simplest, was about competing ideas of America. The question for the Young Irelanders thus became: Which America is Ireland's future?

John Mitchel and Slavery

The Young Ireland generation operated in an American public sphere in which slavery was increasingly the preeminent political controversy. This was not their instinctive political ground. Despite the fact that many of them personally objected to slavery, in Ireland the Young Irelanders had not taken the same abolitionist stance that made Daniel O'Connell— who famously argued that "Ireland and Irishmen should be foremost in seeking to effect the emancipation of mankind"—a global figure in the antislavery movement worldwide.[20] Frederick Douglass, by contrast, in his influential *Life and Times of Frederick Douglass*, remarked that Young Ireland was comprised of "men who loved liberty for themselves and their country, but were utterly destitute of sympathy with the cause of liberty in countries other than their own."[21] As these contrasting comments might suggest, slavery had in fact been a major source of conflict between Young Ireland and their O'Connellite predecessors. Moreover, some Young Irelanders had been happy to take money from slaveholding Irish Americans, whereas the followers of "The Liberator" were not, and O'Connell's lasting reputation in many parts of the world was as much due to his ardent work for the abolition of slavery as it was for repeal of the Union in Ireland.[22] For their part, Young Ireland tended to avoid the issue by arguing that the matter of slavery was not relevant for Ireland, and that abolitionism distracted from their ultimate goal of creating an Irish nation.[23] As a consequence, the topic seldom appeared in the pages of *The Nation*, and, among those associated with the newspaper, views on the issue differed from individual to individual. However, in the United States, where slavery stood at the center of political debate, this studied ambivalence would prove to be an impossible posture to maintain.

Figure 4.1. N. Currier, *John Mitchel: The First Martyr of Ireland in Her Revolution of 1848.*
New York, ca. 1848. Library of Congress Prints and Photographs Division, Washington, DC.

The Young Irelander who took the most firm public stance on slavery was John Mitchel. As early as 1852, Michel wrote to an Irish friend that he believed that "the grandest states & greatest & best nations have been slave holding states & nations."[24] It may well be that, here again, we see the influence of Carlyle (see chapter 1),[25] and it is likely that Mitchel would have been acquainted with Carlyle's argument made in a notoriously offensive pamphlet that if work was a moral good in its own right, then "white Europeans have a moral obligation to force labor from supposedly indolent Africans."[26] This is apparent even in the language in Mitchel's *Jail Journal*, where he writes of slavery in Brazil in a style very similar to Carlyle's. However, Mitchel differed from Carlyle in one crucial aspect, in that initially he pursued this logic to a conclusion that reversed the terms of imperial hegemony: he argued that rebellions by slaves against their owners in Pernambuco earlier in the nineteenth century might entitle them to liberty if repeated to greater success.[27] Of those insurrections, he wrote, "I see no great harm in this: the moment the black and brown people are able, they will have a clear right to exchange positions with the Portuguese race."[28]

Mitchel's apparently contradictory views on slavery go back to the same logic of power that drove him to armed rebellion amid the passive suffering of the Irish Famine. At the core of Mitchel's *Jail Journal* was what amounted to an article of belief: "Success confers every right in this enlightened age . . . success is right and defeat is wrong."[29] As Tony Hale has noted, Mitchel saw slavery as "a punishment for those without the will to assert their 'natural' rights. In this view of things, which Mitchel had originally articulated as a critique of colonialism, chattel slavery is an expression of inferiority in its 'natural' form.'"[30] In Ireland, this led Mitchel to take the raw logic of colonization—which insists that the colonizer's right to power is proven by the exercise of that power—and expose it, stripping it of its pretensions of virtue and turning it on its head, so that the obverse was also true: if Irish people fought for freedom, then they deserved freedom. If we follow through with this line of thought, Mitchel was perfectly willing to countenance a turning of the tables of power when it came to slavery in Brazil.

Once in the United States, however, where debates over the justification of slavery grew far more heated than they had ever been in Ireland, Mitchel appeared to abandon his original logic, and his attitude toward slavery hardened, so that eventually he refused to countenance the idea that slaves could earn their liberty, even by taking up arms.[31] This was far from a popular view in New York. For instance, *The Citizen* published an account of a meeting held by the New York Anti-Slavery Society at which speakers had highlighted some of the fundamental contradictions in Mitchel's stance: "Mr. Mitchel comes over here, and has the reputation of being a brave man; but here, the Irish Apostle is only the slaveholder's Paddy. The Emperor of Russia, even, had liberated some three millions of his slaves. What a contrast between the autocrat of Russia and the slaveholding democracy of the United States."[32] Nonetheless, slavery became an increasingly important issue for Mitchel, and in 1855 he left New York for the South, where his views received a warmer welcome.[33]

From that point on, Mitchel's attitude about slavery became more entrenched as his understanding of race changed. In Ireland, Mitchel often conceived of it as an underlying determinant of nationality; he wrote of "the primitive Irish race, proud, strong and vehement, tender and poetical."[34] Like many Europeans at the time, in Ireland Mitchel had used the term "race" to denote what the Young Irelanders also called "the spirit of the nation," which referred to an underlying collective essence.[35] In this, he was far from unique. Luke Gibbons has remarked that the core Young Ireland idea that the history of their country possessed "the unity and purpose of an epic poem" served as "a cue for *race* to enter the proceedings, securing the image of an embattled people surviving intact and maintaining unity in the face of two thousand years of upheaval, invasion and oppression."[36] To put it simply, the idea of an Irish race papered over the sectarian cracks in Irish history, although, as will become apparent, this expedient had its own pitfalls and would ultimately be modified by Young Irelanders such as Thomas Davis. Young Ireland's nationalism—to use a recent definition put forward by Metodi Siromahov, Michael Buhrmester, and Ryan McKay—understood the nation as "defined by some physical essence."[37] In Ireland, concepts based on a physical essence, a uniquely Irish race, could be subsumed within a historical narrative, and, hence, race could be contained in a concept of nationalism, without forcing its contradictions to the surface.[38] However, after Mitchel moved to the United States, a concept of race that in Ireland had been to a certain extent an instrumental and rhetorical gesture was placed in an entirely different context.

In response, Mitchel retreated into a position that Ivan Hannaford has argued was typical of the period: he came to see race as "immutable major divisions of humankind, each with biologically transmitted characteristics."[39] Like many, Mitchel considered these divisions of humanity not only immutable but also hierarchical. Again, in that moment, this was common intellectual currency with Tzvetan Todorov tracing the idea of a hierarchy of races back to its origins in the eighteenth century: "Faith in a rigid hierarchy of values, at the top of which sits European civilization, is common to many Encyclopaedists."[40] By the mid-1850s, Mitchel had accepted both the reality of immutable racial distinctions and their equally immutable hierarchical relations. Black people, he wrote, were destined to be slaves no matter what they did: "They are born and bred as slaves."[41] In 1855 he wrote to a correspondent in Ireland: "When any of your taunting friends asks you again (as you say they do) 'What do you think of Ireland's emancipation now? Wd. You like an Irish republic with an accompaniment of slave-plantations?'—just answer quite simply—Yes, very much. At least I would so answer—and I never said or wrote anything in the least degree inconsistent with such a declaration."[42] Whereas earlier he had been the most vocal proponent of an understanding of nationhood and the right to self-determination that was based on the belief that people could claim rights by resisting those who sought to take those rights away, now a biological understanding of race effectively subverted this earlier view, so that by the 1850s Mitchel insisted that freed slaves were not entitled to the rights of citizenship, no matter what they did, reversing the position he had held with respect to the rebelling Pernambuco slaves.

Mitchel's views on slavery may not have been unique, but they mattered because of his public profile. Whatever his attitude, he was still John Mitchel, the Young Irelander. This was true even as his support for slavery became extreme even by the standards of the American South; he went as far as advocating the reintroduction of the slave trade from Africa, which since 1808 had been prohibited by the American Constitution.[43] In his enthusiasm for the issue, Mitchel misrepresented his erstwhile comrades. In 1859, writing about "the revival of the African Slave-trade," Mitchel commented that "Wm. O'Brien, though he seems well content with the institution of slavery, hesitates as yet about the actual importation."[44] In fact, O'Brien, had written in 1854 that he "detested the institution," a view he had held for a long time. In Ireland, O'Brien had a reputation for "giving away copies of *Uncle Tom's Cabin*"—an important work of literature that drove support for abolition—to friends and acquaintances.[45]

While Mitchel's proslavery views alienated him from his former colleagues, they made him popular within Southern American political circles that supported slavery. Although Mitchel was not a Catholic and therefore did not face the same barriers as Thomas Francis Meagher when integrating into American society, his decision to leave the main Irish centers of New York, Philadelphia, Chicago, or Boston to Knoxville, Tennessee, in 1856 indicated that, in order to achieve prominence, he felt that he had to appeal to a different cross-section of society than the existing Irish American community.[46] To do so, Mitchel relied upon a tried-and-tested method that he had honed first in Ireland and again in New York: in Knoxville, he joined forces with that city's mayor, William Swan, and established a newspaper, the *Southern Citizen*, to promote "the value and virtue of slavery, both for negroes and white men."[47] In the present context, what makes this enterprise interesting is that the strategies Mitchel used were not dissimilar to those employed by Meagher when he pinned the Irish colors to the flagpole of manifest destiny. Basically, Mitchel encouraged his readers to see Ireland and the Confederate States in a similar light; as one of his nineteenth-century biographers put it, "both were rural societies unjustly oppressed by large, industrializing, foreign powers."[48] Mitchel even wrote that one of key goals of his *Southern Citizen* newspaper was "contending for the South as the Ireland of this continent."[49] His long-standing support for slavery offered him a means to do so, transcending barriers with which many of his fellow countrymen struggled. For instance, he told his friend Mary Thompson of his high standing among elites in the South, that "Southern judges, members of the legislature & no end of Southern Colonels. . . . welcomed me to the South—that they sympathised with me as a patriot & martyr, & admired me as a scholar & a gentleman—that they warmly approved my "conservative" principles (in the matter of slavery)."[50]

Mitchel was not alone in seeing a kinship between Ireland and the American South, or both as nations. As Paul Quigley puts it, for white Southerners from about 1848 until the end of the Civil War, the "grounds of nationhood" shifted.[51] As questions over slavery and abolition edged the South toward secession, white southerners changed their allegiances from the Union to the Confederacy, driven—as many scholars have argued—by a Southern nationalism grounded in support for slavery, rather than for states' rights.[52] These shifting allegiances required a conception of Southern nationality distinct from a wider American nationality, which created an opportunity for a Young Irelander such as Mitchel, who had prior experience in creating a secessionist nationalism. Nor was he alone: other Young Irelanders who took up the Confederate cause include Richard D'Alton Williams and Joseph Brenan, both of whom had joined Mitchel when he had left *The Nation* to found the *United Irishman* in 1848, with Brenan later continuing the paper as *The Irishman* after its suppression and Mitchel's arrest. Once in the United States, both Mitchel and Brenan attempted to use techniques that had been employed by Young Ireland in the 1840s to construct a sense of Southern nationalism, not least in the use of ballads to influence opinion.[53] Brenan even published a poem entitled "A Ballad for the Young South" in which Northern abolitionists were compared to Cromwellian soldiers, "in sanctimonious hordes.[54] Moreover, in titling the poem "A Ballad of the *Young South*," he consciously connected Southern nationalism with Young Ireland.

To the extent that Southern nationalism was founded on racial difference, attempts to align it with Irish nationalism exposed the racial aspect of Young Ireland nationalism that had long simmered as an unresolved contradiction. In the South, many of the political and plantation elites held to the view that Anglo-Saxon or Anglo-Norman heritage made them superior to those of mixed racial and ethnic heritage in the North. Such racial arguments posed a challenge for the Young Irelanders, who wanted to integrate the Irish into white Southern nationalism.[55] Before 1845, a constant theme in Young Ireland poetry and historical writing was the idea that there was an Irish nation that was distinct from Britain because Irish people were Celtic as opposed to Anglo-Saxon. Thomas Davis, in particular, contended that Ireland, where "three-fourths of the people are of Celtic descent," was entitled to independence for this reason.[56] However, even in the 1840s, this argument had problems. As Cian McMahon has shown, a series of editorials in the *Times* in August 1845 that attributed the Famine to the laziness of the Celts revealed a crucial flaw in Young Ireland's race-based thought.[57] If Ireland's Celtic racial foundation made it distinctive, then racial attributes could explain why Ireland, and not England, was suffering from famine. This observation accelerated an awareness of the weakness in relying too strongly on the idea of race. This weakness developed into a distinctive ambiguity—one might even say constructive incoherence—that had emerged in Young Ireland's writing in relation to race in 1844. In the introduction to a collection of his poetry, Davis, for instance, wrote influentially that while Celts and Saxons were essentially different, they could nonetheless live together in harmony, and that an Irish literature and an Irish history would "create a race of men full of a more intensely Irish character and knowledge" that would eventually combine the two.[58] By the same token, we find Davis writing in the poem "Celts and Saxons," published in *The Nation* in April 1844: "If you're to Ireland true, / We heed not blood, nor creed, nor clan."[59] Here, Davis insists on the Celt/Saxon distinction and, in the same gesture, relegates it to secondary importance, where both are subsumed by an "Ireland" capable of accommodating both without overturning the core nonsectarian, nonethnic aspect of the Young Ireland project. In Ireland, Mitchel had subscribed to this position, writing in 1845 that "the several races that now occupy Irish soil, and are known to all the world besides, as Irishmen."[60]

In the United States in the 1850s, however, Davis's old colleague Mitchel adopted a version of the Celtic racial thesis that stripped it of its ambiguity, writing in *The Citizen* in 1856 that "the Scoto-Irish were purely Celtic."[61] In order to reconcile this racial understanding of Irish people with the racial narrative of Southern superiority, Mitchel found himself forced to confront the dominant racial thesis directly; he argued that "American political culture was a Celtic, as opposed to Saxon, inheritance."[62] This was a far from an unproblematic stance. The contradictions in Mitchel's racism became particularly pronounced after the end of the Civil War, in which two of Mitchel's own sons had died fighting for the Confederacy. After 1865, Mitchel became even more severe in his racial views, refusing to accept Black people as equal citizens. Writing in the anti-Reconstruction New York newspaper *Irish Citizen*,

Mitchel declared that having "black barbarians as fellow citizens [imposed a further outrage] upon the already more than sufficiently humiliated community."[63] Part of the force of Mitchel's rhetoric in his journalism of the 1840s, as well as in both his *Jail Journal* (1854) and his polemical history *The Last Conquest of Ireland (Perhaps)* (1861), comes from the way in which he reverses this equation. In 1847, for instance, Mitchel wrote that "as for us expatriated and exterminated Irish . . . our enemy pursues us . . . until Ireland shall become, as Scotland is, a contented province of the British Empire, thoroughly subdued, civilized, emasculated, and 'ameliorated.'"[64] The force of Mitchel's anti-imperial rhetoric comes from being able to subvert—and invert—the language of imperialism itself; to "civilize" is to conquer, while to "ameliorate" is to eliminate, and the distinction between "civilian" and "barbarian" collapses. It is this criticism of the civilizing mission of imperialism that has ensured the endurance of Mitchel's work in Irish anticolonial thought.[65] According to his own earlier logic, the approximately 198,000 Black soldiers who had fought for the Union would surely have disproved the thesis that Black people were inherently submissive or barbaric (even if that misconstrues the term) and thus were entitled to citizenship.[66] Where the Mitchel of the 1840s and of the *Jail Journal* could be, alternately, accommodating of difference or radically subversive by deconstructing the opposition between civilians and barbarians, the Mitchel after 1865 advocated for a rigid hierarchy of race in which a barbarian was a barbarian; what before had been shades of gray became a matter of black and white.

After the Civil War, Mitchel spent a brief period writing for anti-Reconstruction newspapers in New York, leading to his arrest and imprisonment at Fortress Monroe in June 1865, which finally made him reevaluate his involvement in American politics.[67] As Bryan P. McGovern has argued, it was clear that Mitchel's devotion to the Confederacy had its limits, in spite of losing two sons to the cause.[68] In prison, he contracted tuberculosis, which permanently damaged his health. After his release was secured by Fenians and the prominent Irish American Richard O'Gorman, Mitchel traveled from New York to Paris, where he worked as a Fenian agent. While Mitchel would continue to play an important role in Irish nationalist thought, his influence on wider American politics diminished after he settled in France.

Thomas Francis Meagher

Although John Mitchel and Thomas Francis Meagher were colleagues who had been closely aligned on the question of the legitimacy of the use of violence to attain national sovereignty in Ireland, it would be difficult to imagine their positions on the American Civil War diverging more widely. In 1879, late in life, Meagher would call Mitchel the man entitled to be "worshipped as the first citizen of our free and sovereign state."[69] Thirty years earlier, following the 1848 rebellion, they had both been transported to Van Diemen's Land, and later, in New York, they founded *The Citizen* together. This makes it all the more remarkable that during the Civil War the two men took opposite sides. Whereas Mitchel based his support of the Confederacy on his support of slavery, Meagher was equally strident in his backing of the Union; his opposition to slavery may have been, in Ian Delahanty's words, "tepid," but by 1861 his commitment to the idea of the Republic was very public and deeply rooted, and it was on this basis that he set out to recruit for the Union Army.[70]

Figure 4.2. N. Currier, *General Meagher at the Battle of Fair Oaks, Va., June 1st 1862*. New York: N. Currier, ca. 1862. Library of Congress Prints and Photographs Division, Washington, DC.

During the Civil War, Meagher's established reputation as a leader of the Irish American community made him attractive to the Union Army. The War Department considered his first foray into military leadership, as the captain of an Irish Zouave (light infantry) unit at Bull Run, militarily unsuccessful; however, they noticed that he was highly effective in recruiting Irish Americans to the Union cause.[71] This was particularly important because the natural sympathies of many Irish in America were to the Democratic Party; hence, many were "suspicious of a war sponsored by the Republican Party."[72] In order to draw Irish Americans to the side of the Union, in February 1862 Meagher was made a brigadier general of the Irish Brigade, which was composed of five predominantly Irish regiments, including the Sixty-Ninth Infantry Regiment. As an officer, the former Young Irelander—who was allegedly often drunk—lacked strategic and military competence.[73] Nevertheless, Meagher used his carefully fostered reputation as an Irish revolutionary to highlight his commitment to the ideal of the American Republic, which made him a highly effective recruiter.[74] He was also an experienced and persuasive public speaker. In his recruitment work, he emphasized that Irish people needed to defend the American Constitution from those who sought to break up the Union because that Constitution protected Irish Catholics against nativism—an argument to which many Irish Americans were susceptible.[75] Therefore, we find colleagues of Meagher such as Joseph B. Tully, the quartermaster of the Sixty-Ninth Regiment, proclaiming that "it is the duty of every liberty-loving citizen [to] endorse the policy that maintains the laws."[76] The success of such arguments, the promise of a steady paycheck, and the efforts of celebrity recruiters like Meagher all contributed to the enlistment in the Union Army of about 150,000 Irishmen, many of whom volunteered for duty, compared to 25,000 Irishmen who had fought for the Confederacy by the end of the war.[77]

The service of Irish Americans on the victorious side of the Civil War provided them with an opportunity to counter "in blood" some of the narratives that had fueled nativism and anti-Catholic prejudice in the United States. In particular, it responded to the belief that Irish Catholics were "disloyal," and that they posed an inherent threat to American democracy. Meagher, one of the most prominent and vigorous proponents of this powerful counterargument, boasted that "a thousand fields now billowed with Irish graves, [and] declare[d] that love for Ireland blends in ecstasy with loyalty to America."[78] After Meagher's speech, secretary of state William Seward told him in a letter: "I think that the young persons to whom it is addressed may find in its happy expression much encouragement to pursue honourable aims with determination and enterprise."[79] In doing so, Meagher and other Irish American leaders with whom he was aligned "promoted a broader concept of American nationalism that challenged nativism and incorporated immigrants and Catholics based on devotion to the republic, into their definition of the American people."[80] Samantha Bruce has argued that "Irish bravery in service to America" challenged prejudice and improved "the image of the Irish among native-born and Irish Americans."[81] A definition of Americanness based on devotion to American ideals allowed Irish communities to retain their distinctive traditions by making Irish values American values (and vice versa). Meagher was a central figure in articulating this position. In the middle of the Civil War, he wrote a pamphlet that was intended to garner support and recruits for the Sixty-Ninth Regiment, in which he remarked: "At 12 o'clock the Green Flag was planted on the deserted ramparts of the Confederates at Germantown, the Stars and Stripes were lifted opposite to it at a distance of fifteen paces, and between two beautiful and inspiring symbols—the one of their old home and the other of their new country—the 69th passed in triumph."[82] The imagery of the symbols of both Ireland and the United States flying beside one other did more than the immediate pragmatic work of motivating Irish Americans to join the conflict: it provided a lasting symbol of the ideological convergence that made it possible to be both Irish and American.[83]

The obverse of this image of the flags flying side-by-side is the implication that if the Union Army thought it could make use of Meagher, Meagher thought that he could make use of the Union cause. In this respect, the aims of Mitchel and Meagher converge, even if their means could not have been more opposed. Mitchel had attempted to draw the parallel between Ireland and the American South as traditional societies threatened by the same rationalizing utilitarianism, which had produced workhouses in Famine Ireland. Meagher, by contrast, connected fighting for the Union with protecting the ideals of American democracy and liberty, which would eventually extend across the Atlantic to

Ireland, in an expansive, global version of manifest destiny (see chapter 3). Meagher forcefully made the argument that "the Republic, that gave us an asylum and an honorable career,—that is the mainstay of human freedom, the world over—is threatened with disruption. It is the duty of every liberty-loving citizen to prevent such a calamity at all hazards. Above all is it the duty of us Irish citizens, who aspire to establish a similar form of government in our native land. It is not only our duty to America, but also to Ireland. We could not hope to succeed in our effort to make Ireland a Republic without the moral and material aid of the liberty-loving citizens of these United States."[84] Later, Meagher would go even further, asserting that the Irish who had fought in the Union Army actually rendered "moral and material aid" to the cause of Irish independence by reflecting "the radiance of a transfiguration upon Ireland, the enslaved."[85] Just as the 1848 rebellion had never been about achieving a military victory but about reclaiming a moral high ground, almost twenty years later Meagher applied the same narrative to the US Civil War: the Irish men and women who supported the Union Army were, in effect, fighting for Ireland.

As had been the case in Ireland, in the United States, Meagher supported the idea that Irish people could claim the rights of citizenship. For Mitchel (in the 1840s, at any rate), they could do this by fighting directly to dominate; for Meagher, they did this by fighting for the institutions that guaranteed the rights pertaining to citizenship. This argument was especially effective because of the particular window of opportunity offered by the Civil War. As one might expect, the question of loyalty—and its relationship to notions of citizenship and Americanness—was intensified by such a divisive conflict. This fusion of loyalty and citizenship in Civil War America proved short lived, soon to be replaced by universal citizenship with the passing of the Fourteenth Amendment in 1868,[86] which declared that "all persons born or naturalized in the United States, and subject to the jurisdiction thereof, are citizens of the United States.[87] However, the belief would persist that, in fighting for the Union, the Irish units in the Union Army had made a place in the narrative of American history for the Irish in America; not only was Meagher crucial in shaping that narrative, but he would also follow through his position in the immediate postwar period.

Montana

The final chapter in Meagher's career involved a combination of his experiences in Ireland and in the United States. In 1865, when the Civil War ended, he was made acting governor of Montana Territory. Here, as in the war, Meagher embraced a powerfully interventionist national government. Indeed, in terms of the American West, the United States can be seen as an imperial state, with a distant center exerting considerable power over the peripheries through the acquisition of territory and the subjugation of Native Americans.[88] The West was both the real and the imagined epitome of the American commitment to individual rights and private property.[89] It made sense, then, that Meagher saw it as a place in which Irish people, among others, could assert the rights they had earned. Although Montana was not a particularly coveted post, Meagher still used the role to promote the territory as a place where Irish Catholics and other marginalized groups could settle, free from the sectarian prejudices prevalent on the East Coast.[90] As he had attempted to do in Costa Rica, Meagher again engaged in colonialism, this time with Irish immigrants. What is noteworthy is Meagher's contention that Montana was also the perfect place for "the Black heroes of the Union Army": the African American veterans who, he believed, "have not only entitled themselves to liberty but to citizenship," and to settle there as well.[91] He nearly echoed Frederick Douglass, who had written in 1863: "Once let the black man get upon his person the brass letters US, let him get an eagle on his button, and a musket on his shoulder, and bullets in his pocket, and there is no power on the earth or under the earth that can deny that he has earned the right to citizenship."[92] Thus, it was in Montana that Meagher, who had not long before run a newspaper with John Mitchel, came to argue for full citizenship for Black Americans. In short, Meagher saw Montana as a place where all those who believed in, and had fought for, America could exercise the rights for which they had gone to battle.

This is not to say that Meagher's concept of citizenship by the late 1860s was entirely inclusive. For instance, it was highly gender specific, not only privileging masculine martial values but also excluding women, who were forbidden from enlisting in the army.[93] To some extent, Meagher's image of citizenship reflected his own self-image as manly, courageous, and adventuresome; as he told a crowd in Virginia City in 1865, "intellect and manhood" would secure the Montana Territory.[94] Completing this logic, in 1853 he had argued with respect to Ireland that the female contribution to the struggle for Irish independence was the "silent prayer of womanhood."[95] This at least posits some role for women and stands in sharp contrast to Mitchel's notion of slavery, which, in the United States, had cast Black people as submissive and effeminate and, as such, inherently unfit for citizenship.[96]

The issue of gender aside, it was in Montana that we can see the beginnings of an understanding of citizenship based on criteria other than ethnonationalism, put into practice by a former Young Irelander for the benefit of people who were not Irish, including, eventually, the original inhabitants of the territory: a sizeable population of Blackfoot Native Americans. Meagher's initial view of the Blackfoot was that of the colonist. In a letter to his father in 1866, he wrote about the active role he had played in the brutal battles "against the Indians on the line of our Eastern settlements" and expressed his certainty that, after his actions, "no mischief will accrue to the Territory from the spirit that animates the savages on our borders."[97] Effectively, this reflected the civilian/barbarian dichotomy we saw espoused by Mitchel in the context of African Americans: if the Blackfoot were "savages," then they were, by definition, hostile to the American state and, hence, beyond the law. They could only be colonized or eliminated if Montana was to be an integral part of the American state and nation.[98] Eventually, however, even in relation to the Native American population, Meagher would become open to the possibility that citizenship might be earned. Alongside military action, he was happy to use religious institutions to bring the Blackfoot within the ambit of the state and into the nation.

From Montana, Meagher proudly wrote to his father: "The Indians on the West of the Mountains, all of whom are Catholics, and subject to the immediate control of the good Jesuit Fathers—are perfectly inoffensive. . . . Were they all Catholics on this side of the mountains, and subject to the same control, the Territory would have nothing to alarm it, and nothing to interrupt its peaceful and prosperous development."[99] Meagher's comments are particularly relevant when viewed in light of the legal issue of US Native American citizenship. The Civil Rights Act of 1866 declared that "all persons born in the United States,

ONE OF THE WAYS INTO MONTANA.

Figure 4.3. *One of the Ways into Montana*, in *Harper's New Monthly Magazine*, October 1867.

and not subject to any foreign power, excluding Indians not taxed, are hereby declared to be citizens of the United States."[100] Native Americans could become citizens by serving in the military, marrying citizens, accepting land allotments, or by being taxed.[101] Essentially, they could earn their citizenship—which is what Meagher believed about entitlement to citizenship in general.

Yet, for many Native Americans, American citizenship did not have the emancipatory connotations that it did for Irish migrants to the United States. This was because granting US citizenship to Native Americans meant stripping them of their own national sovereignty. This exposes a major contradiction at the heart of how the Young Ireland generation came to see the United States, and, indeed, Australia and Canada, as locations in which people could gain the freedoms that the Young Irelanders sought in Ireland. Their connection of the United

States with universal liberty was ultimately filtered through a (sometimes necessarily) self-interested Irish American lens. In a similar vein, as we have seen earlier, Meagher, and the other Young Irelanders who supported the Union in the Civil War were not motivated by a belief that abolition was morally right. Instead, they based their support on the belief that the Union and the Republic protected Irish people as they sought to integrate into American society. Nevertheless, Meagher, who had gone from fighting colonialism in Ireland to becoming a colonist himself, found himself moving away from an understanding of citizenship based on race towards one based on a broader suite of qualifications. Here, he differed from Mitchel, who, unlike Meagher, held an essentialist conceptualization of race. Both men had cultivated a nationalism in Ireland, where the racial elements of Irish nationalism were subsumed to a wider historical narrative; both carried this view of nationality with them to the United States, where, in a context in which the issue of race could not be avoided, each confronted it differently: Mitchel, by embracing the racial logic in Irish nationalism, and Meagher, by turning toward civic nationalism. In this respect, Meagher's thought can be seen to have drawn on a strand of civic republicanism that David Dwan identified in Young Ireland's thought in Ireland, "in which a life of active citizenship was a necessary condition of self-realisation," capable of existing without the underpinning of race.[102]

Fenianism and Citizenship

In the years preceding the Civil War, Mitchel and Meagher were among the most prominent Irish nationalists in the United States. However, by the war's end, a new Irish nationalist organization with roots in Young Ireland began to assert itself, bringing a different group from within the same generation to prominence. As the 1850s came to a close, Irish nationalism began to manifest itself in the more explicit and direct form of the Fenian Brotherhood, which, rather than the liberalism of the other Young Irelanders, represented a more whole-hearted embrace of American republicanism. Founded in New York City in 1858 by John O'Mahony and Michael Doheny, with the help of James Stephens, the Brotherhood sought to establish a republic in Ireland. As we saw in the previous chapter, Doheny was involved with Young Ireland circles in New York; Stephens and O'Mahony, on the other hand, were out-side of the wider transnational Young Ireland circle of exiles of which Meagher and Mitchel were a part. Following the rebellion in Ireland in 1848, the two escaped to Paris together—an episode recounted in Doheny's *The Felon's Track*.[103] There, they lived in poverty, whereas even those transported to Van Diemen's Land lived in reasonable com-fort.[104] In 1855 Stephens returned to Ireland, and in 1854 O'Mahony moved to New York, where, with Doheny (who was already there), he founded the Emmet Monument Association, a revolutionary soci-ety dedicated to bringing about an independent Ireland, which later merged with a secret organization Stephens had founded in March 1858: the Irish Republican Brotherhood.[105] In 1859, O'Mahony, Stephens, and Doheny became part of a core group in the United States who, led by O'Mahony, established the Fenian Brotherhood, as an organiza-tion intended to complement the Brotherhood in Ireland. Together, O'Mahony, Doheny, and "Stephens formulated what was to be the key strategy of radical Irish nationalism down to the First World War, namely, mobilization of Irish American resources and secret organiza-tion in anticipation of an international crisis that would throw up a powerful anti-British ally."[106]

The Brotherhood owed some of the success of its Irish American project to an early embrace of the transatlantic telegraph, laid in 1865.[107] As an 1866 report in the *Manchester Times* noted, the telegraph served "one great object of the Fenian ambition, by uniting Ireland with America."[108] In doing so, it allowed the Irish nation to expand to in-clude Irish Americans; by extension, the Irish American Fenians could claim a place at the center of the Irish nation. Fenians, who had "sat in deep contemplation, cultivating an anti-British, anti-colonial philoso-phy on behalf of the Irish at home and abroad," could, with the aid of the telegraph, partially erase the physical and mental distance between "home and abroad."[109] Therefore, it should come as no surprise to find that telegraph fees were the Fenians' single largest nonmilitary cost in 1866–67: they spent $741.50 on telegraph fees compared to $701.89 on postage.[110] Using the telegraph allowed them to transmit information to supporters across the United States and in Ireland, thereby further developing—and participating in—an Irish public sphere not necessar-ily tied to the island of Ireland, extending the networks previously established by the Young Ireland generation while in Van Diemen's Land and New York.

The Fenian Brotherhood additionally drew upon already existing Young Ireland networks in the United States. Stephens traveled to Knoxville, Tennessee, to convince Mitchel to write to influential Irish American newspaper publisher Horace Greeley; Mitchel complied, offering to introduce Greely "to you my friend Mr. Stephens, formerly of Ireland, but lately resident in Paris. He has a special object in seeking an interview with you; which he will himself explain."[111] Mitchel noted the fact that Greeley was "still a member of the Irish Directory, and there remains a considerable sum in its hands, placed there for special purposes."[112] The Irish Directory was an Irish American organization that had been founded with the intention of raising one million dollars for an Irish revolution and that had been responsible for funding Mitchel's escape from Van Diemen's Land.[113] Its leadership included Greeley, Judge Robert Emmet, and Judge James W. Wright, among other prominent Irish Americans.[114] Mitchel asserted that "Mr Stephens has himself made great exertions & sacrifices to create & perfect an organisation looking to the . . . revolutionizing of that country [Ireland]," and, as such, the Fenian Brotherhood would be a worthy recipient of support.[115] Mitchel sought to use his influence in the Irish American community to secure funding for the Fenian movement. The relationship between many of the more prominent Young Ireland leaders and the Fenians, however, would soon sour.[116]

The Fenians have been described as "the first large scale channel of Irish American nationalist expression."[117] While the organization had always been, in the words of John Mitchel, "looking to revolution, foreign and home, or left distinctly preparing for that," the Brotherhood served a significant social function for the Irish American community in the United States.[118] The majority of Irish people in the United States who interacted with Fenianism did so through the events like Fenian balls, picnics, and fairs, which were often organized by the Fenian Sisterhood, the Brotherhood's female counterpart.[119] Caleb Richardson has argued that, "for thousands of Irish Americans, Fenianism had as much to do with American citizenship, and participation in American civic and associational life more generally," as it did with Irish nationalism.[120] When Irish nationalism was mentioned in connection with events, it was often in a manner that emphasized American values. One typical example is an advertisement for the Irish National Fair in 1864 that told prospective attendees: "The Fenian Brotherhood are friends of Ireland, thoroughly and truthfully conversant with the wrongs inflicted upon that unhappy Country, and in this behalf make their appeal to America, the refuge of the oppressed of all Nations, whose sympathies have ever generously responded to the cry of the down-trodden liberties of all peoples."[121]

The Civil War contributed significantly to making the Fenians an important Irish American organization. As Patrick Steward and Bryan P. McGovern have noted, both Meagher and Mitchel recognized the role that the military experience gained by Irishmen could potentially play in training Fenian soldiers.[122] As we have seen, this was obviously apparent to a good many ordinary Irish men, for a considerable number joined the armies on both sides. David Brundage has written that "the Union cause naturally drew those with the deepest ideological commitment to republicanism."[123] In 1863, in the midst of the war, the Fenian Brotherhood adopted a new constitution, which modeled the organization's political values on those of the United States, with the goal of creating a "thoroughly democratic, self-governing institution."[124] At a convention in Chicago on 3 November 1863 they declared: "Deeming the preservation and success of the Union of supreme importance to the extension of democratic institutions, and to the well-being and social elevation of the whole human race; it was 'Resolved, that we, the Representatives of the Fenian Brotherhood in the United States, do hereby solemnly declare, without limit or reservation, our entire allegiance, to the Constitution and Laws of the United States of America.'"[125]

Moreover, many Fenians had accepted the arguments made by people like Meagher that military service served as a means of claiming their place within the American nation.[126] Thus, the actions of Civil War veterans who became Fenians and sought to claim a place for themselves within the Irish nation can in many ways be seen as acting in logical concordance with the argument that by being loyal Americans, Irishmen could further the cause of Irish nationalism. When they defended American democracy and republicanism, they did so both because they were committed to them as Americans, and because those institutions had come to occupy a central role in their Irish nationalism. It also helped that these arguments could be made without challenging their claim to American nationality.

As demobilized Civil War soldiers swelled Fenian ranks, the movement grew in strength. The Fenian Brotherhood in Chicago stated explicitly to secretary of state William Seward that "there was not an Irish Regiment in the field that did not owe its organisation to our society, and hundreds of brave men whose lives went out side by side with your countrymen experienced the hope, that when the day of Ireland's trial came, that in that hour America would not forget the many brave Irish heads who marched to death beneath the starry banner."[127] These direct appeals to the American government sought to assert that Fenian and Irish loyalty to the Union substantiated Fenian commitment to American ideals, as a way of facilitating the Brotherhood's integration into an American narrative—in many cases, successfully.

For instance, we can consider the case of Colonel William J. Nagle: a war Democrat who left had left his job in the customs office and joined Meagher's Irish Brigade in 1861. Upon leaving the Union Army, he joined the Fenian Brotherhood and became the military inspector general of the O'Mahony wing of the organization.[128] In 1867 he sailed for Ireland on the *Erin's Hope* in order to aid in the planned rebellion in March, but he was arrested just hours after setting foot on Irish soil.[129] In 1867, Charles Adams, the US consul in London, wrote to Edward Stanley, the secretary of state for foreign affairs in the UK: "I have received from my government very strong instructions to do all in my power on behalf of Colonel Nagle, on account of the services rendered by him and several brothers during the late difficulties in America, as well as of his character as a citizen."[130] That the American government was willing to advocate strongly on behalf of a Fenian was evidence of the poor state of relations between the United States and Britain. More significantly in the current context, the fact that service in the Civil War constituted a justification for doing so indicates that arguments about Irishmen earning loyalty to US through military service were persuasive to many in the American government.

The relative popularity of Fenianism among Irish Americans, whose numerical importance was becoming increasingly important in elections, made them a force for whom it made sense for politicians of all stripes to be at least perceived to be entertaining their concerns. In her study of nineteenth-century American democracy, Mary P. Ryan notes that "Irish nationalism in particular became more robust after the war," in part because it was recognized that in order to court the Irish vote, American politicians would have to court the Fenians.[131] The Brotherhood, however, was spread widely but unevenly throughout the United States. Based around local units known as "circles"—named after prominent figures from Irish history and usually made up of between 100 and 500 members—the Brotherhood was concentrated in areas long settled by Irish migrants.[132] For instance, out of 374 circles, there were 92 in New York, and the new territory of Montana had only 4. At the same time, this geographical diffusion gave the organization political clout not unlike that of a centrally organized political party.[133] In 1865, the Fenian Brotherhood could make an official appeal to president Andrew Johnson for the release of John Mitchel from Fort Monroe in which they emphasized that they "represent[ed] large social classes in thirty States and territories" who had come to Washington, DC, "to wait upon your Excellency and express to you how deeply they feel the act restoring to freedom a man whom they love and venerate for his self-sacrificing devotion to his native land."[134]

This episode encapsulates both some of the problems and some of the opportunities that Fenianism began to present in American politics due to the way the organization cut across the Civil War divide. In the war's immediate aftermath, Johnson, who had been Lincoln's vice president, suggested that a number of Confederates should be hanged for treason.[135] When the prospect arose that Mitchel might be executed for his support of the Confederacy, the Fenians, represented by "Colonel W. R. Roberts, of New York," urged Johnson to dismiss the charge, claiming that, while "they remember nothing of John Mitchel's American career [they] can never forget that he risked all a patriot should for Ireland."[136] If Johnson, a Democrat, were to build up any sort of electoral base for his party, he needed to find causes common to supporters of both the Union and the Confederacy: in this respect, the cause of Ireland was perfect. Johnson quickly changed his tune about Confederate prisoners and "passed out pardons on application."[137] He responded to his correspondent in the Fenian Brotherhood: "As you, sir, delicately re-marked, we could not remember Mr. Mitchel's American career; but we were anxious, as a mark of respect and compliment to the large section of our countrymen with whom Mr. Mitchel was previously identified, to yield to their expressed wishes in that regard."[138] For Johnson, acceding to the Fenian request to release Mitchel served as a fairly easy means of courting the Irish American vote. At the same time, actions such as this led the Fenians to believe they had the support of the Johnson administration.[139] Moreover, the release of Mitchel, and the subsequent naming of Fenian circles after Mitchel, offered Fenians a means of recruiting Confederate veterans to a movement that had been identified hitherto with the Union cause.[140] As David T. Gleeson argues, the "Irish cause had thus become a way for Irish Confederate and Union veterans to reunite."[141] Additionally, it created a position within American culture in which it was possible to begin to heal the divisions caused by the Civil War.

The episode of Mitchel's release fit a wider pattern of Irish nationalism facilitating post–Civil War reconciliation. This included the recognition among Irish nationalist leaders in the North that "throughout the Southern States there is distress, hunger, misery in every form, some at least of which money may relieve. There the pride of the people is broken, their hopes are wrecked, their dearest fondest memories linger over graves."[142] By the same token, the former Young Irelander Richard O'Gorman claimed that "it may be that something in my blood makes it easier to understand and sympathise with the kind of sorrow that now afflicts the Southern communities," drawing upon the feelings that had helped drive Young Ireland toward rebellion: "I am an Irishman and the bitter memories of defeat, the eternal consciousness of subjugation have darkly interwoven themselves into the texture of the Irish character. . . . So it is that sympathy with sorrow is innate to the Irish nature."[143] For all of O'Gorman's talk about "suffering," his charge of "subjugation" addressed itself to landowners and their hirelings, not to the Black slaves who had actually been subjugated and whose suffering was greater than having lost a war. If Mitchel had identified an emotional appeal that could be made to Southerners, positing a natural kinship between Ireland and the Southern states, comments like O'Gorman's suggested that this appeal could persist after the Civil War, *albeit* in a form that did not preclude making common cause with the larger enterprise of the American republic.

The Fenian Brotherhood reinforced its alignment of the cause of Ireland with the ideals of the American republic by proclaiming the same common cause that Meagher had identified in the doctrine of manifest destiny, which sought to spread American liberty and democracy across the world. In a letter written in 1865 on behalf of the active Fenian circle in Chicago, James B. maintained: "We believe that it be so the intention of America that republican institutions should extend and must extend, until mankind the world over shall clasp hands in one holy bond of Brotherhood."[144] The Fenians were thus able to argue that not only were they loyal Americans because of their service in the Civil War; in attempting to bring American democracy to Ireland, they were also acting as enterprising American citizens, fulfilling manifest destiny.[145] Moreover, they adopted the tactics of the most ardent Young Americans—in particular their tradition of filibustering.[146] What other scholars have not noted, however, is that this is part of a wider pattern of thought among the Young Ireland generation. David Doolin contends that "the Fenian Brotherhood took its blueprint from mechanisms deployed in American expansionist practices, specifically, the annexation of Texas in 1845 and the subsequent Mexican American War of 1846–48."[147] Yet the Fenians took more than the mechanisms of American expansionist practices; they firmly believed in spreading American ideals and, in so doing, consciously positioned themselves within a wider American political tradition.

The tradition of manifest destiny in Fenianism was evident in certain events—the first in 1866, when the Brotherhood engaged in a series of raids in British North America. The two most significant happened first in New Brunswick in April and then in Canada West at Ridgeway. In both cases, the Fenians sought either to create an Irish Republic that would eventually be annexed by the United States, or to spark a war between the United States and Britain.[148] Writing of the planned raids, John Mitchel averred that "unless it drags the US into war with England it can only end in defeat to those that engage in it."[149] This view was supported by some American newspapers, which saw the plans for a Fenian raid on Canada as a means of avenging British support for the South.[150]

In fact, reasoning behind the raids had more to do with internal politics within Feniansim itself. The Brotherhood experienced a split in

1866, in which one wing, led by O'Mahony (who had been president of the organization), was deposed by the Fenian Senate and power assumed by another faction, led by William R. Roberts (a future congressman and former colonel in the Union Army) and Thomas William Sweeny (who had risen to rank of brigadier general in the Union Army after service in the Mexican-American War and the Civil War). The Roberts/Sweeny wing sought direct action and, in turn, received most of the money donated by Irish Americans. The turn toward Roberts and Sweeny and away from O'Mahony—who had close ties with Stephens and the Irish Republican Brotherhood in Ireland and whose primary aim was fomenting rebellion in Ireland—was, according to R. V. Comerford, reflective of an organization that increasingly "served the purposes of Irish America rather than the supposed needs of the motherland."[151]

In an attempt to compete for support and money, O'Mahony advanced his own plans for invading British North America at New Brunswick in April. This first raid, which involved over seven hundred Fenians, was quickly subdued by over nine hundred British soldiers deployed from the large garrison at Halifax.[152] The second raid, at Ridgeway (in what is now Ontario), by the more militarily experienced Roberts wing, involved over a thousand Fenians. Here, the Fenian Civil War veterans overcame the inexperienced militias that had come out to defend Canada.[153] They arrived on 1 June, with Sweeny declaring that they had no quarrel with the Canadians: "We are here as the Irish army of liberation, the friends of liberty against despotism, of democracy against aristocracy, of the people against their oppressors."[154] The Fenians positioned themselves as a force intent on spreading American democracy and liberty across North America as well as to Ireland. This time, however, it was President Johnson's decision to avoid being drawn into a war with Britain that scuppered the Brotherhood's plans: the American government cut off the Fenian supply lines, forcing them to retreat.[155] Sweeny was arrested, but soon released and returned to his commission in the US Army. Effectively, the Fenian raids compelled the American government to balance strong domestic support for Fenianism with the threat posed by nonstate actors seeking to take control of American foreign policy. The American response in June 1866 forced support for further raids of British North America to the periphery of the Fenian Brotherhood. Nevertheless, as the Brotherhood's focus shifted to Ireland, their activities in North America would soon be the least of the US government's concerns.

As William B. West, the US vice-consul to Dublin, warned in October 1865, "This Fenian mania has, I regret to state, induced a great many of our adopted citizens to visit this country [Ireland], of which there can be little doubt, and many of them are now suffering most severely, and, I might add, justly punished for their folly, in abandoning the comforts and happiness of their American homes for the insane project of aiding revolution here."[156] The numbers of naturalized American citizens who traveled to Ireland to take part in a Fenian rebellion in the mid-1860s was small, but large enough to be a concern. While the US vice-consul may have considered the Fenian plan for rebellion an "insane project," the participation of American citizens could create a very awkward situation. Prior to naturalization, Irish people in the United States had been British citizens, and so, as West highlighted, "British law does not admit any renunciation of allegiance by a native-born subject found in the United Kingdom."[157] Hence, an Irish person found to be involved in rebellion in Ireland could "be tried and punished as a *British subject*" for treason, even though such individuals, if naturalized, were also legally American citizens.[158] Such a scenario could potentially open up a larger can of worms, for British claims of perpetual allegiance had been disputed in the United States since the American Revolution, when the thirteen colonies repudiated their allegiance to the Crown. The American position was that "individuals had the inherent right to change their political allegiance."[159] While this had long been assumed to be the case, it was only in 1868 that Congress would pass the Expatriation Act by which it was formally codified; in 1865, however the issue was not only live—it was also unresolved. Consequently, the possibility of American Fenians launching a rebellion in Ireland threatened, as Lucy Salyer's recent study shows, to trigger "a revolution in the law of citizenship."[160]

Illustrating the complexity of Young Ireland's engagement in American culture in the second half of the nineteenth century, the American Consul in Dublin (and West's immediate superior) at the time was also a former Young Irelander and Fenian, James Cantwell. In 1859 Cantwell had helped to establish the Fenian Brotherhood in Philadelphia, where he had become a successful merchant.[161] After the 1848 rebellion, he had fled to America with John Blake Dillon and remained friendly with P. J. Smyth and John O'Mahony.[162] He was appointed US consul in Dublin in 1863,[163] although this is something the few biographies of Cantwell fail to mention.[164] Cantwell's appointment was important, though, because it not only demonstrates yet again how former Young Irelanders were able to find places of influence in the countries where they went into exile after 1848; it also more specifically suggests both the reaches of Fenian influence, and the ways in which that influence operated. In a 1863 letter to John Blake Dillon, another former Young Irelander who had climbed the political ladder, Meagher wrote: "Isn't it glorious! You Lord Mayor of Dublin, and honest old Cantwell Consul of the United States of America!"[165] Meagher went on to boast that "soon after receiving Cantwell's note, asking me to use my influence in procuring the appointment for him, I wrote to Mr Seward on the subject; and in reply I received the enclosed very agreeable despatch. I wish I had kept a copy of my letter to the Secretary of State. It was a model of the most refined, brilliant, and persuasive enthusiasm."[166] For his part, secretary of state William H. Seward wrote in the early 1860s that "changes will be made whenever Irish citizens shall agree in what they recommend to be done" regarding the appointment of US consuls to Ireland, and whether or not they should be affiliated with the Fenians.[167]

This kind of maneuvering in the background on the part of former Young Irelanders forms an important part of the context for the rebellion that the Fenians planned in Ireland for March 1867. A group of forty American Fenians sailed to Ireland to take part, although thirty-two of them were arrested soon after they arrived in Cork. These arrests, along with British plans to execute some of those who had been involved in the rebellion, sparked a strong reaction in both Ireland and the United States. Seward wrote to Charles Adams, the son of president John Quincy Adams and American ambassador to the UK, stating that "the judgement of mankind is that in revolutionary movements which are carried on by large masses, and which appeal to popular sympathy, capital execution of individuals who fall within the power of the government are unwise and often unjust."[168] He underscored that the arrest and possible execution of American citizens was likely to inflame public opinion in the United States and emphasized that "such severity, when practiced upon a citizen of a foreign state, excites a new sympathy by enlisting feelings of nationality and patriotism."[169] Here he referred both to the potential response of Irish nationalist opinion as well as to the wider potential reaction to the perceived ill treatment of US citizens, which could result in American public support for confrontation with the UK. Through expatriation, the Fenians had successfully made Irish nationalism into an American issue.

Nonetheless, in the 1870s, the United States and Britain inched toward reconciliation. Republican president Ulysses S. Grant enforced American neutrality, declaring that "there would be no more diplomatic wrangling to free Fenians."[170] This détente led in 1870 to refinements to the US Naturalization Act and the Anglo-American Treaty, which stated that "British subjects who have become, or shall become, and are naturalized according to law within the United States of America as citizens thereof, shall, subject to the provisions of Article II, be held by Great Britain to be in all respects and for all purposes citizens of the United States, and shall be treated as such by Great Britain."[171] The organization to which Young Ireland had given birth—the Fenians—had inadvertently forced the United States and the United Kingdom to define the question of citizenship that had preoccupied Young Ireland, compelling the two countries to define who counted as an American citizen, and how that citizenship would be recognized in international law.

Conclusion

American nationalism, Gary Gerstle argues, has two ideological pillars: one civic, the other racial.[172] As white Europeans, the Irish could and did utilize American racial nationalism to their advantage. Mitchel's secessionism and virulent racism can be considered evidence of this taken to the extreme.[173] It was in the field of civic nationalism, however, that the Young Ireland generation would make its greatest impact. Eric Foner has claimed that, "for North and South alike, the war's legacy was fraught with ambiguity," and that this ambiguity suited many Young Irelanders.[174] Crucial events like the race riots in New York—which, in the eyes of their American compatriots, tarred many Irish

Americans with the brush of disloyalty—were quickly forgotten in an act of "collective amnesia," as part of a wider "anachronistic reading back of national unity in a grand cause."[175] Post–Civil War politics allowed Irish Americans, through narratives of their service in the Civil War, to reposition themselves as the strongest defenders of the Republic and to make the argument that Fenianism continued this tradition of defending democracy and liberty, thereby framing Irish Americans as consummate civic nationalists.[176]

The Fenians ably exploited that period in the 1850s and 1860s, when the question as to who was and who was not an American citizen was debated with particular vigor. They were able to do so because the understanding of American citizenship, and its relation to Irish nationalism, had been shaped by members of the Young Ireland generation—and not just those actively involved in the Fenian movement itself. The concerted effort to define a place for Irish people, as Irish Americans, as citizens of the United States, was typified by two different but interlinked understandings of citizenship, held, respectively, by John Mitchel and Thomas Francis Meagher. At Meagher's funeral, in New York in 1867, one orator, the former Young Irelander Richard O'Gorman, told the gathered crowd that Meagher had been "faithful to the flag he followed—the flag of the republic which gave him a welcome and a home; loyal and faithful not in seeming or in words alone, but in the deeds of earnest devotion and sacrifice of self, wherein men put to hazard what men most prize on earth, ease and pleasure, and liberty and life."[177] In saying so, O'Gorman neatly encapsulated the conviction—so central to Meagher's political philosophy—that citizenship was earned.

At one level, Mitchel held to the same belief, declaring in his memoir of another Young Irelander, Thomas Devin Reilly: "If you cannot take liberty, never ask it, or receive it."[178] That both Mitchel and Meagher thought that those rights could be earned through physical force gave a particularly masculine tinge to their conception of citizenship. This had the obvious effect of excluding from full citizenship those who, for legal and cultural reasons, could not claim their place in the nation. It is on this point that the two men differed. For Mitchel, race became a disabling qualification for citizenship that, by definition, could never be overcome. For Meagher, citizenship as a means through which Irish

Catholics could be integrated into the American national project placed Irish Catholics' "sacrifice of self" at the center of a narrative of national salvation, which in turn created a space through which future generations could inscribe themselves into a broader American story. Ultimately, he extended the principle to all, including the Native American population. As such, the differing trajectories of Meagher and Mitchel led to two contrasting ways of understanding the contribution of Irish nationalism in the United States to the discourse of rights during the Civil War and, by extension, to the concept of citizenship—one with the potential to be truly emancipatory, the other compromised by its enmeshment in attitudes about race.

5

Canada, 1857–1867

In 1857, having escaped from Ireland to the United States following the failure of the 1848 rebellion, Thomas D'Arcy McGee, after spending time in Boston, Buffalo, and New York City, moved to the Province of Canada. After Confederation in 1867, the province—present-day Quebec and Ontario—would join with New Brunswick and Nova Scotia and New Brunswick to become Canada.[1] In Montreal, McGee set up a newspaper, was elected to the Legislative Assembly, earned a law degree, and became a key figure in the negotiation of Canadian Confederation. Throughout his time in Canada, McGee returned to ideas formed in Ireland in the 1840s. Shortly after his arrival in Canada, McGee returned to writing poetry, as he had done for *The Nation* twenty years earlier, publishing a collection of *Canadian Ballads and Occasional Verses*, which he addressed to "the younger generation of Canadians." McGee told his readers: "We shall one day be a great northern nation, and develop within ourselves that best fruit of nationality, a new and lasting literature."[2] To the very end, the idea of the nation as a cultural entity was at the core of McGee's work. In the Canadian context, where loomed the twin republican bogeymen of the United States and Fenianism, McGee leaned into liberalism and nationalism and rejected his earlier republicanism. Meanwhile, parts of the Young Ireland movement to which he had belonged had evolved into Fenianism, to which he would grow implacably opposed, and in 1868 he would be assassinated by a Fenian, James Whelan.[3]

McGee navigated Canadian politics in the 1850s and 1860s by engaging with debates over democracy and Confederation. Through his engagement with these debates, we can interrogate McGee's understanding of democracy and its relationship to minority rights, which he identified primarily with the demands of the Roman Catholic community. In so doing, he—and a group of likeminded Irish Catholic leaders—sought to carve out a place for Irish Catholics in Canadian society by formulating a new Canadian nationalism, enabled by new communications technologies, that sought to overcome sectarian, linguistic, and ethnic divisions in British North America.

The politics and society in the Canada that McGee entered in 1857 were in turmoil, enflamed by a raging debate about democracy in particular. Canada was the product of a Union between two colonies, Upper Canada (Canada West, Ontario) and Lower Canada (Canada East, Quebec).[4] In 1837, there had been rebellions in both driven by the demand for increased democratic rights.[5] This posed a challenge, because the population in the predominantly Catholic and Francophone Lower Canada, which had a sizeable Anglophone minority, was greater than that of the predominantly Protestant and Anglophone Upper Canada. Moreover, in the early nineteenth century, many in Lower Canada had begun to self-identify as part of a distinct French Canadian nation.[6] In order to ensure that Britain would not have a colony with a French-speaking majority in North America, the colonies were joined in 1841, which created a state with two nations recognized as linguistically, religiously, and culturally distinct (First Nations were largely ignored): Francophone Canada East and Anglophone Canada West, each of which had an equivalent number of seats in both the Legislative Assembly (the lower house) and the Legislative Council (the upper house).

The 1850s and 1860s saw significant demographic changes, which upset the assumptions that had underpinned the Union of the Canadas. Canada West was in the midst of economic expansion and a massive influx of migrants.[7] This meant that the Union, which had initially been intended to ensure an Anglophone majority, had resulted in Francophone voters wielding more power per vote than Anglophone voters. In Canada West, this caused resentment among reformers organized under George Brown, who bristled at the notion that taxation there was subsidizing an economically lagging Canada East, while many in Canada East sought the return of local control over their cultural institutions.[8] Such demographic changes sparked a debate over how responsible government and democracy should work, and how that government would be financed, that by 1864 had escalated to a constitutional crisis. The solution—Confederation, which created a federal state, with a balance of powers among the constituent provinces—

ultimately came to include the Maritime Colonies of New Brunswick, Nova Scotia, and Canada, which, collectively, had been known as British North America.[9]

The increasingly aggressive nature of American expansionism, brought into sharp focus by the Fenian raids of the 1860s, drove many to question whether British North America should form one single state in order to best resist American pressure. In 1865, Étienne-Paschal Taché, joint premier of Canada, wrote that "if the opportunity [Confederation] which now presented itself were allowed to pass by unimproved, whether we would or would not, we would be forced into the American Union by violence, and if not by violence, would be placed upon an inclined plain which would carry us there insensibly."[10] The unspoken premise here was that being "forced into an American Union by violence" would entail a break with the British Empire, whereas the majority of politicians in British North America felt that the link with the British Empire was valuable and should be maintained and strengthened by whatever means necessary.[11]

During these years of internal political change in what would become Canada, large numbers of Irish people were migrating to British North America. While precise figures are difficult to ascertain, it has been estimated that approximately 403,509 people migrated from Ireland to Britain's North American colonies in the 1850s and 1860s.[12] However, it is unknown precisely how many stayed, because the cost of traveling to British North America was less than it was to the United States; thus, many Irish people went there first and then moved south. Nevertheless, of those who did move to the Canadas, many were Catholic and found themselves in a country where English-speaking Catholics were a "double-minority."[13] In other words, they were part of a minority of Catholics in the Canadas as a whole, and, as English speakers, they were a minority within the Catholic Church in Canada, the majority of whom were Francophone. Even among Irish people in Canada, Catholics were outnumbered by Irish Protestants by about two to one.[14]

In this respect, Montreal, the city in which McGee first settled, would prove pivotal in the direction that his political thought would take: it was a microcosm of the challenges faced by Canadian Catholics, and of the role of minorities in Canadian politics in general. Since the Treaty of Paris in 1763, when France handed over most of its North

American colonies to Britain, Canadian politics has been shaped by competing minorities. Majority Francophone and Catholic Montreal on the banks of the St. Lawrence was the industrial and commercial heart of Canada.[15] Moreover, most of the city's considerable wealth was concentrated in the hands of a Protestant Anglophone minority.[16] In this social stratification, the Irish, whose ranks had been swelled by Famine migration in the 1840s, occupied an unusual place.[17] Like the Francophone majority, they were largely Catholic and predominantly working and middle class, yet, like the Anglophone minority, they were English speaking.[18] However, Irish Catholics often found themselves in conflict with French Canadian Catholics, which posed challenges for McGee and others who sought to build a multiethnic Canadian coalition.[19] The Anglophone and Francophone Catholic communities were relatively separate. For instance, Montreal had two Catholic Basilicas—St. Patrick's, for the predominantly Irish Anglophone Catholics, and Notre Dame, for the Francophone community. The divisions between Catholics in Montreal might suggest a city—and, by extension, a state—fraught by religious division; indeed, it would be remiss to ignore the significant tensions between Irish and French Catholics, especially within the hierarchy of the Catholic Church, as well as between working-class Irish and French Canadians.[20] However, at least politically, as Irish Catholics occupied a fast-growing third group, Montreal was also an environment that compelled many Irish Catholics to engage in McGee's form of pragmatic pluralism to secure their own place in society.[21]

Thomas D'Arcy McGee in Canada

In spite of the challenges posed by these divisions, McGee believed in the potential of Canada to become a place where, unlike in the United States, Catholics could achieve religious equality. True to form for a Young Irelander abroad, McGee's first endeavor upon his arrival in 1857 was to establish a newspaper, the *New Era*, whose prospectus declared that its title was "an indication of the time of its birth. This magnificent Province has evidently arrived at such an era:—steam by land and sea; the sub-Atlantic telegraph; the probable annexation of a habitable region, larger than France and Austria combined; are acts which must give their own character to the times in which they occur."[22] McGee saw the society he had joined as one where it was possible to contribute to its development. "In the onerous future," he continued, "which is to see the fair promises of the present fulfilled or marred; Journalism will play an important part; and we desire to have a share however small, in the labours and duties it imposes."[23] In spite of McGee's excitement about its potential, Canada was an unusual destination for a former Young Irelander: it had neither the republican appeal of the United States, nor the reputation for radical politics, or the wealth of gold rush Australia. As such, McGee had no access to the networks that other members of the Young Ireland generation did upon arrival in Australia and the United States; both Duffy in the former and Meagher in the latter tapped into vigorous and robustly funded political organizations that considered their reputations as rebels against the British Empire to be an asset. The absence of a Young Ireland network in the Canadas meant that McGee had to create his own network by drawing on the wider Irish diaspora.

Before McGee's arrival in Montreal, he made contact with Irish Catholic newspaper editor James George Moylan, who had been the Washington correspondent of the *New York Daily Times* from 1852 to 1854. He continued to work for the newspaper until he moved to Guelph in Upper Canada in 1856, when he was appointed a professor of classics and English literature at a Jesuit college in Guelph, about one hundred kilometers west of Toronto. In 1859, Moylan left Guelph to buy the Toronto-based *Catholic Citizen*, which had been critical of McGee. In 1859 he renamed it the *Canadian Freeman*—presumably evoking the Irish *Freeman's Journal*—and transformed it into a publication very much in line with McGee's thought.[24] McGee met Moylan in 1850 when Moylan invited McGee to engage in a speaking tour of Canada.[25] McGee wrote to Moylan on Easter Monday, 1857, before traveling to the Canadas, about his intention of founding a newspaper: "I mean to call it the *New Era*—to make it tri-weekly; strictly secular." He told Moylan that he planned to devote part of it to literature, in a strategy clearly reminiscent of *The Nation*.[26]

Throughout McGee's time in Canada, McGee and Moylan remained close, and the *Canadian Freeman* often reflected McGee's views, as Moylan had intended.[27] In 1861, for instance, McGee wrote to Moylan that "if I were in your place, editorially, I would commence a series of strong, preparatory articles, on who keep the 12th [by taking part in Orange Order parades on July 12], calling on your correspondents everywhere to send you the names of those politicians who abet and encourage the next parade, though they many not overtly join in it, themselves."[28] McGee felt that "to know that they were so watched just now, would exercise a salutary influence on the pre-Orange public men, of all parties."[29] This sits somewhat oddly with McGee's stated belief in the first issue of the *New Era* that "questions strictly, or mainly, RELIGIOUS—unless forced upon the Press, under political or partisan pretences,—ought, it seems to us, to be carefully avoided by the secular Journalist."[30] However, an important distinction must to be made here: McGee's belief was not necessarily that religion should be excluded from the public sphere, but, rather, that sectarianism had no place in politics. Given that McGee, while in the United States, had been particularly virulent in his ultramontanism (as we saw in chapter 4), to the point of being anti-Protestant, this marked a considerable shift in his worldview. In that first edition of *New Era*, he went on to argue that "as of all Freedom's gifts to man, none is so dear as the free domain of his own conscience, we shall cordially concur with whatever party in the Province can give the best guarantees that the freedom of conscience, which now so happily characterizes Canada, shall perfectly be preserved."[31]

It did not take McGee long to make the logical move from working as a campaigning journalist to entering electoral politics. On 15 October 1857, he declared his intentions to run for office to Toronto alderman and lawyer John O'Donohoe, who was prominent among his local Irish Catholic community: "The real object of my friends is to keep my name before the city constituency, with a view to the next election. They think they can by good management seat me as one of the three representatives of Montréal. So far they are unusually unanimous, and I believe, if they continue so, they can do what they promise."[32] To this end, a public subscription was organized to support McGee's run for a seat in the Legislative Assembly of the Canadas.

This subscription was successful among the Irish community in Montreal in part because McGee cultivated a sympathetic media audience and edited his own newspaper, which meant that he could advance his opinions on a number of issues of concern to the Irish community in the Canadas. Foremost among these was the issue of separate schools for Canadian Catholics.[33] McGee argued that the government system of schools in Canada-West was "unequal and unjust," as their teaching staff and administration was dominated by Protestants.[34] Both McGee and O'Donohoe believed that separate educational institutions for Catholics would remedy these problems. Moreover, McGee considered the question of Catholic education to be about respecting Catholics' right to educate their children as they saw fit and guarding against the discrimination by Protestants that he had experienced in Ireland (and, in a different way, in parts of the United States).[35] In advancing the argument that Catholics had a right to choose where their children were educated, McGee could present himself as a leader of the Irish Canadian Catholic community—an argument he framed within a discourse about equality and justice: "Justice between class and class, and Province and Province, between creed and creed, between man and man."[36] Extending this principle, he proclaimed that "this [equality and justice] must constitute the glory, the safety, and the strength, of this new country," and, in doing so, he presented separate schools as more than a singularly Catholic concern, but one that applied to the Canadian state.[37] McGee, who was himself devoutly religious and had shown a distinctly ultramontane streak of orthodoxy during his time in the United States, had come to believe that denominational schools actually encouraged a diversity of thought that countered "an all-devouring uniformity," and that what he had encountered as unthinking democracy in the United States resulted from its system of common schools.[38] In short, by the time he took up office in Canada, McGee had made the journey from championing almost theocratic ultramontanism to valuing religious equality in a context of religious plurality, a value he would place at the center of his vision of Canadian state-building.

McGee's election to the Legislative Assembly of the Canadas in December 1857 presented him with a conundrum. Canadian politics was divided into two main factions: the Liberal-Conservatives under John A. Macdonald, and the Reform Party under George Brown. Macdonald was closely affiliated with the Orange Order and generally unfavorable to denominational education; Brown was strongly in favor of representation by population, which would have seen Catholics concentrated in Canada East politically disadvantaged, and he appeared downright hostile to the idea of separate schools. Such was the level of Catholic animosity to Brown on this count that the *True Witness* wrote that the Catholics of Montreal should "reject with every mark of honest scorn and indignation everyone who makes common cause" with "a dirty fellow like George Brown."[39] McGee, however, seeing Macdonald's connections with the Orange Order as the more intractable problem, initially sided with Brown and the Reform Party, believing that he could convince him to waver on the issue of separate schooling. To his credit, McGee persuaded Brown of the merits of an education system based on the Irish national school system—whereby mixed education existed in theory, if not in practice—and that it could work in Canada.[40] Although the Reform Party would lose its position in government before such reforms could be enacted, and the Catholic hierarchy and the Catholic press would become increasingly alienated by McGee's membership in the Reform Party, McGee remained personally popular and electorally successfully in Montreal. Moreover, in 1862, when the Reform Party returned to power, McGee was appointed president of the Executive Council.[41]

While a member of the Legislative Assembly, McGee shocked the Irish community when he threw his support behind "representation by population," which he felt "could not be long resisted."[42] It would involve changing from a political system in which Upper and Lower Canada each had the same number of seats to one in which seats were distributed across the entire Confederation according to population. In supporting this, he drew the ire of the Catholics, who, as already noted, were a minority in Canada; they felt that such a move would open them up to attack by Protestants and the Orange Order, who would command a significant numerical advantage overall. McGee drew significant criticism from people like George Clerk, founder of the *True Witness*, who wrote "strongly condemning the declaration," on the grounds that a Protestant majority would be likely to discriminate against Catholics.[43] McGee, however, did not waver, as he believed that the inevitable consequence of denying democratic rights would be "dissolution of the Union" of the Canadas.[44] With sufficient constitutional safeguards, he maintained, representation by population was possible in a manner that would be safe for minority groups and smaller regions, and that "territory as well as number, and nationality as well as territory must be represented if we are to continue as a unitary body."[45] The surest way to make those provisions was supporting and shaping representation by population to ensure that it had adequate safeguards. This was not simply a philosophical position; it concerned the survival of the state. As with the question of Catholic schools, McGee placed the question of equal rights at the core of his understanding of politics, at the same time framing his position within a certain political pragmatism.

In May 1863 McGee left the Reform Party over the refusal of its new leader, Sandfield Macdonald, to support federalism. He continued in politics as an independent before crossing the floor in October 1863 to the Liberal-Conservatives, where he found himself grappling with the inevitable tensions and compromises of trying to maintain a position founded on equality in a political world whose modus operandi was a transactional sectarianism.[46] As Elsbeth Heaman wrote about John A. Macdonald, "Whenever Macdonald wanted to woo a given community, he would teach them to demand group rights by organizing politically."[47] From the outset, McGee had not been adverse to courting the Irish Catholic vote along similar lines, but his alliance with Macdonald meant that he was now a member of a party organization that expected such an approach to group demands, and McGee recognized that this entailed an organized transactionalism among the Irish Catholic community. "If the Catholic strength elects in one a Conservative, & in another a Reformer on merely personal grounds," he wrote to Moylan in 1861, "instead of two friends you will have, politically none."[48]

By the time he joined the Liberal-Conservatives, McGee enjoyed a position as the preeminent Irish Catholic politician in Canada; moreover, in joining the party, he found himself in the company of not only Macdonald but also George-Étienne Cartier, arguably the foremost French Canadian politician of his time. In joining forces, McDonald, Cartier, and McGee brought together three groups in Canadian society—Anglophone Protestants, Anglophone Catholics, and Francophone Catholics—under a single party banner. This was a delicate enough balance in its own right; it was made even more precarious in the tumultuous environment of Canadian politics in the 1860s. The Liberal-Conservatives and the Reformers were closely balanced, making it difficult for either party to win an outright majority, which meant in turn that governments were unstable and regularly fell.[49] This was symptomatic of a wider malaise in the Province of Canada. In 1864, a little over a year after McGee joined the Liberal-Conservatives, George Brown started to argue for a federal Canada as a means to end the political deadlock: this would enable representation by population, while ensuring that Canada East would have its own majority Francophone legislature, assuaging concerns of Anglophone domination. With the support of Cartier and of Macdonald as prime minister, a unity government was put into place, and the proposed federation became a larger union of British North America that was intended to include the Maritime provinces of New Brunswick, Nova Scotia, and Prince Edward Island.[50]

McGee had been one of the earliest proponents of Confederation in Canada. The year he arrived in Canada, he used the *New Era* to lay the "intellectual foundations for Confederation."[51] On 8 August 1857, he wrote an editorial titled "Confederation of the Colonies" that declared: "We must ultimately come to a federal union."[52] In a Canadian context, McGee's early support for Confederation was somewhat unusual, because he saw Confederation as a project both of state- and nation-building. This is at odds with its traditional portrayal by Canadian historians, such as P. B. Waite, who argued in 1962 that Confederation had a "fundamentally empirical character."[53] In addition, E. R. Black has contended that "Confederation was born in pragmatism without the attendance of a readily definable philosophic rationale."[54] In 1861 McGee wrote, "We have acres enough, powers mechanical and powers natural; and sources of credit enough to make out of this province a great nation" and went on to assert that Confederation would create "a greater British North American State, existing under the sanction, and in perpetual alliance with the Empire, under which it had its rise and growth."[55]

It was at conferences in Quebec and Charlottetown in 1864 that the details of Confederation were conceived. These conferences brought together in one place Brown, Macdonald, and Cartier, along with McGee and Alexander Galt, the conservative politician from Sherbrooke in Lower Canada who had long supported Confederation. Elsbeth Heaman writes that, "together, these men represented effective political power in Canada. If they could agree, then the deal would pass."[56] What is striking about these five men is that three of them represented minority communities: McGee and Galt the two Anglophone minorities in Canada East, and Cartier the Francophone Canadians who would become a minority in Canada following Confederation. It was largely because of this strong presence of minority representatives that Confederation became strongly focused on minority rights.[57] For instance, at the Quebec Conference, McGee made the statement that "if Canada went into this union she went into it mainly with a view to promote the common prosperity, to secure the common safety and to establish the common liberties of all British North America."[58]

At Quebec, McGee secured commitments that enshrined the Catholic right to separate denominational schools, which would become part of the final agreement on Confederation—a point that McGee made specifically. At the Confederation debates he argued that the new constitution would protect "the rights and privileges which the Protestant or Catholic minority may profess as to their denominational schools."[59] He frequently used the concept of minority rights in advocating for Confederation in the 1860s. In 1865, he told an audience at St. John's that, "so long as we respect in Canada the rights of minorities, told either by tongue or creed we are safe."[60] In the first instance, McGee saw rights as protected by the state. In line with other nineteenth-century liberals outside of the United States, McGee viewed rights as invested in communities—be they religious or linguistic—rather than in the individual.[61] In connecting the security of minority groups with Confederation, he charged the Canadian state with endowing those rights and, in so doing, played an important part in making Confederation a process "profoundly shaped by liberalism."[62]

McGee also engaged forcefully in other debates about Confederation, not least those of an economic nature. For instance, in July 1863, McGee gave a speech at Temperance Hall in Halifax in which he laid out five key arguments for Confederation. His first two focused on credit and tariffs: many in Canada West saw Confederation as a means of ending fiscal transfers to the less prosperous Canada East.[63] McGee, too, engaged with taxation and fiscal issues, realizing that, were Confederation to happen, it needed a solid fiscal base: "*First.* There is the argument from Association. What is taught us by the whole history of our times? That the greatest results are produced by the association of small means. . . . Is it not the union of our joint credit, skill, and resources for the accomplishment of a common purpose which singly none of us, nor all of us, can hope to effect?"[64] In speaking of a Union of joint credit, McGee engaged directly with the idea that Confederation would create a state with a large enough taxable base to raise debt, which would enable it to finance large infrastructure projects such as the proposed intercontinental railway, which was a prime demand of the Maritime Provinces, who felt geographically isolated from the larger Canadas. "*Second*," McGee continued, "there is the commercial argument. Why should we, colonies of the same stock, provinces of the same empire, dominions under the same flag, be cutting each other's throats with razors called tariffs?"[65] In rejecting interprovincial tariffs in favor of a selective protectionism for all of Canada, McGee made a broad case for Confederation.[66]

It was perhaps in the Maritimes that McGee made his most crucial contribution to the cause of Confederation. He was the member of the Canadian delegation at Quebec who had engaged the most with the Maritime Provinces; in 1862 and 1863, he embarked on a number of tours of the provinces, where he spoke at length about his desire to bring about Confederation. In that same July 1863 speech, he spoke of how a united British North America would attract more immigrants, and he referred to the need for sustaining a sense of the common good: "There is what I shall call the patriotic argument—the argument to be drawn from the absolute necessity of cultivating a high-hearted patriotism amongst us provincialists . . . we must stand or fall together, if war comes."[67] The very fact that McGee sought to directly connect with groups of voters in the Maritimes was significant. For one thing, Confederation could not happen without Maritime engagement. Yet his effort also spoke to an attempt to cultivate an inclusive identity and a sense of greater patriotism in British North America. In approaching Maritimers first through newspapers and then in speeches throughout British North America, he courted popular opinion, which indicates that McGee and others paid more attention to the influence of popular opinion on politics than some historians have acknowledged.[68] This, perhaps, was most evident in McGee's last argument for Confederation: "*Fifth* (and for the present lastly). There is the argument of political necessity, arising from the state of our next neighbours."[69] Of all the means of whipping up considerable public anxiety that served to advance the cause of Confederation, this, arguably, was the one that McGee was best qualified to use, if only because the main American threat to British North America in the 1860s came from those of his colleagues among the Young Ireland generation who had joined the Fenians.

McGee and Fenianism

McGee believed that the United States and what in 1863 he described (in sharp contrast to his old colleague Thomas Francis Meagher) as "their ravenous 'manifest destiny' [ideology]" posed a threat to Canada and to the civic and political rights McGee felt that it guaranteed.[70] In 1862, at the height of the Civil War, he told the Irish Protestant Benevolent Society: "I do not believe that it is our destiny to be engulphed into a Republican union, renovated and inflamed with the wine of victory, of which she now drinks so freely—it seems to me we have theatre enough under our feet to act another and a worthier part; we can hardly join the Americans on our own terms and we never ought to join them on theirs."[71] McGee was tapping into fears that had a basis in reality: a long history of concerted efforts by both Americans and some Canadians to annex Canada to the United States.[72] The Civil War amplified these fears, as many Canadians, despite supporting abolition, sympathized with the Confederacy and saw the war as further proof of the United States' aggressive nature, and its desire to impose its will on smaller states.[73] Although McGee strongly supported the North, he was concerned that many Northerners sought to annex Canada; therefore, he sought to ensure that the Canadian state was strong enough to resist an attempt at annexation, whatever the war's outcome.[74] When combined with a fear that the conflict could spill over into Canada, the Civil War provided a powerful mobilizing argument for a Canadian federal union.[75]

The end of the Civil War in 1865 sharply intensified rather than reduced these threats, and the Fenians would play a role in bringing them to the fore of Canadian thought. Because the Fenian raids of the 1860s caused three British North American Provinces to see Confederation as a means of strengthening their defenses, they "helped to turn the tide in favour" of a federal state in Canada.[76]

Figure 5.1. *Battle of Ridgeway, C.W.* Buffalo, NY: Sage, Sons, ca. 1869. Library of Congress Prints and Photographs Division, Washington, DC.

In fact, the raids did cause consternation in British North America. The Fenians had clearly stated that "the true road to Irish nationality" was "by way of Canada" being annexed by the United States, and they sought to bring this about by force.[77] The first raid, on Campobello Island in New Brunswick, led by John O'Mahony in April 1866, was quickly dispersed by the Royal Navy, who dispatched six warships from the large garrison at Halifax. This was followed by another raid between 31 May and 2 June 1866 at Ridgeway, led by William R. Roberts, in which battle-hardened Civil War veteran Fenians faced off against an inexperienced and mostly volunteer Canadian militia, who only succeeded in resisting the incursion with the support of the US government, which cut off the Fenians' supply lines.[78] This led the governor-general, Charles Stanley Monck, an Irishman, to write to the secretary of state for the colonies of the UK in 1866, expressing his fear that the Fenians would soon launch a large-scale attack on Canada.[79]

The changing nature of the Fenian threat meant that it remained a topic of conversation throughout the 1860s. Even after Confederation, in 1868, the Fenian threat still loomed large in Monck's correspondence: "The Canadians are working themselves into a state of excitement at the prospect of a Fenian raid."[80] The fear generated by the raids greatly contributed to the mixture of fear and idealism that Jerry Bannister has identified as shaping the processes of nation-building in British North America.[81]

The Fenian raids brought the looming threat of the United States, and the possibility that it could attempt to annex Canada, into sharp focus for Canadians.[82] For McGee, such a danger highlighted his reason for feeling that nationalism was important to securing the Canadian border. In formulating this logic, he clearly differentiated between Confederation as a political arrangement and Canadian nationalism as a cultural phenomenon. For instance, McGee asked why men who had been sent to guard the frontier would fight: "For what do good men (who make the best soldiers) fight? For a line of scripture or chalk line—for a pretext or for a principle?"[83] He continued: "What is a better boundary between nations than a parallel of latitude, or even a natural obstacle?—what really keeps nations intact and apart?—a principle."[84] Here, McGee made explicit the importance of nationalism to Canada: he contended that Canadians needed a common vision of their country's future in order to ensure that it did not become a part of the United States. Such a vision manifested itself in practical terms in the form of the plan for Confederation. Speaking in the Legislative Assembly, McGee declared that "we on this side, Mr. Speaker, propose for that better future our plan of union."[85] While it was important to formulate this plan, McGee also argued that an emotional attachment to Canada on the side of the people was essential for the success of state formation: "When I can hear our young men say as proudly, 'our Federation' or 'our Country,' or 'our Kingdom,' as the young men of other countries do, speaking of their own, then I shall have less apprehension for the result of whatever trials the future may have in store for us."[86] Such sense of nationality would be grounded in the defense of Canadian liberties that were understood to safeguard all Canadians, regardless of religious or ethnic affiliation. "I think I may say," McGee wrote in 1865, "that wherever the flag above us is at stake—wherever our community is in question—we will be found by word and deed to shed the last of our Irish blood in defence of the inestimable liberties we enjoy, in common with all classes of Her Majesty's Canadian subjects."[87]

Fenianism presented a considerable challenge to McGee's vision of a pluralist Canadian society, not least because it heightened already existing tensions between Irish Catholics and Irish Orangemen. Perhaps not fairly, but also not unreasonably, Irish Catholics in Canada began to be perceived as potential Fenian sympathizers, a perception heightened by the presence of a small number of Fenians who lived in and were active in Canada, as opposed to attacking it from the United States.[88] McGee had warned of this in 1861: "In Canada, with men of all origins and all kinds of culture, . . . if we will carefully convey across the Atlantic half-extinguished embers of strife in order that we may by them light up the flames of our inflammable forests—if each neighbour will try not only to nurse up old animosities, but to invent new grounds of hostility to his neighbour."[89] McGee was not alone in this position. Commenting on the Fenians in 1867, the Conservative *Montreal Gazette*—which was edited by Brown Chamberlin, who had been decorated for fighting the Fenians—declared that they "endeavour[ed] to introduce into Canada one of the wickedest conspiracies that were ever formed against the peace of a nation."[90] Like McGee, the *Gazette* claimed that Fenianism in Canada was particularly egregious because Irish Fenians in Canada were living in and attacking a society in which "Irishmen in Canada have no grievances to complain of. They stand on a perfect equality with all other races."[91] In threatening "the whole structure of the government under which some millions of people enjoy freedom, peace and prosperity," McGee believed that the Fenians would endanger the rights and freedoms of everyone in Canada.[92] In a private letter to Moylan in 1865, McGee wrote that "genuine religious equality, strong in the Colonies, must come sooner or later, by the mere effect of time, prevail in Ireland, & that was the main stake, for which our fathers fought and now it is within our reach."[93] He cautioned, however, that "we have in the way, the worst obstacle, the Devil has ever invented for the Irish, an irreligious revolutionary society, in which patriotism takes the garb, of indifference or hostility to religion. This is the enemy of the Irish cause in our time."[94] In this, McGee was in line with the influential Irish archbishop (and soon-to-be cardinal) Paul Cullen, who held a strong view that Fenianism was irreligious,[95] and who used his considerable sway over the English-speaking Catholic Church in Canada to propagate this view.[96] Partly as a consequence, the Catholic hierarchy in Canada largely condemned Fenianism,[97] putting religious pressure on Irish Catholics to dissociate themselves from the Fenians.[98] Therefore, by 1865 McGee had placed considerable distance between himself and his erstwhile colleagues.

McGee argued to the Earl of Mayo in 1868 that "we are loyal because our equal civil social and religious rights are respected by this government, in theory and in practice. Were it otherwise, we would be otherwise."[99] McGee considered Canada a place in which the rights of Catholics were protected, and, as a result, the Canadian state had earned his loyalty. For McGee, and many other Canadians with a liberal concept of rights, the republicanism of the Fenians was incompatible with how their understanding of how the state should operate in Canada.[100]

McGee and Qualified Democracy

After Confederation in 1867, partly in response to the challenge that Fenianism posed to his position, McGee wrote his seminal "Mental Outfit of the New Dominion," in which he declared that, while "the onwards march of political democracy is a fact equally apparent, it is by no means clear to myself, for one, that religion will wield diminished power."[101] This became, for him, the crux of the political question facing Canada: how to balance democratic rights with religious freedom. This was important for McGee not only because of the importance he attached to his own principles but also because—at the time, far from uniquely—his political views were heavily tinged with what Paul O. Carrese has called "sustainable liberalism," which holds that democracy "needs guidance from religious faith," in particular from Christianity.[102] In Canada, where the influence of religious faith on the state was widely accepted, this was an easy sell, although McGee, like many other Catholics in North America, made little mention of the increased role for the Church in politics that the Holy See sought in the 1860s.[103] Left to its own devices, democracy was a far more dangerous creation. Like Duffy in Australia, McGee feared that the individualism he saw accompanying democracy would lead to a loss of moral compass; religion, like nationalism, he believed, served to counter this individualism.

McGee had been arguing to Canadian audiences the need for a democracy with checks and balances since at least 1862. In an influential speech before the Irish Protestant Benevolent Society, McGee told his listeners that Canadians were "heirs of one seventh of the continent—inheritors of a long ancestral story,—and no part of it dearer to us than the glorious tale of this last century,—warned not by cold chronicles only, but by living scenes, passing before our eyes, of the dangers of an unmixed democracy,—we are here to vindicate our capacity, by the test of a new political creation."[104] That "new political creation" was Confederation. The process of creating a federal state in Canada—where provincial boundaries were drawn specifically to create a plurinational state—with a French-speaking linguistic and Catholic religious majority in Quebec, was part of a wider process of tempering the power of the majority to discriminate against minority groups.[105] This was fundamentally different from the United States, where the Senate and the powers of state governments vis-á-vis the federal government were meant to prevent what many feared might be a tyrannical federal government, or the domination of one particular region.[106] In the United States, the view prevailed that rights were vested in the individual, whereas, in Canada, rights were invested in groups.

The qualified democracy that McGee proposed would take a form advocated by other key figures in the Confederation debates, a mixed constitution that retained the monarchy as well as a limited franchise. However, they understood the challenges that a multinational federation presented, and that, as such, the building of a Canadian state required popular consent.[107] On the one hand, this may sound opposite to the direction taken by McGee's erstwhile colleague Meagher, who, in his embrace of Young America, aligned himself with a political and cultural ideology determined to put behind it all traces of the British political system, in particular its monarchical and aristocratic elements. While McGee's language is much more conciliatory to the British system, he recognized, as Meagher did, that he was in a different set of circumstances: "This is a new land—a land of pretension because it is new; because classes and systems have not had that time to grow here naturally. We have no aristocracy but of virtue and talent, which is the only true aristocracy, and is the old and true meaning of the term."[108] In the end, this position would lead him to support the appointment of a hereditary Senate, which would act as a check on the House of Commons, just as the elected House would act as a check on the appointed body.[109]

McGee came to this understanding of democracy through his reading of Alexis de Tocqueville's *Democracy in America*. Tocqueville's influence is evident in a letter from McGee to Charles Gavan Duffy (who at this point was minister for lands in Victoria), published in 1863 as a pamphlet entitled *The Internal Condition of the American Democracy Considered.*[110] The pamphlet expressed McGee's concerns about the United States, which acted as a foil to Canadian development: "However the people of the States may choose to read the lesson of their late experience, I sincerely trust, my dear Duffy, you will agree with me when I say that to Irish settlers in British colonies, and other Irishmen about to emigrate, it ought not to be an example and a warning given in vain."[111] McGee argued for separate denominational schooling, for maintaining a connection with Britain, and for developing a distinct Canadian press. McGee wrote: "My Dear Duffy,—It is now nearly twenty years since we canvassed together the merits of the late Alexis De Tocqueville's work, "Democracy in America." . . . When the complete work fell into our hands, we adopted most of his well-weighed and well-worded conclusions, or dissented from them, when we did dissent, not without a respectful hesitation and regret."[112]

McGee used all full nineteen pages of *The Internal Condition of the American Democracy Considered* to argue that, since Tocqueville had written *Democracy in America*, his worst predictions about American democracy had come true. Rather than a synthesis of religion and political liberty, the desire for equality had created a society in which "the fine points of the individual had been filed down."[113] For McGee, who (as we saw in chapter 3) was concerned with Irish people losing their Irishness in the United States, and who based his conception of rights on group rights, which meant recognizing distinct groups within society, such a position was particularly egregious. Furthermore, McGee had direct experience of the United States, having spent time there twice. Initially, he was inspired by American republicanism and then disillusioned by nativism; therefore, he did not approach Tocqueville merely from a theoretical point of view. More significantly, we know that in the same month as Confederation, McGee was urging John A. Macdonald to read Tocqueville; in an unpublished letter of 18 October 1867, McGee wrote to McDonald offering to lend him his copy.[114] It should come as no surprise that McGee would press a copy of *Democracy in America* on Macdonald at this crucial juncture, for, in the opening pages of *The Internal Condition of the American Democracy Considered*, McGee told Duffy that while "the rise of the American democracy was natural and inevitable,"[115] it was equally the case that, as Tocqueville had argued, if left unchecked it would lead to a "tyranny of the majority."[116] This, in a phrase, captures McGee's deepest concern.

McGee saw "universal democracy"—which for him meant a democracy without constraints on the power of the majority—as inextricably linked to American expansionism. In a warning to the Canadian Legislative Assembly of 9 February 1865, he stated that "if we are to have a universal democracy on this continent, the Lower Provinces—the smaller fragments—will be 'gobbled up' first, and we will come in afterwards by way of dessert. Confederation will enable us . . . to resist the spread of this universal democracy doctrine."[117] In McGee's mind, opposition to the spread of universal democracy to Canada was central to opposition to "union with the United States."[118]

McGee delivered his warning against universal democracy in terms calculated to appeal to Orangemen and to indicate his softening stance toward the Order by the mid-1860s. "The idea of a universal democracy in America," he asserted, "is no more welcome to the minds of thoughtful men among us, than was that of a universal monarchy to the mind of the thoughtful men who followed the standard of the third WILLIAM in Europe.'"[119] This appears to vindicate Phillip Buckner's argument that "it has long been known that the Fathers of Confederation were not democrats."[120] We do need to be careful, though, while reading McGee cautioning against the bogeyman of universal democracy, for, as Janet Ajzenstat has noted, "if we believe parliamentary government is liberal democracy, then we must conclude that the Fathers [of Confederation] are democrats—democrats as we use the word in our own day."[121] It was not democracy per se that worried McGee, any more than it did Tocqueville; instead, as Ajzenstat argues, it was a democracy incapable of accommodating Canada's various geographical, linguistic, and ethnic differences.[122]

The concern that an unrestrained democracy in Canada could prove dangerous to the balance between the different religious and ethnic groups, which, given that Confederation emerged partly as a response to representation by population, was urgent for McGee and his contemporaries. As Victor DeSelva writes about democracy in Canada, "The great danger for Canadian society is that French and English will deny each other mutual recognition, treat one another as strangers, and destroy the country."[123] McGee's response to the idea that Canadians might no longer recognize each other's rights involved the creation of a new, culturally based Canadian nationalism that superseded individual ethnic identities. For McGee, "a Canadian nationality, not French-Canadian, nor British-Canadian, nor Irish-Canadian—patriotism rejects the prefix—is, in my opinion, what we should look forward to,—that is what we ought to labour for, that is what we ought to be prepared to defend to the death."[124]

Canadian Nationalism

In 1861, in an attempt to distance himself from an already threatening Fenianism, McGee dismissed his Young Ireland past, claiming that "politically, we were a pack of fools; but we were honest in our folly; and no man need blush at forty for the follies of one-and-twenty."[125] "Pack of fools" or not, McGee's response to the challenges faced by British North America in the 1860s revived a version of the ideology that he had helped to formulate twenty years earlier when he wrote for *The Nation*.[126] On 1 July 1867—the day on which the Act of Union brought together Canada East, Canada West, Nova Scotia, and New Brunswick as a single state—McGee powerfully articulated a vision of a Canadian future in a lecture given to the Literary Club entitled "The Mental Outfit of the New Dominion," later printed in full in the *Montreal Gazette* and subsequently published as a pamphlet.[127] In it, McGee argued for a distinctive Canadian tradition of thought.[128] English books, he wrote, "bearing traces of controversies or directed against errors or evils, which for us hardly exist," and, as such, they could not form the intellectual basis for a Canadian nationality.[129] McGee insisted that because of the large and culturally distinctive community of French Catholics, models created in other societies could not be simply imported wholesale; indeed, such attempts could be ruinous to any attempt to create a unified state.

In the same speech, McGee stated that "our mental self-reliance is an essential condition of our political independence."[130] He felt that the new dominion needed to establish its own press if it wished to become a nation—again repeating an argument that had been made and won in Ireland with *The Nation* and that he also advanced in his 1858 book *Canadian Ballads and Occasional Verses*, which he addressed "to the young people of Canada."[131] McGee contended that "we shall one day be a great northern nation, and develop within ourselves that best fruit of nationality, a new and lasting literature."[132] In putting together his *Canadian Ballads*, McGee drew directly on cultural strategies he had used in Ireland, including the efficacy of the ballad as a popular form of communal literature.[133] Here, as in Ireland, McGee placed narrative at the center of his nationalism. Elsewhere, McGee's reworking in a Canadian context of the cultural nationalism formulated in Ireland in the 1840s is even more explicit. For instance, he finished his "Mental Outfit" with the lines "Oh brave young men, our hope, our pride, our promise, On you our hearts are set,—In manliness, in kindliness, in justice, To make *Canada* a nation yet!"[134] Here he paraphrased Samuel Ferguson's "Lament for Thomas Davis," first published in the *Dublin University Magazine* in 1847.[135]

McGee may have been able to transfer a line from Ferguson's poem into a Canadian context; however, aspects of the nationalism that he had espoused in Ireland could not be imported quite as easily. Specifically, whereas in Ireland in the 1840s McGee had relied upon Irish history to make the argument that nationality bound together the Irish people, in that the inhabitants of Ireland shared the same story, this would be a difficult case to make among European settlers in Canada, where the soil of history was thinner, and where the histories of individual ethnic groups varied considerably. Nonetheless, McGee did make the attempt. In *Canadian Ballads* McGee published three poems that venerated early European explorers and settlers in Canada; in them, figures such as Jacques Cartier and Sebastian Cabot appeared as heroic figures bringing Catholicism and, with it, civilization to the Canadian wilderness. In "Jacques Cartier" he imagines Cartier telling his French compatriots when he returned home:

Of the Algonquin braves—the hunters of the wild,
Of how the Indian mother in the forest rocks her child;
Of how, poor souls, they fancy in every living thing
A spirit good or evil, that claims their worshipping
Of how they brought their sick and maim'd for him to breathe upon,
And of the wonders wrought for them thro' the Gospel of St. John.[136]

As Katrin Urschel has observed, McGee sought to create "a national identity at the intersection of Christianity and Canadian history, thus replicating an imperial ideology."[137] From today's perspective, there are clear problems with this enterprise of creating a mythic history predicated upon the conquest of the First Nations as heroic. One might think of John Mitchel's vigorously satirical use of the verb "civilise" in the context of the Irish Famine, in characterizing mass starvation as a product of "British civilisation."[138] By the same token, McGee's attitude to the First Nations peoples—that they were in need of redemption in the form of Christian conversion—is effectively the same as Meagher's attitude to the Blackfoot nation he encountered in Montana.

Even without drawing attention to the limitations of McGee's project in such a context, he faced a far more immediate problem in trying to repeat the effect of the ballad history of Ireland in Canada: once the First Nations were effectively placed outside of history, there was not a lot of Canadian history left to work with. After writing about Cartier and Cabot, McGee appears to have exhausted his supply of suitable early European heroes in Canada upon which he could build a Canadian nationality. The paltry number upon which he could draw presented a challenge, because, as McGee himself acknowledged, "where men are born in the presence of the graves of their fathers, for even a few generations, the influence of that fact is great in enhancing their attachment to that soil."[139] In Canada in the 1850s and 1860s, it could not be assumed that settlers of European descent lived anywhere near "the graves of their fathers."[140] This was problematic for McGee, who had argued in response to Fenianism that "our first duty is to the land where we live and have fixed our homes, and where, while we live, we must find the true sphere of our duties. While always ready therefore to say the right word, and to do the right act for the land of my forefathers, I am bound above all to the land where I reside."[141] The challenge was to find as a reason as emotionally compelling to commit oneself to "the land where I reside"—a reason not purely transactional—as the reasons that existed to commit oneself to "the land of my forefathers."

To his credit, McGee seems to have registered the contradiction that emerged in attempting to create a Canadian history myth that ignored the First Nations people: he attempted to find a place for them in his poetry. As his biographer David A. Wilson has noted, in poems such as "Artic Indian's Faith," McGee wrote a form of verse history that placed "'aboriginal tribes" at the heart of Canadian history—or, at least, at the heart of McGee's understanding of that history—and allowed him "to insist that they were an integral part of the country's identity."[142] Admittedly, much of this poetry relied on the romanticizing and the patronizing tropes of the noble savage that considered First Nations peoples as part of a landscape that had to be tamed.[143] What is more, McGee's admiration for the spirituality of the First Nations was always framed by a belief that they would be brought into the fold, and that their religious beliefs could be reconciled to Christianity. This can be seen as part of a wider process that Lisa Phillips and Allan McDougall have identified in which "First Nations connections with the land were eventually erased [or at the very least appropriated] and replaced with social reconstructions that fit with the contemporary values."[144] This is precisely what McGee does in "Arctic Indian's Faith":

> That Spirit we worship who walks, unseen,
> Through our land of ice and snow;
> We know not His face, we know not His place,
> But His presence and power we know.[145]

As well as providing McGee with the basis to write a version of Canadian history that inscribed religious feeling into its earliest inhabitants—and into the landscape—the First Nations provided him with a neutral ground of identity, whereas any other figure from Canadian history, such as Cartier or Cabot, would be strongly identified with one or another ethnic group. In spite of this, the problem persisted for McGee that the First Nations peoples could not form the basis of an identity for a nation-state that was actively dispossessing them.

In the "Spirit" that "walks, unseen,/ Through our land of ice and snow," we glimpse yet another strategy that McGee employed to adapt his Young Ireland strategies of cultural nationalism to Canadian conditions.[146] If Canada was lacking in history (or, at least, what a nineteenth-century European would recognize as history), it was over-supplied with geography; as David A. Wilson has suggested, geography came to play the role in his Canadian writing that history had played in his Irish work.[147] Thus, we find him writing in 1860 in the same florid prose with which he had praised O'Sullivan Beare in Ireland twenty years earlier: "I see within the round of that shield, the peaks of the Western mountains and the crests of the Eastern waves—the winding Assinaboine, the five-fold lakes, the St. Lawrence, the Ottawa, the Saguenay, the St. John, and the Basin of Minas."[148] If he imagined Irish nationality as a parade of historical events (to take the titles of some of his ballads, "The Battle of Clontarf," The Landing of the Normans," and "Sir Cahir Doherty's Message")—he imagined Canada as an un-folding vista of landscapes.[149] This was, perhaps, the most enduring element of his Canadian cultural nationalist production, and one has only to look at the refrain that became the Canadian national anthem in 1980 to see its legacy: "O Canada! Where pines and maples grow, Great prairies spread and lordly rivers flow, How dear to us thy broad domain, From East to Western sea! Thou land of hope for all who toil! Thou True North, strong and free!"[150] By defining Canada primarily as a geographic rather than as a racial or historical community, McGee articulated a vision of a Canada that could be adapted to accommodate a wide variety of people and, as such, was essential to the creation of a pluralist Canadian nation.

McGee and Communications Technologies

The other way in which McGee compensated for the absence of a use-able common European history in Canada was to construct a Canadian nationalism that was forward looking and embraced new technologi-cal possibilities. In this vein, in 1867 McGee asked his audience "to consider now, on the eve of our first Dominion Parliament, with what intellectual forces and appliances, with what kind of mental com-mon stock, we are about to set up for ourselves, a distinct national existence in North America."[151] In a speech in the House of Assembly in Quebec on 2 May 1860 of "our march towards nationality" described by David Wilson as "the most eloquent expression of British North American Nationalism ever made," McGee put forth his vision of a Canadian nationality.[152] He stated, "I see in the not remote distance, one great nationality bound, like the shield of Achilles, by the blue rim of ocean—I see it quartered into many communities—each disposing of its internal affairs—but all bound together by free institutions, free intercourse, and free commerce."[153]

Herein lay the core of McGee's proposal for binding Canada together. "Free commerce" would be enabled by measures such as a common external tariff that would encourage economic development within the states, making the new state economically viable.[154] "Free intercourse" would be facilitated by the development of a railway and other transport routes linking the Canadian Provinces. "Free institutions," such as an independent press and denominational schools, would create a pluralist society, which meant that minorities like Irish Catholics would, unlike those in the United States, be able to participate actively in civic and political spheres. As Peter Russell has noted, this combination of "the principles of pluralism and pragmatism that McGee wrote about and spoke about so eloquently, and in which he came to believe so fervently, were essential to the successes of Confederation."[155]

One of the things that comes through most clearly in McGee's Assembly speech of 2 May 1860, is that—as had been the case with the Young Ireland generation in Ireland in the 1840s—his political vision in Canada in the 1860s had been made possible in part by new communications and transportation technologies. For McGee, the creation of an equitable national culture that would serve as the basis for a successful state depended upon recognizing the power of these technologies and making use of them accordingly. In *The Internal Condition of American Democracy*, McGee asked Duffy to "imagine what a power for evil an able man, without a conscience, may derive sitting behind an untaxed penny press, driven by steam!"[156] He saw the press and democracy as more than inextricably linked; they were similar, in that an unregulated press was like universal democracy, capable of running roughshod over minority rights; therefore, he favored the development of an indigenous Canadian press "free from the license which too often degrades and enfeebles the authority of the free press of the United States."[157] He advocated instead for a "higher style of newspaper," which he felt was the responsibility of journalists and the reading public.[158]

The creation of a distinct Canadian press with the means to distribute newspapers throughout the entire territory faced considerable physical challenges, based on the country's huge land expanse, which prevented the rapid communication of and debate about news and ideas and in this way might frustrate the rise of national (in contrast to regional) public opinion. Transport links joining Canada and the United States, as well as the Maritimes and the United States, were already reasonably strong through existing railroads and a series of canals (which, ironically, had been built with extensive government support). By contrast, travel between Canada and the Maritime Provinces required either travel by ship through the St. Lawrence River, which froze in the winter, or by means of an arduous overland crossing. Thus, information and printed material could travel more easily from the United States to British North America and Canada than it could within Britain's North American colonies. Therefore, McGee and others felt that it was a "political necessity" for the two parts of British North America to be connected by rail if the British Empire in North America was to avoid "annexation" by the "aggressive movements" of the United States.[159]

McGee's cultural nationalist understanding of politics meant that he became a key advocate for a railway linking Montreal and Halifax as part of the process of Canadian state-building. While the idea had been debated vigorously in Nova Scotia for much of the 1850s, McGee was one of the first Canadian politicians to connect the construction of the aptly named Intercolonial Railway with Confederation, and he believed that it would be central to the success of Confederation.[160] McGee argued that "the very Intercolonial Railroad, of which I am by-and-by to speak, is a proof of the absolute necessity of intercolonial association. Canada cannot build it alone; you cannot do it without Canada."[161] In making such an argument, McGee ensured that the construction of a transcontinental railroad became a key condition of Maritime participation in Confederation. Consequently, one of the key resolutions of the Quebec conference was that "the General Government shall secure, without delay, the completion of the Intercolonial Railway from Rivière-du-Loup through New Brunswick to

Truro, in Nova Scotia."[162] The centrality of communications technology to the idea of the nation was something McGee had learned in the 1840s in Ireland, where much of the effectiveness of Young Ireland could be attributed to the efficiency with which they ensured the availability of *The Nation* around the entire island, not just in Dublin. The difference between Ireland and British North America, however, lay in scale. The vast and sparsely populated geographical expanses meant that the considerable cost of the construction of railroads often had to be borne by the state (whereas in Britain and the United States, this was not the case). The railway networks that *The Nation* used to make sure that copies arrived in Cork or Belfast did not need the same level of state support that it would take, for instance, to ensure that a train ran from Halifax to Montreal, or Montreal to Edmonton; hence, if the nation as McGee understood it required an effective communications network, in British North America the construction of railways required, as A. A. Den Otter has written, "the mechanisms of an interventionist state."[163]

By the 1860s, however, technologies of communication had developed significantly since the days of *The Nation* in the 1840s. The most dramatic development of the period occurred in June 1866, when the first successful telegraph cable became operational, connecting Europe and North America through Valentia Island in Co. Kerry and Heart's Content in Newfoundland (a cable in 1857 had broken within its first weeks of operation).[164] "We are in telegraphic communication with Ireland," the *New York Times* exclaimed.[165] To use Jürgen Osterhammel's phrase, this "great new medium with a globalizing effect"—which produced near-instantaneous communication between Britain, British North America, and Ireland—fundamentally altered the political space in which McGee was operating.[166] As Duncan Bell has argued, "Conceptions of time and space structure the way in which ideologies and theories articulate political projects"; whether this was within the British Empire, as in Bell's formulation, or, more broadly, in a global context, changes in communications technologies altered the "imaginative limits" of the state.[167] Not least, it gave the project of empire central nervous system, enabling a communicative space that finally mapped onto the political, geographical, and cultural parameters of the British Empire.[168]

From very early on, and before most other commentators, McGee grasped the political significance of the telegraph for the project of state-building in British North America, not least for the means it provided to create a North American state that could continue to draw on the resources of the British Empire. No longer an outpost, the telegraph had the potential to make Canada part of a larger entity. Writing in the *Ottawa Times* in August 1866, he declared that "intentions and demands of men can be transmitted, by this means, at a rate of 280,000 miles in a second of time—from London to Ottawa, once in the wires in about the 90th part of a second. As the mean difference of time between Ottawa and London is about five hours . . . it follows that a direct message started from there at 12 o'clock practically might be read here at 7—sharp, or, apparently, five hours before the message had taken shape in the mind of the sender."[169]

In August 1866, when fears that the Fenian raids of April and June of that year would escalate in intensity, this was more than an abstract idea for McGee. In case of war, immediate communication between London and Ottawa was not simply a technological marvel, but a strategic game-changer: "When we have Woolwich and Portsmouth, and Downing Street within an easy forenoon's reach of us, it is perfectly evident that we have all the resources of the Empire not only theoretically, but practically at our back, in any just defensive war, which we may be forced to face."[170] Indeed, the Fenians provided (an unintended) impetus for the telegraph's further development in Canada by spurring construction by the Canadian government of a second line between Kingston and Montreal in April 1866, specifically to ensure that they could quickly marshal soldiers to respond to any future Fenian raid.[171]

Beyond this practical use, however, the transatlantic telegraph contributed to Canadian nationality by consolidating a link with Britain that, paradoxically, was seen as a distinctive marker of identity. As J. M. Bumsted has noted, "Canadian nationality would be somehow inseparably entwined with Imperial enthusiasm and loyalty."[172] What is more, this cut across the divisions in Canadian society: a "strong tie with Britain," and, in particular, British institutions, was a matter of importance for Anglophone Canadians, many of whom saw themselves as British; for Francophone Canadians who saw those institutions as protecting

them from the excesses of the Anglophone Canadians; and for Indigenous Canadians, whose limited rights were guaranteed by treaties with
the Crown rather than with local Canadian institutions and who also
turned to the larger entity for protection.[173]

The Limits of Irishness

When McGee praises the transatlantic telegraph for putting the British
Army in London on call in Ottawa, it is worth remembering that he
had ended up in Canada in the first place because he had to flee Ireland for advocating armed resistance to that same army. For some time
before the Fenian raids of 1866, McGee had been attempting to put his
Young Ireland past behind him, even as it continued to form the bedrock of his cultural capital. In 1865, in a printed copy of a speech that
he had given in Wexford, Ireland (the speech actually given was different, but it was the printed copy that was read in North America),[174] he
rejected the idea that revolution was ever a legitimate response, commented that Young Ireland had been a "pack of fools," and described
what he saw as the buffoonish Fenians as "Punch and Judy Jacobins."[175]
In Montreal in January that same year, he accused the Fenians of being
the greatest barrier to progress in Ireland, imploring an assembled audience at the St. Patrick's Society, an Irish fraternal organization, to "purge
your ranks of this political leprosy; weed out and cast off those rotten
members who without a single governmental grievance to complain of
in Canada, would yet weaken and divide us in these days of danger and
anxiety."[176]

Speeches like these pushed to a breaking point the tension between
his identity as an Irish rebel and the form that his political views were
taking as they adapted to the religious and ethnic pluralism of Canada.
"When you were editor of *The New Era* you were as big a rebel as ever
uttered alive," J. J. Sullivan wrote to him in 1866. "What were you but
a rebel when you called the English flag the 'pirate Union Jack,' the
robber of the high seas."[177] However, after establishing McGee's former
nationalist credentials, Sullivan continued: "You turncoat, do you think
that we the citizens of Montréal are fools or that we have no memories?
and you turn round and call the Fenians a lot of rascals . . . because they
are trying to free themselves from the yoke of England."[178] He then

made a direct threat, stating that the Fenians "will give you something that you will recollect, and which will not go down with you quite as well as the dinner that you received."[179]

At the same time, it is important to recall that back in 1847 McGee had been one of the most ardent speakers among the deputation of Young Irelanders at the public meeting in Belfast's Music Hall, attempting to convince members of the Orange Lodge that their best interests were served by aligning themselves with *The Nation*. A little over twenty years later, after an outburst of anti-Confederation sentiment in Nova Scotia, when prime minister John A. Macdonald dispatched McGee to find a solution, McGee wrote back to suggest that in Nova Scotia "both Masonic and Orange influences of the right kind, might be brought to combat these republican tendencies," which he felt were behind the anti-Confederation sentiments.[180] One satirical publication from Montreal took particular umbrage at this: "A boy from the *Nation* sayin a kindly word of Orangemin and Prosbeterans! What would poor Duffy think if he was listenin to you on Tuesday last?"[181] Certainly, for a public figure whose reputation still referenced his involvement with Young Ireland to be making overtures to the Orange Order must have seemed like a betrayal of his earlier principles; however, it is also consistent with McGee's advocacy of a political culture founded on parity of esteem. "Orangemen were an important and indispensable element in the consensus which brought about Confederation," he insisted, and, as a consequence, he could not ignore them.[182] What is more, as David Wilson has pointed out, "the central tenets of McGee's new nationality were shared by many Canadian Orangemen," and this extended to such practical considerations as "east-west railway development and selective protectionism."[183]

In some respects, McGee's political evolution provides us with a limit case in the transnational politics of Young Ireland. From his own perspective, McGee's efforts to help create in Canada a state in which the rights of Irish Catholics could be protected was entirely consistent with his political goals in Ireland in the 1840s; a line connects the McGee who reached out to Orangemen Belfast in 1847 to the McGee who suggested that Orange support could save Confederation in Spring, 1868. However, for those who had adopted the identity-based cultural politics he had been so instrumental in forging, the actions and alli-

Figure 5.2. James Inglis, *Cortège Funèbre Lors des Funérailles de l'Honorable Thomas D'Arcy McGee.* Library and Archives Canada, James Inglis Fonds, c083423.

ances he made in pursuit of those ends in Canada amounted to apostasy. The full extent of the danger of McGee's willingness to cast aside his own mythology became apparent later in 1868: on 7 April, arriving back at his boardinghouse after a parliamentary debate that went past midnight, McGee was shot in the neck by a Fenian, Patrick James Whelan. He died at the scene. Although spies asserted that the Fenian leadership condemned the murder, many of its rank and file felt that McGee had reaped what he had sowed. His assassination convulsed Canadian politics, and McGee's detractors rushed to condemn his murder. It is estimated that over eighty thousand people lined the streets of Ottawa—at a time when the city's population was just over one hundred thousand—as his funeral cortege passed through.[184]

Conclusion

Only hours before his assassination, McGee delivered what was to be his final speech in the House of Commons. In its closing lines, he spoke in defense of Confederation and told the House that he was one "who have been, and who am still, its warm and earnest advocate speak here not as the representative of any race, or of any Province, but as thoroughly and emphatically a Canadian, ready and bound to recognize the claims, if any, of my Canadian fellow subjects, from the farthest east to the farthest west, equally as those of my nearest neighbour."[185]

In his speech, McGee encapsulated the ideas at the core of his Canadian nationalism. He strongly articulated a distinctive Canadian nationality, but he left its content largely open ended, evoked in vague geographical terms, reduced to "east" and "west," both horizons beckoning toward some hopeful future. Underlying his rhetoric, however, is a consistent position: that the concept of the nation must be expansive enough to enable the creation of a state that would protect minority rights, even if that meant putting limits on what he called "universal democracy" and "republicanism." To this end, he told the House, he had contributed to the first Constitution ever given to a mixed people, in which the conscientious rights of the minority are made a subject of formal guarantee."[186]

6

Australia, 1856–1872

In 1856, immediately upon arriving in Melbourne, Charles Gavan Duffy told an audience assembled to greet him that

> I had hoped to-night to speak of the future destiny of these countries; not only of the political liberty in store for us, but of the precious opportunity we enjoy in a new social experiment of adopting whatever is best in the habits of kindred nations, and rejecting whatever has proved dangerous or deleterious; till a national Australian character grows, which, once created, will probably prevail on the shores of the Southern Ocean after the last stone of this city has crumbled into dust.[1]

From one perspective, this was the Charles Gavan Duffy the crowd had come to see. To anyone who had followed Duffy's writings and speeches as a Young Irelander in Ireland, much of this was familiar: the belief in a future that included "political liberty," and the assertion that the foundation of the nation was a national "character," an ineffable force more permanent than the stones of the city and, by extension, the state itself. They would have every reason to expect as much; Charles Gavan Duffy's credentials were impeccable. He was one of the founders of *The Nation* and had subsequently been tried (and acquitted) three times for his involvement in Young Ireland activities. Unlike Mitchel or Meagher, he was not deported, so he remained in Ireland after the rebellion of 1848 and was elected to the House of Commons in 1852 for the Independent Irish Party. It was not until 1856 that a combination of a weak economy in Ireland, his frustration with Irish politics, and the material attraction of gold-rush Australia carried him to the newly created colony of Victoria, which had separated from New South Wales in 1851.

However, if we look more closely at his speech, we see that it differs from his Young Ireland writings in one obvious and important way: now the "future destiny" of which he speaks is to be found "on the

shores of the Southern Ocean." What we see here is a confident assertion of the claims of settler colonialism, mingled with the politics of
cultural nationalism as it took shape in Ireland in the 1840s. What will
become apparent as we trace Duffy's career in Australian politics is the
addition of a political stance best described as liberalism, both to his
nationalism and to his newfound embrace of settler colonialism. For
Duffy, this was not incompatible with either of the two other strands in
his political makeup, although it would produce its own challenges and
contradictions, particularly in relation to the situation of the Aboriginal peoples of Australia. From his Melbourne speech onward, Duffy
would be involved in forging a liberal Australia, which allows us to
see him in the context of a growing body of literature that argues that
liberalism and settler colonialism often went hand in hand.[2] If we take
the two primary flaws in recent work on liberalism and empire identified by Duncan Bell—namely, "a tendency to overlook the significance
of settler colonialism and over-reliance on canonical interpretations of
liberalism"—then Duffy and the wider Young Ireland generation in
Australia offer an excellent means through which to study the practice
of liberalism in the context of settler colonialism.[3]

In 1871 Duffy was elected premier of Victoria, and he began to argue
for what would become the Federation of Australia, insisting that the
state should create the conditions and institutions of a nation, which
would facilitate nationalism. In turn, nationalism would create mature,
responsible individuals, who would sustain liberty and support the state
for its role in creating the conditions in which liberty was possible. In
Australia, class and sectarian differences posed less of an existential question for the Young Ireland generation than they did elsewhere, rendered
less pressing by a combination of the social and economic upheavals of
the gold rush, an influx of European radicals, vast expanses of land available for white settlement, and little external threat of invasion. This created the conditions for a "new social experiment" that finally combined
republican and liberal conceptions of rights with a nationalism along the
lines that they had envisaged for Ireland. This chapter explores how the
Young Ireland generation navigated Australian politics in the 1850s to
1870s. It shows their fervent belief that nationalism would create Australians who could be trusted to act in service of a common interest, which
would make a democratic Australian state viable.

Melbourne, Victoria

By the time Duffy arrived in Melbourne, a network of Young Irelanders had begun to form in Australia that, over the course of the
1850s and early 1860s, would include the former editor of the *Galway
Vindicator* Edward Butler, Kevin Izod O'Doherty, and the poet Mary
Anne Kelly. Central to the attraction of Australia—and specifically
of Victoria—during this period was the gold rush. In those years, the
population of Victoria mushroomed, from 77,345 in 1851 to 540,322
in 1861.[4] This increase was largely driven by the arrival of immigrants,
many from Ireland, looking for opportunities in the decade after the
Famine. Although outnumbered by men, considerable numbers of
women migrated as well, drawn by the less rigid social structures of
colonial society, which offered opportunities not available in Europe.[5]
Irish migrants would likely have been enticed by newspapers, which,
like the *Irish Examiner* in 1852, told their readers that "the Australian
papers teem with news from the gold districts, with accounts of new
diggings and rich fields, of large quantities of gold."[6] Irish newspapers
widely reported "the continued and increasing prosperity of the colony
of Victoria, and of the Australian colonies."[7] For example, *The Nation*
noted that "the most marvellous accounts are hourly received as to the
vast extent and inexhaustible richness of the Australian Diggings. New

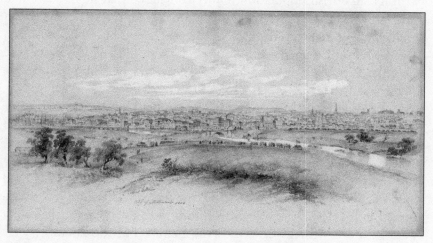

Figure 6.1. Albert Charles Cooke, *City of Melbourne, 1858*. State Library of Victoria, 1662471.

mines are discovered every day, and the wealth realised by individual diggers [unsettled gold prospectors] is extraordinary."[8] With the prospect of gold diggings "unlimited in extent and inexhaustible in their treasures" and the attendant boomtown economy, it was little wonder that Victoria appeals to Irish immigrants in the 1850s.[9]

However, in Victoria itself, residents expressed concern that the gold rush was bringing in "all the reckless vagabonds from all parts of the world,"[10] and that the rapid expansion of an unsettled population in the gold fields would create what the *Melbourne Daily News* described as "a most lawless state of society . . . , and that crimes of every description will abound."[11] In response, dedicated efforts were made to create a civic and cultural sphere in Victoria—specifically in Melbourne—that would counter the ill effects of the gold rush on Victorian society. This led to an impressive spate of institution-founding (helped, it must be admitted, by the wealth generated by the very goldfields that were the source of the anxiety). The University of Melbourne was founded in 1853 with support from the Catholic and Anglican bishops.[12] It was soon followed by a public library in Victoria, funded by the state and intended as a national institution in 1856.[13] As Ann Curthoys and Jessie Mitchell have observed, Victoria in the 1850s was "an environment that fostered literacy, education and political liberalism and radicalism."[14] Therefore, when it came to choosing between Melbourne or Sydney, with its large Irish population, Duffy concluded that he had come to see "many reasons for preferring Melbourne. From the spirit of the men I had encountered, and the tone of the people and of public meetings, and the Press, it seemed certain that Victoria would take the lead of the Colonies in public spirit and courageous experiment. This was a motive all but irresistible."[15]

The political sphere in Victoria was also broader than in Ireland or Great Britain. Universal adult male suffrage by secret ballot was enacted in 1856, the year of Duffy's arrival; in 1857, the requirement that members of the legislative assembly be property owners was abolished. Duffy had successfully lobbied for this, asking, "Was Victoria likely to hold the foremost place she ambitioned in the march of freedom if she continued to maintain this system?"[16] From 1859, elections for that body were held every three years; in 1870, members of the assembly were granted a stipend, which meant that it was no longer necessary to have private wealth in order to sit as an elected member.[17] While most British commentators, including liberals, were critical of democracy there, Victoria actually compares favorably to the United Kingdom, where, in 1856, approximately one in every five men could vote, a property qualification for MPs remained on the Statute Book until 1858, and MPs would not be paid until 1911.[18] What is more, Victorian residents were well aware of the extent to which their political rights greatly exceeded those afforded to people in England. In 1858, one of the main Melbourne newspapers, *The Age*, made the statement that "among the chief advantages coveted by civilised and intelligent men, are political power and independence. The people of Victoria have had the rare fortune to obtain . . . the right of Manhood Suffrage."[19] However, a major reason for advocating such relatively generous democratic rights in Victoria were the people in the goldfields, who constituted the majority of Victoria's population and who were not shy about pushing their grievances and their demands for representation to the fore.[20]

The most spectacular manifestation of democratic agitation in the goldfields occurred in the territory just outside the boomtown of Ballarat on 30 November 1854: what became known as the "Eureka Stockade," a rebellion in the goldfields, driven by a combination of anger at increases in golddigger licenses to a maximum of £1 a month (in effect, a tax) at a time when the right to vote was restricted solely to property owners, who in many cases paid comparatively less actual tax.[21] This, the rebels said, instantiated taxation without representation, as the diggers were, by and large, not landowners. Peter Lalor emerged as a leader among the miners: an engineer and brother of the Young Irelander James Fintan Lalor, who had been associated with John Mitchel's militant *United Irishman* newspaper in Dublin in 1848 and whose support for large-scale Irish land reform made him one of the most radical members of the group at the time of the 1848 rebellion.[22] Several Chartists joined Peter Lalor—notably, Tom Kennedy and John Basson Humffray—as well as other European radicals like Raffaello Carboni, who had been involved in the Young Italy movement in the 1840s (and who would later write an influential account of the Eureka Stockade).[23] Under Lalor's command, the diggers built a makeshift stockade at Eureka and began to train in military tactics. The stockade lasted for two days before, on 3 December 1854, a combination of soldiers and policemen stormed it, leaving twenty-two people dead.[24] Therefore, while we should of course be mindful that "the first Parliament that met under Victoria's new constitution was alert to the democratic spirit of the goldfields," we must also recognize that contained within that "spirit" was the spirit of the European and Irish militant movements of the 1840s.[25]

The O'Dohertys in Brisbane

From the middle of the 1850s until the end of the 1870s, a considerable Young Ireland network existed in Australia that extended well beyond the group forcibly based in Van Diemen's Land early in that period. Among them was Kevin Izod O'Doherty, who, upon his release from Van Diemen's Land, briefly and unsuccessfully prospected for gold in Bendigo, Victoria, before returning to Europe.[26] Facing poor financial prospects there after he received his medical degree, he moved back to Australia and settled in Brisbane with his wife, the poet Mary Anne O'Doherty (née Kelly), who had written in *The Nation* as "Eva of *The Nation*."[27]

In his early years in Australia, Kevin Izod O'Doherty established himself as a leading surgeon,[28] but he soon gravitated back to politics and was elected to the Legislative Assembly in August 1867.[29] His views often mirrored those of other Young Irelanders in Australia in their emphasis on the importance of education—of reading in particular—for the development of a democratic state. For instance, O'Doherty became involved in the establishment of a museum and in plans to build a library in Brisbane in 1871—although, unlike in Melbourne, the library was not built.[30] He also served on the board of the nondenominational Brisbane Grammar school, but he opposed bills that sought to remove funding from denominational schools, in a move echoing Thomas D'Arcy McGee's stance on that particular issue in Canada.[31] Moreover, like the other former Young Irelanders, he remained part of a globalized Irish nationalist politics. In 1883, O'Doherty presided over an Irish Australian convention held in Melbourne at which John Redmond spoke to over 150 delegates from across Australia and New Zealand.[32]

Brisbane did not, however, have the cultural, economic, or political vitality of Melbourne or Sydney.[33] Mary Anne O'Doherty, who in the 1840s had been among the most popular of *The Nation* poets, wrote a number of poems that described her difficulty in adjusting to life in Queensland,[34] including a poem simply entitled "Queensland":

> In virgin freshness calm and bland . . .
> No old tradition's magic lies . . .
> There is no heart within thy breast,
> No classic charms of memory hoary,
> No footprint hath of old Time imprest,
> On thee of song or story.[35]

One senses here that "bland" is not a complimentary term. The cultural nationalism of Young Ireland had been deeply rooted in a sense of history, and, even in the midst of active political careers, Thomas D'Arcy McGee would find time to write *A Popular History of Ireland from the Earliest Period to the Emancipation of the Catholics* in 1863, while John Mitchel would write a two-volume *History of Ireland from the Treaty of Limerick to the Present Time* in 1869, as well as a biography of the seventeenth-century figure Aodh O'Neill in 1845. Queensland was a land with neither "charms of memory" nor "old traditions"—clearly a problem for a poet who in Ireland had been part of a concerted effort to cultivate a conception of an Irish nation based on its "mystic stories of ages gone."[36] At the same time, this sense of disconnection was part of a wider trend in Australian society at the time, when individuals who had been separated from their homes and the communities of origin that determined their identities found that they could reinvent themselves and their politics.[37] In her poem "Ad Astra," Kelly continued developing the theme of the absence of a past upon which to draw:

> Thou hast no token from the shadowy land,
> The storied past, heroic and sublime;
> No sacred lore or cryptic myth of time,
> Nor print of footstep on thy golden sand.
> Blank, mute, and barren—earth and sea and sky—
> On thee are writ no records proud and high.[38]

"Ad Astra" concludes on a more upbeat tone than "Queensland." In a trajectory that echoes other Young Irelanders in Australia, Kelly comes to see that because Australia's past lacked the imaginative resources from which to forge a sense of nationality, that hole could be filled by identifying Australia with the future:

> Australia Felix, born to name and fame.
> Onward to starry heights thy path doth tend,
> As flame shoots upward, so must thou ascend
> To noble impulse and heroic aim.
> And reach at length thy glorious destiny
> A place amongst the nations, proud and free![39]

In promoting a forward-looking nationalist agenda, in which the solidarities that bind the nation together lie in the future and not in the past and "its dead," Kelly did what others of the Young Ireland generation would do elsewhere in the world. Faced with circumstances that differed from those in which her political formation had been grounded, she adapted while maintaining the core belief that a nation is shaped by its "spirit"—which, in this case, happened to be oriented toward the "starry heights" of the future, rather than the lost glories of the past.

In terms of creating a compelling national narrative, Kelly met with some success; her Australian poetry was as popular in Australia as her Irish poetry had been in Ireland, and both were carried to the United States by the networks of print that the Young Ireland generation utilized so adeptly, with an edition of her poetry published in 1877 in San Francisco.[40] Like her husband, Kelly's contribution to the formation of the state in Australia may have been relatively modest (compared to, say, McGee's involvement in Canadian Confederation); however, it does provide yet another instance of the ways in which political and cultural strategies that had been formulated in Ireland in the 1840s could be adapted and reapplied in very different contexts.

Duffy in Australia

It was into this context of an Australia in flux, in which there were demonstrable opportunities—political and personal—for former Young Irelanders, that Charles Gavan Duffy moved to Melbourne.

Unlike O'Doherty, however, Duffy had been actively courted to come to Australia by the Irish community, specifically on the promise that he would play a central role in "assist[ing] in the furtherance of progressive and liberal legislation for this our adopted land."[41] The Hibernian Australian Catholic Benefit Society invited Duffy specifically so that "in the future as in the past [he would] show the Irishmen of this Country that they can be true to the Principles for which their Fathers fought and suffered in Ireland, and at the same time law-abiding Citizens of this free and fair land of Australia."[42] The illuminated addresses presented to Duffy upon his arrival emphasized that "we are convinced that the people of no Country can boast a more earnest solicitude for the amplest popular rights and fullest Civil and Religious Liberty."[43] Their desire to "increase the measure of those inestimable blessings" can be seen in the money that locals (mainly but not exclusively from the Irish community) raised to ensure that Duffy could take an active role in Victorian politics.[44] Ultimately, this amounted to £5,016, considerably more than the £2,000 required for Duffy to "get his qualification" to run for a seat in the Legislative Assembly.[45] Those who raised the money were already familiar with Duffy, because as an Irish MP he had played an important role in guiding legislation concerning Victoria through the Houses of Parliament in London. It was for this reason that, as the Irish-born politician (and later premier of Victoria) John O'Shanassy put it, "the first proceeding of the People of Victoria after Charles Gavan Duffy had sought the shelter of that Constitution which he helped to obtain for them, was to secure him the Property Qualification."[46]

Duffy's political credentials made him attractive to a broad range of Australian liberals outside of the Irish community as well. For instance, Sir Henry Parkes—who would go on to spend more time as premier of New South Wales than anyone else in history, and who would be the person to push through Australian Federation in 1901—wrote favorably of Duffy in *The Empire* before his arrival. He stated that "we cannot enter into the national sympathies which tinged the political creed of the Young Ireland party, but we, in common with thousands in every part of the world, watched the extraordinary struggles of 1848 and 1849 with an interest which could not resist the fascinations of intellectual power so remarkable all through that strangely-chequered and unfortunate movement."[47] Parkes expressed the view that "men of every faith, and entertaining sentiments the most diverse and opposite, warmed to the heroic eloquence" of the Young Irelanders.[48] However, he also argued that "the vigorous writing, which has characterised *The Nation* throughout its existence, is not the highest quality of Mr. DUFFY."[49] For Parkes, Duffy's appeal lay not in the cultural nationalist legacy his movement had left in Ireland but in the skills he demonstrated in organizing Young Ireland, and in the proposals for reform that he had advanced in his native country.

Indeed, although Duffy moved to Victoria (rather than New South Wales, as Parkes had hoped), this prediction turned out to be accurate.[50] Duffy, as the only person in the Victorian Legislative Assembly with experience at Westminster, on which parts of the Victorian system had been modeled, was often called upon to give advice on parliamentary procedure.[51] There was in this, of course, a certain irony: an Irish nationalist being charged with ensuring that Victoria, a British colony, could follow Westminster's parliamentary rules. Yet Parkes also contended that "those who have most closely observed his public life, have recognised in him a projective human talent."[52] The phrase "projective human talent" suggests that what Parkes saw in Duffy was both an ability to organize and a respect for democratic institutions that could be applied in a variety of contexts—"projected," as it were. As this chapter will argue, Parkes's contemporaries widely shared this view.

When he arrived, Duffy would have been aware of the tumult on the goldfields, and it is likely that it reinforced his belief in the fragility of the state, even in Melbourne. However, he would always be adept at turning a challenge into an opportunity. Shortly after arriving in Melbourne in 1856, he took the position that if future Eureka Stockade rebellions were to be avoided, the solution was to be found in forging an inclusive Australian nationalism. "As a national Australian character grows," he told his audience in his 1856 speech in Melbourne, "it will probably prevail on the shores of the Southern Ocean after the last stone of this city has crumbled into dust."[53] Duffy's speech thus extended beyond a view held among radical Australian politicians that groundwork for "the great national movements of the Australian future" was being laid.[54] In his vision of a national spirit enduring "after the last stone of this city has crumbled into dust," he posited the nation-state as not simply one possible expedient political formation among others, and that "national character" has a noncontingent nature that will last. From that point on, he would be consistent in arguing for Australian Federation, becoming "the most vociferous advocate of federation in the late 1860s," according to John Manning Ward, thereby moving the conversation about federation from its position as a commercial and administrative endeavor to "the level of a surging national endeavour."[55] To this end, on 23 May 1862, at a committee convened by Duffy with the intention of establishing a roadmap to federate Australia, he said that "we shall best set ourselves right with the world by uniting our strength and capacity in a common centre."[56]

Beyond his deeply rooted faith in the nation as an entity that would endure through time, Duffy argued for Australian federation on pragmatic grounds that in some ways echo the arguments his erstwhile colleague Thomas D'Arcy McGee made during those same years in Canada. Writing in 1867, Duffy envisaged a "European war, for which every continental power in Europe is preparing," and into which he felt Australia would inevitably be drawn if it could not "effect a federal union of the Australian colonies before the European war."[57] This came at the height of British fears of a war with France over Belgian neutrality.[58] Federation, Duffy felt, would allow Australians a degree of separation from Britain that would enable them to remain neutral and, consequently, unscathed. The fear that Australia might get involved in a European war was not just Duffy's. In 1853 *The Argus* had written: "We state our belief that, at no time since this colony was first settled, was there greater probability of a war in Europe, in which the whole civilised world may be forced to take a part."[59] However, this line of argument was made by a minority of commentators and was largely unconvincing, because, as several of Duffy's colleagues pointed out (including Richard Baker, the attorney general of South Australia), Australia was simply too far from Europe for any country to consider invading.[60] A committee of the parliament in Victoria found that no other nation "could possibly attempt to land a body of troops in Australia for the conquest of Australia, except possibly the French."[61] In this sense, Australia's geographical position made Duffy's arguments moot, until an increasingly expansive Japan in the late nineteenth century raised the specter of an invasion from Asia.

Duffy found support for Federation in a fellow Young Irelander, Edward Butler, who in 1853 had moved from Ireland to Sydney, where he took up a post with Parke's newspaper, *The Empire*. This was another of those ironies with which the careers of Young Irelanders in Australia are rife: a former rebel against the British Empire writing for an Australian newspaper called *The Empire*. It is perhaps a measure of the extent to which Parkes was able to see past the specific circumstances of Butler's political career in Ireland that he developed a friendship with him. Butler, for his part, threw himself into the fight for responsible government in New South Wales, and he became a prominent figure within the liberal movement in New South Wales. Butler wrote to Duffy that "I cannot imagine how any person could have an objection to the Federal scheme."[62] Yet Butler was aware of the challenges that lay ahead in this particular political battle, admitting that "the one objection" he could see was "that when a permissive or enabling statute were obtained it would be likely for a long time to come no practical results."[63] Beyond such technical impediments, Butler shared with Duffy a foundational conviction of the importance of cultural nationalism; the Australian people had to first of all feel that they were Australian. He was concerned, he wrote, that "the colonies do not appear to be awake upon this matter of federation. Here in New South Wales there is no major public opinion upon the subject if indeed there is any public opinion at all."[64] After identifying the lack of public support for Duffy's scheme of federation, Butler then argued that politicians would "with their endeavours to get into public office or to keep themselves there" be unlikely to support such a large reform without public demand to do so.[65] Essentially, the problem was how to make a population into a polity.

Land and Colonialism

Throughout Duffy's Australian career, the discussion of Federation would remain largely confined to the political elite. The issue of the distribution of land, however, touched all aspects of Victorian politics and society. This presented Duffy with a situation in which his Irish experience was germane, for land ownership and nationality were inextricably interwoven in Ireland. Upon his arrival in Australia,

Duffy emphasized his role in "the Tenant League, of which I was one of the founders."[66] Whereas the issue in Ireland with land lay primarily with heredity ownership, Australia had the opposite problem: there, wealthy squatters had taken advantage of the inability of early colonial governments to control vast tracts of land and had settled there without the explicit approval of the colonial government. By the end of the 1840s, approximately seventy million acres had been commandeered by fewer than two thousand squatters.[67] As the decades passed, their entitlement to the land would be recognized by law, culminating in Victoria in the Land Act of 1860, which made squatters leaseholders and thus consolidated "the pastoral monopoly" that they held.[68] Duffy sought to counter this; just as the Tenant League in Ireland had taken up the cause of small farmers, in Australia Duffy worked to reform the Land Acts in Victoria to facilitate property ownership for a comparable social group.

In his efforts on behalf of Australian land reform, Duffy was helped by Moses Wilson Gray, who had accompanied him to Australia in 1856. In Ireland, Gray had moved in similar social and political circles as Duffy and had been one of the proprietors of the *Freeman's Journal* during the 1840s. In spite of his newspaper interests, Gray's main concern was land reform. He had traveled earlier to the United States and Canada and in 1848 returned to Dublin, where he published a pamphlet, *Self-Paying Colonisation in North America*.[69] After moving to Victoria, Gray founded the Victorian Land League, which advocated change in land distribution in Victoria and opposed the monopolization of land by squatters.[70] Duffy claimed that the Victorian Land League was partly his idea, and his prominence as a land reformer meant that in the O'Shanassy ministries in 1858–59 and 1861–63, Duffy was made minister in charge of the Lands Department.

For Duffy and others, ownership of land was intricately connected with democracy. The Land League sought to mobilize their supporters with the cry "A vote, a farm, a rifle."[71] For the Young Ireland generation who, in Ireland, had understood democracy in line with their contemporaries as "opposition to oligarchy or privilege," opposition to the monopolization of land, then, was a natural position to take.[72] Indeed, Duffy's *Guide to the Land Law of Victoria* featured a section about "checks on monopoly" in land holding.[73] When Gray ran for election to the Legislative Assembly in 1859, he stated that he aimed "to Open the Country to the Man of Small Means."[74] This intertwining of democracy and land came about as a result of the introduction of universal manhood suffrage in 1856. In Duffy's case, it has been argued that much of his support base in Australia was comprised of those who had been enfranchised by the recent reforms, but who did not own land.[75] This would explain why promises to reform that system of landholding were a key aspect of Duffy's appeal to voters.[76]

Duffy believed that "a yeoman proprietary has long been recognised as the safest basis on which a state can rest," and he advanced this idea in a pamphlet in 1862, when he was president of the board of Land and Works.[77] In arguing for a yeoman propriety, he placed himself directly in opposition to Edward Gibbon Wakefield, an English liberal whose writings, as James Belich has noted, largely reflected public opinion on colonization in Britain.[78] Wakefield wrote frequently about colonization in Australia, where he advocated the creation of a society like that of rural England, with large estates, "high farming," and plentiful, cheap labor, in order to maximize profits.[79] Having seen the Irish version of this unravel grotesquely in Famine Ireland in the 1840s, Duffy and the Young Ireland generation formed part of a wider movement at the time who rejected Wakefield's model, turning instead to the American and Canadian system of "Homestead Act" settlement, which favored smaller, landowner-operated farms. Here, Duffy embraced the form of liberalism most famously advocated by John Stuart Mill, with whom we know he corresponded.[80] Writing about Ireland,[81] Mill had advocated for a peasant proprietorship, arguing that a system of large landowners was "the grand economical, as well as moral, evil of Ireland."[82] Duffy, too, believed that the purpose of land ownership was not necessarily to maximize the return on capital, but to provide a basis for civil and moral growth. He thought that a more equal division of land was essential to the survival of the Australian state. He wrote, "It has been the habit of late to speak of our era of prosperity in the past tense; the time was (it is said) when such and such successes might have been achieved."[83] He rejected such an understanding of Australian history and argued that "when every temperate, industrious man may take for himself a home," then the future of Australia would be secure.[84]

For Duffy, then, smallholders were at the core of Australian society—not just in the present, but in the future. This connected the issue of landholding to the question of nationality. "The next generation, I am persuaded, will look back with similar feelings upon the opportunities we possess at this moment, when the pith and marrow of the world-famous Australian soil, ribbed with gold, is thrown open to all, at a cost which the humblest may reach."[85] Duffy connected the distribution of land with the "national interest," writing that "the humblest shall reach it is our highest national interest at present."[86] Moreover, when the Land League used the motto of "Advance Australia" and rallied around the Southern Cross flag, they underlined the symbolic links between land-holding and a nascent Australian national identity.[87] In a country whose "prosperity" remained "subject to fluctuations and panics whenever a rich reef [gold-bearing quartz vein] is discovered in another colony, or even in another hemisphere," land ownership served as a means of "fasten[ing] the industrious population to the soil by the potent tie of ownership."[88] Therefore, Duffy argued, the distribution of land was essential to Australian nationalism and democracy.

To this end, in 1862 Duffy pressed for the introduction of a Land Act, which sought to allow the purchase of land by the smallholders central to his policy. His legislation aimed to "throw open to all adult males and single adult women" the ability to select land for purchase.[89] However, Duffy's act was largely ineffective, and most of the squatters bought back the lands they were already occupying. Echoing Young Ireland criticisms of Irish people who had not supported the 1848 rebellion, Duffy contended that the act failed because "the very class for whom we legislated sold their inheritance for some paltry bribe."[90] Nonetheless, there would be other efforts to regulate the sale of land in Victoria, with previous and subsequent acts or amendments in 1860, 1862, 1865, and 1869. The sheer quantity of legislation on the issue suggests that Duffy was not the only person to struggle to control the squatters. Brendon Kelson and John McQuilton have suggested that "the Land Acts were nothing less than one of Australia's most ambitious attempts at social engineering," which sought to create "a colony of small farmers."[91]

It is in the intersection of land ownership, settlement, and nationality that we begin to glimpse some of the blind spots in the Young

Ireland concept of a nonsectarian, nonethnic nationalism when transplanted to Australia. Settlement was crucial to the Young Ireland generation's nationalism in Australia, and in Canada, and, for Meagher, in Montana, because it "emphasised the creation of new societies, not the control of old ones. It had no moral superiority over Empire." However, as James Belich reminds us, "it tended to displace, marginalize and occasionally even exterminate indigenous peoples rather than simply exploit them."[92] When we apply scholarship on empire more broadly to the Young Ireland generation, we see that they were, at the very least, complicit in the process of subimperialism, whereby the colonial population—often without the explicit approval of the Colonial Office, in the case of existing imperial structures—engaged in and directed territorial expansion and consolidation. The most common form of subimperialism would be found in settler colonialism, and subimperial settler colonialism was at the heart of the policies that Duffy advocated and imposed. Duffy's subimperialism created a fundamentally different power dynamic than more conventional patterns of imperial settlement. The decentralized nature of the decision to colonize and to annex new territory meant that the subimperialist colonists were often at odds with the metropolitan elite in London, who were reluctant to commit to (and to pay for) further colonial expansion.[93] This conflict between the wishes of the Colonial Office and those of the colonists impacted the power dynamic within the empire. Those who had settled the new areas without much support from the metropole often felt that they owed little allegiance to the political wishes of politicians or administrators on the other side of the world. Likewise, many in London were happy to allow colonies to chart their own course when it came to expansion and settlement, provided that it did not pose a threat to prosperity of the metropolitan center. For instance, in 1870 Duffy wrote to John Dunmore Lang that "the Colonial Office in later times seems to be quite in accord with you as to Australian independence. They are ready to shake hands and part and are a little impatient perhaps that we delay too long."[94] From this perspective, the position of a figure like Duffy becomes increasingly contradictory: as a lifelong Irish nationalist working to support and encourage colonial expansion in Australia in ways that did not offend the interests of the Colonial Office.

We can put this in context by noting that Duffy's 1862 Land Act, and his intention to distribute land to smallholders, was only possible because Britain had adopted a land policy in Australia (similar policies were key parts of colonialism elsewhere) that treated all land on the continent as terra nullius—unowned land—and hence effectively granted the Crown the right to distribute it.[95] This treatment of Australian land conveniently used the absence of European concepts of property ownership in Aboriginal culture to gloss over the fact that much of the land in Australia was already in use prior to the arrival of Europeans on the continent. The basis of the principle that Australian land was effectively unowned until claimed by a settler often rested upon principles that were not simply racialized in the sense that they failed to recognize Aboriginal understandings of the relationship between humans and the land. More often it was specifically and narrowly defined in racial terms in which, as Penelope Edmonds puts it, "the Anglo-Saxon race was providentially entitled to settle unlimited territory and that this race possessed a specific vocation in human history."[96] Like the American idea of manifest destiny, which was so influential for Meagher in Montana, European settlement was thought by many in Australia to be divinely ordained, and the task for Irish Australians was to ensure that they stood on the right side of that ordinance. As such, Duffy's department got involved in making maps to carve up indigenous land, building roads to allow selectors access to those lands, and encouraging settlement. This meant that Duffy was therefore actively and intensely involved in the dispossession of Aboriginal lands.

Moreover, the distribution of land played an important role in another element of racial politics in Australia: the debates about the place of Chinese migrants in Australia. Although Duffy left Australia before these debates intensified (and he did not say much at all about migration from Asia while he was there) and had died by the time the infamous "White Australia policy" was enacted in 1901, it is important to consider how elements of his (and others') thinking can be seen in the ideological underpinnings of this racialized immigration policy. The centrality of land, for example, to political personhood saw Chinese migrants—who were often viewed as coolies or servile laborers and characterized as unmanly people incapable of the decision-making required for self-government—contrasted against independent white migrants who were building farms.[97] Similar arguments were made in other areas in which Duffy (and many of his contemporaries) placed significant emphasis on the concept of Australia as a forward-thinking country that promoted equal rights and opportunities; however, this concept of "equal rights and opportunities" could facilitate racist ways of thinking. In the case of "White Australia," it was the supposed threat to these liberal concepts by Asian migrants that was often used to justify support for White Australia policies.[98] Therefore, while Duffy was not necessarily a proponent of these policies, the paradoxical legacy of his thought can be seen within them.

At the same time, we can glimpse more radical potential in Duffy's thought, commensurate with his formative experiences in Ireland during the Famine. In 1859, Duffy made the unusual step of allocating 4800 acres to thirty-two heads of household of the Aboriginal Kulin Nation at Nak-krom on the Goldburn River.[99] In justifying this, he argued that "it is the opinion of myself and my colleagues, in the highest degree desirable to give aborigines some choice of escaping the ruin and destruction which have fallen on so many of their race."[100] Ultimately, after Duffy completed his tenure, the Kulin Nation lost their lands to squatters.[101] However, in considering Aboriginal people in his land reforms, Duffy was not only doing something unusual in Victorian politics; he was also making a potentially radical gesture, which acknowledged what Anne Curthoys and Jessie Mitchell call "indigenous agency."[102] In the eyes of many early nineteenth-century liberals, property ownership was essential in order to enter freely into exchange and to participate actively in politics; hence, in granting land to the Kulin Nation, Duffy effectively acknowledged Aboriginal people as political persons.[103]

Duffy's actions can be understood in the context of Young Ireland thinking with reference to an episode a few years earlier in 1859, in which the former Young Irelander Patrick O'Donohoe, editor of the Hobart-based newspaper the *Irish Exile and Freedom's Advocate*, began to campaign for the rights of the Aboriginal population in Van Diemen's Land.[104] In its first issue, the newspaper declared that it would not "pander to power, or to shrink before oppression, but will be ready to defy tyranny in every form and all its places, and to sustain the oppressed of every clime, creed, and colour."[105] O'Donohoe's universalist approach to rights was uncommon in the period, and his political views in relation to the Aboriginal peoples grew more explicit as he spent more time in the colony. By September 1850, O'Donohoe pointedly asked the free settlers who claimed that it was their birthright to live in Van Diemen's Land, where "the copper coloured natives, with their hearts full of red blood, to whom, and to whom only, this sunny land appertained," had disappeared.[106]

Whether in attempting to make land ownership possible for small holders, or granting land to Aboriginal peoples, Duffy imbued the process of settling the Australian landscape with a deeper meaning, and he consistently spoke of Australian settlement as part of a civilizing mission.[107] In this respect, his political vision in Australia differed from the position he held in Ireland. In Australia, Duffy focused his nationalism on questions of rights and governance and did not seek to spark an Australian literature as McGee did in Canada. Even when in his memoirs Duffy praises the Australian landscape as "seamed with gold, fanned with healthy breezes, and bathed in a transparent atmosphere like the landscapes of Guido," what he sees is the possibility of creating an ordered and prosperous pastoral society, not the romantic Canadian wilderness that McGee evoked. Duffy wrote, "The newcomer can scarcely look upon these charming landscapes without seeing them in imagination studded with warm farmhouses, with here and there the sparkling villas for which they seem to be expressly framed; but a generation must pass, fertile in wise laws, before we shall see these results."[108] For him, the establishment of an organized, liberal society was possible in Australia, but only if the land's natural bounty could be directed by wise governance. In short, settling and ordering the landscape was for Duffy the spine of the Australian national narrative, not the cultivation of an historical narrative, as had been the case in Ireland.[109]

Democracy in Victoria

On 19 June 1871 Duffy became premier of Victoria, only to be ousted almost exactly a year later, on 10 June 1872, after the coalition he had established fell apart.[110] Duffy placed the blame for the collapse of his government squarely on squatters who were opposed to his land policies and on wealthy merchants who opposed his vision of a society composed of smallholders. Reflecting on his time in government, Duffy later wrote: "The immense interests at stake in the question of who should possess the public territory, . . . created classes ready to spend profusely, and to exhaust their very considerable interest in damaging the Government. During the recess the fire of their journals was fierce and incessant."[111] Yet, in the support that he received from the electorate, Duffy's saw "a convenient mode of reply" to the squatters and the wealthy merchants that were opposed to him. This "popular sympathy with the Government expressed itself in invitations to banquets in all the great towns of the colony in succession, and on all the great goldfields."[112] Duffy saw these invitations as vindicating his political vision for Victoria. This banqueting tour, which Sean Scalmer has described as "significant to the development of electioneering internationally," was a crucial but underacknowledged element of Duffy's style of governing and consensus-building.[113] It involved Duffy and his administration visiting eleven county centers across regional Victoria, stopping at each for a banquet at which they would make speeches and announce policies. In doing so, Duffy bypassed the legislature and appealed directly to electors in a manner that prefigures British prime minister W. E. Gladstone's style of campaigning, which he would develop from 1876.

This caused considerable consternation among Duffy's detractors, who objected both to the nature of Duffy's engagement with the public and to its populist contents. In the words of the *Bendingo Advertiser*, "For a period we must expect to be doomed to a persistent harping on the Duffy string."[114] The paper, fearing that the banquets would be the first step toward demagoguery, wrote satirically that "we blindly pledged ourselves to worship" Duffy.[115] Again prefiguring many of the criticisms that would be made of Gladstone,[116] they believed that such a method of conducting politics would lead to the end of representative democracy and its replacement by a dangerous "government by the people."[117] However, Duffy's decision to take politics directly to the people demonstrated a wider concern for democratic institutions, with one speaker declaring that the banquet "was intended to support and strengthen a Ministry which had endeavoured to give effect to the principles of democracy."[118] As such, it was consistent with his belief that a situation containing wide discrepancies in the number of electors

SIR CHARLES GAVAN DUFFY, SPEAKER OF THE VICTORIAN ASSEMBLY.

Figure 6.2. *Sir Charles Gavan Duffy, Speaker of the Victorian Assembly.* Melbourne: May & Ebsworth, 1877. A/S01/09/77/84.

between one one-member constituency and another was "an artificial system" whose "inequalities," Duffy contended, had to be amended "without any unnecessary delay"—his argument mirroring the Chartist demand for "equal electoral districts."[119] Unlike Thomas D'Arcy McGee, his colleague in Canada, Duffy had few qualms about what McGee referred to as "universal democracy" and seems to have been inclined to push democratic reform as far as he could. However, he and McGee kept company in holding to the principle they had both supported in Ireland in the 1840s: that the institutions of the state must be rooted in a sense of national feeling. As stated by one of the banquet speakers, "All present that evening had met, not as English, Irish, or Scotchmen, but as Australians, for the time had now arrived when they must raise their own flag."[120] In Duffy's mind, men united by a common nationality could be trusted to make decisions that were guided by common national interest, as opposed to self-interest.

Catholic Politics

In 1863, when the O'Shanassy Ministry fell, Duffy took a brief hiatus from Victorian politics, having served in the Legislative Assembly for long enough to earn a pension of £1,000 a year. After a few years, he returned to the fray because of a debate in 1867 about denominational education—the same issue that had so exercised McGee in Canada. This debate about the role of government in education, which been simmering for much of the 1860s, came to a head in 1867, when George Higinbotham introduced a bill that would make Victorian schools state controlled and nondenominational.[121] When Duffy had first arrived in Melbourne in 1856, he had declared, "I cannot see what any man, high or low, wise or foolish, can hope to gain in the long run by setting Protestant against Catholic, and Catholic against Protestant." For this reason, he might have seemed like the ideal supporter for Hinginbotham's proposals.[122] Here, again, however, we see the limits of Duffy's inclusive national vision: the prospect of nondenominational education proved anathema to him, as well as to the Irish Catholic hierarchy in Australia and to Irish Catholics more broadly.[123] For his part, Kevin Izod O'Doherty in Brisbane refused to serve on the royal commission on education because it proposed to remove government support for nonvested schools, despite being on the first board of the nondenominational Brisbane Grammar School.[124] In spite of their support for nonsectarian politics in Ireland and for secular education as essential to creating an Irish nation free from sectarianism, the majority of the Young Ireland generation in Australia, like McGee in Canada, strongly supported segregated education.

In 1869 Duffy wrote that Catholics had "a peculiar interest in the education question," reasoning that "we [Catholics] are labouring in some of the humblest and most labourious employments, [because] we have been debarred from education by iniquitous laws in our own country [Ireland]."[125] The system of common schooling had failed in Ireland, he argued, because it merely reinforced state discrimination against Catholics—which, incidentally, was diametrically opposed to the argument for nonsectarian schooling made by Young Ireland in Ireland.[126] In Victoria, Duffy reversed his Irish position and advocated for separate Catholic schools. While he contended that "there is no place on the face of the earth where Irish Catholics are so independent as a body or as individuals" as Australia, he maintained that there is "as much bigotry here as at home."[127] As a result, like McGee, he came to believe that Catholic education stood as a bulwark against that discrimination and insisted that Irish Catholic schools should remain independent. Another way in which we can read Duffy's actions, however, is that denominational education was popular among Catholic voters, and Duffy was never less than a canny politician. Moreover, in Victoria, unlike in New South Wales or Queensland, the Catholic Church and the Anglican Church stood together in their opposition to state-funded common schools, which were supported by Baptists, Congregationalists, and religious skeptics.[128] This meant that Duffy could present his support of denominational education as nonsectarian and so could argue (as McGee had done in Canada) that religious toleration was an Australian national characteristic, demonstrated (with only slightly convoluted logic from Duffy) by cross-denominational support for denominational schooling. As we unravel the arguments here, it might be tempting to see Duffy's advocacy of denominational schooling as contradictory to his liberalism; however, it is unlikely that Duffy himself would have acknowledged the contradiction. He was a Catholic in Australia, where the Catholic Church had embraced liberal democracy.[129] He was far from unique in this respect; we should remember that, as Eugenio Biagini has argued, liberalism had a long tradition among Irish Catholics, many of whom also advocated for separate schools.[130]

Whether the question was land reform or denominational schooling, the real issue for Duffy always came back to nationality, which formed the basis of his enduring political relationship with Henry Parkes, who became premier of New South Wales for the first time on 14 May 1873. Both men held a similar vision for Australia in which, as Parkes wrote to Duffy in 1870, the inhabitants of Australia, "whether English or Irish, Protestant or Catholic," could be "one Australian people."[131] In that same letter, Parkes told Duffy that they shared a common enemy in "the false light of men who were not more my enemies than the enemies of your 'race', but who could do nothing without using the Irish people. They have used them for their own scandalous and disastrous purposes."[132] Underlying those principles, however, were ideas that Duffy had developed in Ireland and could implement in an Australian context, including land reform and democracy. Duffy and Parkes maintained a friendship and correspondence throughout both of their lives,[133] and in 1874, when Duffy was clearing out his archive, he offered Parkes part of his autograph collection, selecting in particular for his Australian colleague documents from Ireland in the 1840s. In doing so, he asked him specifically: Would he "care to have the Young Irelanders—Meagher, Smith O'Brien, McGee?"[134]

Conclusion

In the years that followed, Duffy's influence on Australian politics would be profound, even though his actual term as premier of Victoria lasted only one year. He was knighted in 1873 and continued to play a prominent role in the political life of Australia until 1880, when he left Victoria for the South of France, where he died in 1903. In 1901, Australia was federated in terms that can be traced back directly to the liberal circles of which Duffy had been a part between the 1850s and the 1870s. Sir Henry Parkes, for instance, was largely responsible for the act in 1901 that produced Australian Federation, and it was through his and others' accomplishments that Duffy's earlier work on federation continued to be acknowledged. In a speech to the Victorian Parliament in 1890, Parkes praised Duffy's role in the process of Australian nation-building by saying that Federation "was the child—the fondled child—of the greatest men we ever had in any of the colonies," among whom he included Duffy.[135] More than any one specific measure, Duffy brought to Australian politics a continuing demonstration that, regardless of the context, the core issue was nationality.

Duffy's political thought was more than simply a pragmatic response to the radicalism on the goldfields; his nationalism was accompanied by a nuanced embrace of liberalism, which allowed him to advocate for separate Catholic schools. Concurrently, he got involved in state-backed processes of colonialism and settlement that allowed Australians to create a distinct Australian nation, grounded in the belief that if he could "fasten the industrious population to the soil by the potent tie of ownership," it would make them into Australians who would support and develop a liberal state.[136] In an argument that had been made in

Ireland at the time of the Famine in relation to small farmers—and that would be repeated in relation to the Irish Land Acts of the late nineteenth and early twentieth century—Duffy believed that once Australians had been tied to the soil, nationalism could ensure that they were guided by a common interest in the emerging democracy. However, as was the case for his colleague Meagher in Montana, this particular vision only held if it ignored the situation of the indigenous peoples, who already occupied the land that was being settled and to which titles were being granted. Nonetheless, it was the relative success of this particular combination of political ideas that led Duffy, fighting for his political career in 1872, to tell the Legislative Assembly: "You have got possession of political power, you have got control of the country, almost for the first time, take care it is not snatched from you, for oh, my friends, this is a country worth fighting for."[137]

Conclusion

Afterlives

In "September 1913," William Butler Yeats wrote:

> Yet they were of a different kind,
> The names that stilled your childish play,
> They have gone about the world like wind.[1]

More than just the Young Ireland generation had "gone about the world like wind." With them they took ideas that they had formed in Ireland, which they adapted and reimagined in response to, and in order to help shape, Australia, Canada, and the United States. In each location they played a pivotal role in the emergence of new national communities and of new states. While individual Young Irelanders took different paths, from the Fenianism of John O'Mahony to the loyal service to the Crown of Sir Charles Gavan Duffy, many of the ideas that influenced their career choices came from the same source. By studying them as a group—as a generation—this book proposes a new understanding of their political thought and legacy, both in Ireland and in the wider world.

At the core of the Young Ireland generation's political thought, from their early days in Ireland and throughout their political careers, was the idea of the nation as the fundamental category through which society was organized. The nation was important to them because they saw as damaging the tendency to withdraw into the smallest and most parochial set of short-term interests and concerns and believed that only the nation could give them a broader perspective, essential for both economic development and independence.[2] In 1880, reflecting on his life, Charles Gavan Duffy wrote of the 1840s as "a period to which may be traced, as to their fountain-head, many of the opinions now universally current among the Irish people."[3] He went on to say: "We desired to make Ireland a nation."[4] While the nation that the Young Irelanders envisaged would have been manifested by the independent Irish state they failed to create in their lifetimes, their conception of nationality per se not only had enduring appeal but would also prove transferable to very different social and political contexts. It was built on the development of a compelling (in the case of Ireland, historical) narrative that was posited as the "spirit of the nation" and that offered a place within this narrative to anyone willing to embrace it. In this, it was distinctive in a number of aspects. For one thing, it was not civic nationalism, because it did not rely upon institutions or adherence to political ideals, nor was it an ethnic nationalism, relying on race and language, although it absorbed elements of both—indeed, elements of both would remain latent within it, capable of being activated in certain contexts. This openness of form, and its capacity for accommodating economic and ideological contradictions, was central both to its enduring appeal in Ireland, and to its flexible applicability abroad.

In the United States, the Young Ireland generation found success inscribing themselves into a wider narrative of American nationalism. Returning to Gary Gerstle's conceptualization of the two ideological pillars of American nationalism, one civic and the other racial, the Young Ireland generation incorporated elements of both in their arguments, with varying degrees of emphasis. Mitchel's racial nationalism, which he mobilized in the cause of the Confederacy, and Meagher's contrasting civic nationalism, which he advanced in the cause of manifest destiny and the Union, may have seemed like polar opposites in an American context. However, these two coedited a newspaper (in New York) and shared the same political formation. Together, they helped to write a flexible, multivalent Irishness into a larger American national story.[5] While in doing so they were not unique, they were instrumental in providing an intellectual argument for integrating Irish people into a future-oriented Young American narrative. What is more, they had the revolutionary pedigree to make such an argument credible, and in their own persons they embodied the narrative upon which their idea of the nation was founded.[6]

In Australia and Canada, where their revolutionary pedigree was often more of a hindrance than a help, the Young Ireland generation were compelled to create their own forward-looking nationalism, working from the same premises they had forged in Ireland. Charles Gavan Duffy, Thomas D'Arcy McGee, and other Young Irelanders saw Canada and Australia not simply as successful colonies, but as potentially distinct nations with the British Empire. While in Ireland they had based their nationalism on a monumental past, they could not do so in the new countries. Instead, they developed a nationalism whose narrative projected forward in time, rather than back, to a future in which the state afforded protections and rights to minorities, especially Irish Catholics like themselves. This maintained the idea of a national "spirit," but in open ended terms. Even in poetry, when McGee or Mary Anne Kelly, respectively, attempted to write a Canada or an Australia defined by geography, they did so in a context of continual expansion, which projected the national space into the future.

Such a future-oriented view of nationalism lent itself particularly well to the broader context of settler societies such as Canada, Australia, or the United States, where settler colonialism "emphasised the creation of new societies," and the Young Ireland generation sought to shape those societies in forging (or, in the case of the United States, reshaping) new national identities.[7] However, this inevitably imbricated the Young Irelanders in the same processes of colonialism and settlement that they had attacked so bitterly in their Irish historical narratives. In spite of this, each of the figures studied here was to some extent responsible for the systematic dispossession of indigenous people, of which Meagher's persecution of the Blackfoot Nation was the most dramatic manifestation.

Nonetheless, at the core of the national identities that they sought to create, the ideological bedrock of most of the Young Ireland generation was almost always the values of European liberalism, with the great exception being John Mitchel. While he was the most radically anti-imperialist of the group, in that he saw liberalism simply as a tool of imperial power, he was also the one whose political thought was most clearly shaped by racist assumptions. Indeed, Mitchel's rejection of liberalism was central to his inability to embrace colonialism in the same manner as his peers. Otherwise, for most of the core of the Young Ireland generation abroad—Meagher, Duffy, McGee, and O'Brien—an embrace of liberalism, and the colonialism that accompanied it, was central to their political thought. Moreover, as many of them were Irish

Catholics who had moved to societies in which they were minorities, the focus of nineteenth-century liberalism on group rights and on the rights of minority groups provided them with a vocabulary through which they could argue for the creation of a society that would accommodate them in a way that had never been possible in the sectarian culture of mid-nineteenth-century Ireland. Furthermore, in Ireland, the basic liberal premise that the people, through the nation, conferred legitimacy on government served as a central part of their argument for independence. Once abroad, this argument allowed them to justify their rebellion in Ireland, even in Australia and Canada, where attachment to empire meant that their republicanism was not universally popular.

The liberalism of the Young Ireland generation was marked by a doctrine they formulated in an Irish context in the 1840s, which held that the rights implied in citizenship were contingent on active participation in the political process. In Ireland, this had been a cornerstone of an argument intended to mobilize the Irish population to the cause of Irish independence. Transplanted to the United States, it became a means by which Irish people—of which they were exemplars—participating in the political cultures of their new homes effectively proved the entitlement of Irish people to the rights and protections of citizenship, their understanding of which was consistent with their nationalism. If a nation could be created by embracing a national narrative, then citizenship could be contingent on participation in the political process.

Both American republicanism and European liberalism focused on the state as the driving force of change in history—a concept the Young Ireland generation embraced. Central to their attempts to create national identities was the process of state-building. From the outset, in Ireland, they had maintained that "national government [was] indispensable to individual prosperity."[8] Young Ireland had sought to create an independent Irish state, which could guarantee the economic prosperity and good government required to make the Irish nation sustainable. While they failed in that goal, once abroad they renewed their focus on the importance of the state in nation-building. In Canada, McGee helped craft state institutions in such a way that ensured the protection of minority groups, allowing him to create a Canadian nationalism in which minority groups were not threatened. Indeed, McGee's nationalism required the use of instruments of state, principally the financing of railways and taxation, to create a single Canadian national community. In Australia, Duffy saw the distribution of land by the state as essential to "fasten[ing] the industrious population to the soil by the potent tie of ownership."[9] Duffy believed that once Australians had been rooted in the soil, they would embrace a national Australian future, which would in turn ensure that they were guided by a common interest—thus, again, confirming the centrality of the state in creating the conditions necessary for nationalism. In the United States, Meagher in particular saw the route to the American national community through citizenship as the process through which the state regulated relations with the individual. He encouraged Irish people to fight for the Union, both to defend the state and to claim their place within it. Here we have another instance of a member of the Young Ireland generation seeing the state as the principal guardian of a vigorous national identity.

A political doctrine that places participation at the heart of the individual's relation to the state must engage with the nature of democracy. The Young Ireland relationship to democracy in Ireland has been characterized as a "nervous fascination," oscillating between advocating for it and seeing it as a threat to the nation; however, in the societies to which they moved, almost all of the group adopted the belief in the inevitability of the spread of democracy.[10] In Australia, Duffy and the Young Ireland generation formed part of wider movement of European radicals who had migrated there and shaped a society significantly more democratic than the Europe they had left, in terms of extending the democratic franchise.[11] Likewise, in Canada, debates about Confederation—in which McGee was actively involved—were partly a response to demands for representation by population.[12] Within these societies, the Young Ireland generation contributed to the formation of democratic states by helping to shape a democracy that was responsive to a minority—the Irish Catholics, the ethnic group that they represented. However, because they framed this argument in terms of the rights of minorities in general, it would have repercussions beyond the Catholic community. Underlying their arguments was the view that a people united by a common nationality could be trusted to make decisions that were guided by a common national interest, as opposed to a self-interest. Ultimately, most of the Young Irelanders—excepting Mitchel—came to see protection of minority interests as a key factor in a wider national interest. This combination of nationalism and democracy was a hallmark of the Young Ireland generation's influence on colonial politics. In the United States, too, nationalism and democracy were intimately connected, particularly evident in the Young American nationalism that aligned closely with that of Young Ireland and held to the idea of manifest destiny, and the belief that American democracy was divinely ordained to spread across the world. The Young Ireland generation's interpretation of the concept took it beyond its original parameters, which were generally expansionist, within the context of North America, and extended it to encompass a narrative of the inevitable spread of democracy to Ireland; hence, within this future-oriented narrative, American expansionism became the promise of future Irish independence.

This complex mix of ideas shows itself to be interrelated here: manifest destiny was inevitable, yet it required work and sacrifice to be achieved. This became the view that the spread of American democracy would bring independence to Ireland, but only if there were Irish participation in politics from abroad. In part, this new transnational consciousness was the product of new forms of communications technology, which enabled the Young Irelanders to engage in Irish politics from abroad in a way that they could not have done otherwise. It has been argued that "the principal way in which technology influences human actions is that it alters the array of choices and possible courses of action open for someone."[13] For the Young Ireland generation, "the growth of communications in the nineteenth century had the practical effect of diminishing space as a differentiating criterion in human affairs."[14] In Van Diemen's Land, the Young Irelanders had begun to establish a globalized Irish nationalism, shaped from outside of Ireland, through letters and newspaper articles. By the time that they arrived in other parts of Australia, British North America, and the United States, the Young Irelanders were well practiced in engaging with the Irish public sphere from abroad. Mitchel's *Jail Journal*, written about his exile to Van Diemen's Land and first published in New York, quickly became one of the "central works in the Irish nationalist canon."[15] Likewise,

Thomas D'Arcy McGee would receive a rapturous reception "among his townsmen" when he returned to Ireland in 1865 as part of a Canadian government delegation—which tells us that he was still very much a part of the Irish public imagination, even seventeen years after his departure.[16] The opening of a successful transatlantic telegraph cable in 1866 once again impacted the ability of the Young Ireland generation to shape an Irish nationalism from abroad, allowing Irish Americans to participate actively in the Irish public sphere. The Young Ireland generation's effective exploitation of the technology served as a template for later waves of Irish nationalists.

Ultimately, this book puts forward the argument that the Young Ireland generation had a profound influence on the development of states and nations in Australia, Canada, and the United States. This formative role was in part fortuitous: after a particularly intense political formation, they left Ireland following the failed rebellion of 1848 on the wave of a great diasporic migration and found themselves in societies that, in the 1850s and 1860s, were, in their respective ways, already embroiled in their own intense debates about the shapes of their respective futures. The Young Ireland generation's nationalism, forged in Ireland, was uniquely suited to reimagining in other contexts. This they did with gusto—in the United States, by connecting their nationalism with that of Young America, and, in Australia and Canada, by cultivating new, forward-looking nationalisms. Collectively, by focusing on the development of broadly inclusive nationalisms that protected minority rights, the Young Ireland generation laid the foundation for the development of pluralist states of the type they had envisaged for Ireland, even if true pluralism in those states would not be realized for many years. In continuing to engage with Irish nationalist politics from outside of the island of Ireland, they expanded the Irish public sphere in ways that would be picked up and extended by successive generations of Irish nationalists. Some sought to influence Irish politics directly from abroad, but others did so more subtly. The "powerfully mobilizing rhetoric for the next century" that Young Ireland provided Irish nationalism, however, was not simply about Irish nationalism or identity.[17] Rather, it contained ideas that rippled out from Ireland and were refracted back. Further research could trace where the activities of the Young Ireland generation around the world rebounded and shaped political thought in Ireland in the twentieth century. These ideas, exchanged to, from, and within the societies to which Young Ireland went, were imbued with understandings of democracy, liberalism, and the place of minorities that had been developed in the context of the radically democratic "new social experiment[s]"—to use Charles Gavan Duffy's words—in which the Young Ireland generation were involved beyond the island of Ireland.[18]

ACKNOWLEDGMENTS

This project was originally conceived on a balcony overlooking Nova Scotia's Northumberland Strait in the summer of 2014. Since then, I have accumulated many debts in the process of turning it into the book that you see before you. First and foremost, it would not have been written were it not for the encouragement, guidance, and considered input of the series editor Kevin Kenny, my editor Clara Platter, Emily Shelton, Martin Coleman, and all at NYU Press.

I owe a great deal to my PhD supervisor, Professor Eugenio Biagini, for his advice, his ideas, and, most of all, his kindness during the early years of this project in Cambridge. Without his guidance, this book would certainly be a great deal poorer. I would likely never have been a historian were it not for some excellent teachers—in particular, Derek O'Donoghue. Likewise, at Maynooth, Oxford, Trinity College Dublin, and Cambridge, I had the immense good fortune to be taught and challenged by brilliant scholars, who gave their time generously to an eager young scholar.

Financially, this work was made possible by a Travelling Studentship from the National University of Ireland, for whose flexibility and understanding I will always be grateful. Smaller grants, too, from the Canada-UK foundation, Sidney Sussex College, and the Faculty of History at the University of Cambridge paid for the many archival visits needed to complete this project. This book is the product of a research trip that spanned the globe. The assistance of the librarians and archivists at the National Library of Ireland, Trinity College Dublin, Library and Archives Canada, the University of Toronto, Dalhousie University, the Library of Congress, the National Archives of the United States, The University of Rochester, the New York Public Library, the American Irish Historical Society, Yale University, the Catholic University of America, the State Libraries of Victoria and New South Wales, the National Library of Australia, and the British Library have been invaluable. So have the librarians at Sidney Sussex College and the University of Cambridge.

A project with such an international scope would have been an isolating experience were it not for my own transnational network: John, Andrew, John, Sam, Sandra, Jinal, Tristan, Vedran, Gabriele, Martina, Ivan, and Bethan, as well as my Canadian grandparents, Rose and Howard, to whose steady supply of cookies the completion of this book owes much. Likewise, my new colleagues in the Department of Foreign Affairs have been immensely supportive. And, finally, to the Morash family; Aoife, Dara, Lindsay, and of course, my parents, Ann and Chris, to whom I owe everything.

NOTES

INTRODUCTION

1 Justin Trudeau, speech at Dublin Castle, 4 July 2017.

2 President of Ireland, Michael D. Higgins, speech to the Parliament of Western Australia, Perth, 10 October 2017.

3 Higgins, 10 October 2017.

4 Remarks by the president at Irish celebration in Dublin, Ireland, White House Office of the Press Secretary, 23 May 2011.

5 Quinn and Murphy, "O'Mahony, John"; Jenkins, *Irish Nationalism and the British State*, 97.

6 Duffy, *Young Ireland*, v.

7 *St. Paul Press*, 3 August 1865.

8 Bell, *Reordering the World*, 33.

9 Moyn, "Global Intellectual History," 13.

10 Jackson, *Ireland 1798–1998*, 53; Foster, *Words Alone*.

11 Thomas Francis Meagher to John Blake Dillon, 22 September 1863, Thomas Madigan Collection, Thomas Francis Meagher Papers, New York Public Library.

12 Duffy, *Young Ireland*.

13 Jaeger, "Generations in History"; Comte, *Cours de Philosophie Positive*, 442–43.

14 Quinn, *Young Ireland and the Writing of Irish History*, 1.

15 Pilcher, "Mannheim's Sociology of Generations," 489.

16 Foster, *Vivid Faces*.

17 Edmunds, "Introduction," 18.

18 Bartlett, *Ireland*, 278.

19 Hutchinson, *Dynamics of Cultural Nationalism*, 105.

20 Rapport, *1848*.

21 Davis, *Poems*, 73.

22 Kiberd, "Thought Revival," 58; Foster, *Yeats: A Life, Vol. 1*, 122; Howes, "Introduction," 5; Alison, "Yeats and His Politics," 44; Yeats, *Tribute to Thomas Davis*, 12.

23 Hart, *IRA and Its Enemies*, 207.

24 Foster, *Words Alone*, 50–52.

25 McConville, *Irish Political Prisoners*, 417.

26 Roberts, *Chartism*, 196.

27 Morash, "Rhetoric of Right," 217.

28 Kymlicka, *Multicultural Citizenship*, 50–51.

29 Farrell, "Irish Rebel, Imperial Reformer," 71.
30 Kerber, "Revolutionary Generation," 33.
31 Koditschek, *Liberalism*, 176; Sullivan, "Liberalism and Imperialism."
32 Bell, *Reordering the World*, 366.
33 Mitchel, *History of Ireland, Vol. 2*, 455.
34 Mitchel, *Last Conquest of Ireland (Perhaps)*, 192.
35 Stafford, *Literary Criticism of Young America*; Bancroft and Reynolds, "Its Wood";
    Danto, *Encounters and Reflections*.
36 Howe, *Ireland and Empire*, 49.
37 Dwan, "Romantic Nationalism," 736.
38 Curthoys, "Advent of Self-Government," 161; Blainey, *History of Victoria*, 50.
39 Curthoys, 161.
40 Heaman, *Tax, Order, and Good Government*, 32; Wilton, *Popular Politics and Political
    Culture*, 8.
41 Ajzenstat, *Once and Future Canadian Democracy*; Constant and Ducharme, eds., *Liber-
    alism and Hegemony*; Bélanger, Coupal, and Ducharme, eds., *Les Idées En Mouvement*.
42 Wilentz, *Rise of American Democracy*, 796; See also Tilly, "Reflections," 42; Hall,
    Ikenberry, *State*, 40–41; and Conway, *War, State and Society*, 275.
43 Balogh, *Government Out of Sight*.
44 Edling, *Revolution in Favor of Government*.
45 Hirota, *Expelling the Poor*.
46 Balogh, *Government Out of Sight*; Edling, *Revolution in Favor of Government*; Rao,
    "New Historiography."

I. IRELAND, 1842–1848

1 *Nation*, 15 October 1842.
2 *Nation*, 15 October 1842.
3 *Nation*, 15 October 1842.
4 Kelly, "Address to the Women of Ireland," 502.
5 Davis, Rollenston, eds., *Prose Writings of Thomas Davis*, 225.
6 "Prospectus of the Nation," in Sillard, *Life of John Mitchel*, 3.
7 Ting, "Social Construction of Nation," 466.
8 Maxwell, *History of Trinity College Dublin*, 199.
9 Davis, *Prose Writings*, 225.
10 Duffy, *Young Ireland*, 55.
11 Molony, "Davis, Thomas Osborne."
12 Dickson, *Dublin*, 308.
13 Young Irelanders who were lawyers: Michael Joseph Barry, Edward Butler, Sir
    Charles Gavan Duffy, Moses Wilson Gray, Thomas D'Arcy McGee, Richard
    O'Gorman, and Sir Bryan O'Loghlen.
14 Duffy, *Young Ireland*, 47.
15 Young Irelanders who were journalists: Patrick James Smyth, Gearld Henry Supple,
    John Donnellan Balfe, Sir Charles Gavan Duffy, Michael Joeseph Barry, Edward

Butler, Margaret Callan, Michael Cavanagh, Daniel Holland, Thomas D'Arcy Mc-
Gee, and John Mitchell.

16 Kilfeather, *Dublin*, 106.

17 Dickson, *Dublin*, 309.

18 *Dublin Penny Journal*; *Irish Penny Journal*; Benatti, "Irish Patriots and Scottish Adventurers," 43; "Reports, Abstract, Ireland, 1841."

19 Hayley, "Reading and Thinking Nation," 31–32.

20 Habermas, *Structural Transformation of the Public Sphere*, 182.

21 North, *Waterloo Directory*, 112.

22 McCaffrey, *Daniel O'Connell*, 12.

23 McGee, *Historical Sketches of O'Connell*, 5.

24 *Nation*, 7 October 1843.

25 MacDonagh, "Age of O'Connell," 160.

26 For examples of the speeches at such events and the reasoning behind them, see
Huish, *Memoirs*, 723; and O'Connell, "Catholic Association Meeting."

27 MacDonagh, "Age of O'Connell," 160; Bartlett, *Ireland*, 267.

28 Speech to an aggregate meeting on 18 September 1810, in O'Connell, *Select Speeches*,
19.

29 O'Connell, "In Favour of the Repeal of the Union," delivered at Mullaghmast,
Ireland, in September in 1843, in Jennings, *World's Famous Orations*, 196.

30 O'Connell, *Select Speeches*, 140.

31 *Nation*, 7 October 1845.

32 Rynne, "Young Ireland and Irish Revolutions," 5.

33 MacDonagh, "Age of O'Connell," 164.

34 Hoppen, *Governing Hibernia*, 108.

35 Kenealy, *Great Irish Famine*, 182.

36 *Nation*, 3 December 1842.

37 *Nation*, 15 April 1848.

38 Dwan, "Civic Virtue in the Modern World," 47.

39 *Nation*, 26 November 1842, in Dwan, 47.

40 *Nation*, 12 February 1848.

41 Quinn, *Young Ireland*, 1.

42 Madden, *Ireland and Its Rulers*, 304.

43 Moody, *Davitt and Irish Revolution*, 38.

44 Walker, *Parliamentary Election Results*, 77–79.

45 "Prospectus of the United Irishman," in McGovern, *John Mitchel*, 70.

46 Rapport, *1848*, chap. 7.

47 Rynne, "Young Ireland and Irish Revolutions," 23.

48 Gellner, *Nations and Nationalism*, 55.

49 Leerssen, *National Thought in Europe*, 161.

50 Anderson, *Imagined Communities*, 47. For a summary of the criticism leveled against
Anderson's work, see Hamilton, "New Imaginings," 73–89; for a different approach,
see Yakobson, *Nations*, 12.

51 Briggs and Burke, *Social History of Media*, 92.

52 Duffy, *Young Ireland*, 18.

53 Daniel O'Connell to W. J. Fitzpatrick, 26 July 1833 in W. J, Fitzpatrick, *Correspondence of Daniel O'Connell*, 377.

54 Daniel O'Connell to the Dublin Pilot on the Reform Bill, Autograph Letters, Daniel O'Connell, 1131.d.46, British Library.

55 Simes, "Ireland," 128.

56 Leerssen, *National Thought in Europe*, 162.

57 Ó Gráda, *Ireland before and after the Famine*, 31.

58 *Nation*, 20 May 1848.

59 *Nation*, 20 May 1848.

60 Anderson, *Imagined Communities*, 36.

61 Gráda, *Great Irish Famine*, 40.

62 *Nation*, 8 November 1845.

63 *Nation*, 8 November 1845.

64 Anderson, *Imagined Communities*, 47.

65 Andrews, *Newspapers and Newsmakers*, 15.

66 Innis, *Empire and Communications*; Innis, *Bias of Communication*, 116.

67 "Prospectus of the Nation," in Sillard, *Life of John Mitchel*, 3.

68 Gellner, *Nations and Nationalism*, 1.

69 Anderson, *Imagined Communities*, 6.

70 Duffy, *Thomas Davis*, 216.

71 Duffy, ed., *Voice of the Nation*, iii.

72 Hayley, "Reading and Thinking Nation," 33.

73 Sperber, *Popular Catholicism*, 277; Weir, *Secularism and Religion*, 79.

74 Hogan, "Lost Hero of the Past," 131–46.

75 Leersen, *Remembrance and Imagination*, 22; Stöter, "Grimmige Zeiten," 173–80.

76 Clark, *Iron Kingdom*, xxiii.

77 Clark, xxiii.

78 Davis, *Literary and Historical Essays*, 246.

79 Davis, 246.

80 Benner, "Nationalism," 41.

81 Herder, "On Diligence"; Herder, "Treatise," 114.

82 Davis, *Literary and Historical Essays*, 173–74.

83 Davis, 173–74.

84 Freifeld, *Nationalism and the Crowd*, 176.

85 Levinger, *Enlightened Nationalism*, 203.

86 Suphan, ed., *Herder's Sämmtliche Werke*, vol. 17, in Berlin, *Three Critics of the Enlightenment*, 189.

87 Davis, *Literary and Historical Essays*, 174–75.

88 Doyle, "Language and Literacy," 363.

89 Penet, "Thomas Davis," 441.

90 Duffy, *Young Ireland*, 95.

91 Doyle, *History of the Irish Language*, 125.

92 Aughey and Oakland, *Irish Civilization*, 113.

93 Quinn, *Young Ireland*, 60.

94 Dwan, *Great Community*, 23.

95 Anderson, *Imagined Communities*, 34.

96 *Nation*, 24 December 1847.

97 *Nation*, 24 December 1847.

98 For the full list, see Quinn, *Young Ireland*, 203–4.

99 Morrow, "Thomas Carlyle," 662.

100 Huggins, "Strange Case of Hero-Worship," 330.

101 Duffy, *Conversations with Carlyle*, 4.

102 Duffy, 4.

103 Morgan, "Poetry of Victorian Masculinities," 203.

104 O'Sullivan Beare, *Historiae Catholicae Iberniae Compendium*; O'Sullivan Beare, *Patritiana Decas*; O'Sullivan Beare, *Ireland under Elizabeth*.

105 McGee, *Irish Writers of the Seventeenth Century*, 33

106 Forster, "Johann Gottfried von Herder."

107 Mitchel, *Life and Times of Aodh O'Neill*, v.

108 Mitchel, vii.

109 Mitchel, vii.

110 Mitchel, vii.

111 Mitchel, viii.

112 Quinn, *Young Ireland*, 74.

113 *Nation*, 30 November 1844.

114 Hutchinson, "Cultural Nationalism," 81.

115 Leersen, *Remembrance and Imagination*, 149.

116 Cairns and Richards, *Writing Ireland*, 35.

117 Andrews, *Newspapers and Newsmakers*, 27.

118 *Spirit of the Nation*, vi.

119 Baycroft, "Introduction," 2.

120 MacCarthy, *Definitions of Irishness*, 148.

121 Duffy, *Ballad Poetry of Ireland*, 78.

122 Davis, *Poems*, 9.

123 *British Magazine* 32, 1847.

124 *Living Age* 18, 1848.

125 Meagher, "Sword Speech," delivered in Constitution Hall, Dublin, 20 July 1846, in Jennings, *World's Famous Orations*, 215.

126 Wall, "Rise of a Catholic Middle Class," 94; O'Neill, "Bourgeois Ireland," 524.

127 Kiernan, "British Isles," 10.

128 Mitchel's father was a prominent Presbyterian who seceded from the Church to found the Remonstrant synod.

129 *Nation*, 25 January 1845.

130 Ó Gráda, *Ireland*, 166.

131 Brown, *Politics of Irish Literature*, 56.

132 Mitchel, *Irish Political Economy*.

133 *Irish Confederation*, 23.

134 Yaffey, "Friedrich List," 84.

135 Davis, *Victorians and Germany*, 377 Daly, *Industrial Development and Irish National Identity*, 5; List, *National System of Political Economy*, 230.

136 *Nation*, 29 October 1842; 29 April 1843; 15 October 1844; 26 October 1844; 6 September 1845; 4 October 1845; 11 October 1845; 30 May 1846; 21 August 1847.

137 *Irish Confederation*, 23.

138 Bielenberg, *Ireland and the Industrial Revolution*, 180.

139 *Irish Confederation*, 23.

140 *Irish Confederation*, 4.

141 *Irish Felon*, 24 June 1848.

142 *Irish Felon*, 24 June 1848.

143 Bew, *Ireland*, 217.

144 William Smith O'Brien, "First Letter to the Landed Proprietors of Ireland," 17 November 1846, in O'Brien, *Reproductive Employment*, 8.

145 Lalor, *Rights of Ireland*, 19; *Irish Felon*, 24 June 1848.

146 *Irish Felon*, 24 June 1848.

147 Duffy, *Spirit of the Nation*, v.

148 *Irish Confederation*, 24–25.

149 Gray, "Great Famine," 664; see also Fitzgerald, "Irish Demography since 1740," 59.

150 Gray, 665.

151 Delaney, *Curse of Reason*, 3.

152 *Nation*, 1 November 1845, in Delaney, *Curse of Reason*, 93.

153 Miller, *Emigrants and Exiles*, 300.

154 Cíosáin, "Famine Memory," 107.

155 Mitchel, *Last Conquest of Ireland (Perhaps)*, 219.

156 Duffy, *My Life in Two Hemispheres*, 274.

157 Duffy, 274.

158 *Irish Confederation*, 29.

159 Bew, *Ireland*, 178.

160 Thomas Francis Meagher, "Irish Pauperism Out-door Relief Music Hall Dublin 7th April 1847," in Meagher, *Speeches*, 121.

161 Mitchel, *Last Conquest of Ireland (Perhaps)*, 317.

162 Lloyd, *Irish Culture and Colonial Modernity*, 97.

163 Riall, *Garibaldi*, 1.

164 Meagher, *Speeches*, 121.

165 Mitchel, *Last Conquest of Ireland (Perhaps)*, 151.

166 Barrett, *History of the Irish Confederation*, 17.

167 Jenkins, *Irish Nationalism and the British State*, 97.

168 Bartlett, *Ireland*, 298.

169 Morash, "Rhetoric of Right," 217.

170 Duffy, *Conversations with Carlyle*, 132.

171 McConville, *Irish Political Prisoners*, 417.

172 Dudink, Hagemann, and Tosh, *Masculinities in Politics And War*, 17.

173 Quinn, *Young Ireland*, 7.

174 Duffy, *Young Ireland*, iii.

2. VAN DIEMEN'S LAND, 1848–1856

1 Mitchel, *Jail Journal*, 223.

2 O'Donohoe, *Commentary on Teetotalism*, 4–5.

3 Reynolds, *History of Tasmania*, 24.

4 Brand, *Convict Probation System*, 6.

5 "Australian Convict Records: Tasmania," State Library of South Australia, guides. slsa.sa.gov.au.

6 Glover and MacLochlainn, eds., *Letters of an Irish Patriot*, 16.

7 Goodway, *London Chartism*, 91; Ní Úrdail, "Cork Scribe in Victorian London," 231.

8 McConville, *Irish Political Prisoners*, 97.

9 Mitchel, *Jail Journal*, 223.

10 Jenny Mitchel to Mary Thompson, 21 July 1851, Letters from Mrs. John Mitchel, 1851–55, New York Public Library.

11 Lawson, *Last Man*; Tatz, *With Intent to Destroy*, 79; Kiernan, *Blood and Soil*, 266–90.

12 Madley, "From Terror to Genocide," 78.

13 Reynolds, *History of Tasmania*, 144.

14 Mitchel, *Jail Journal*, 263.

15 McConville, "Gentlemen Convicts," 63.

16 Davis, *William Smith O'Brien*, 20.

17 Henry Grey to John Russell, "Colonial Matters; Mitchel Should Be Sent to Van Diemen's Land with Ticket of Leave," 20 July 1848, Papers of Lord John Russell, Personal Collections, PRO 4098–6803/Fonds PRO 30/22, National Archives of the United Kingdom.

18 "Treatment of Mr. Smith O'Brien," 14 June 1850, House of Commons Debate, *Hansard Parliamentary Debates*, vol. III cc1231–4.

19 William Smith O'Brien, "Journal III, Port Arthur to Journal IV, 1, New Norfolk," 6 November 1850–1 January 1851, Papers of William Smith O'Brien, MS 46,822/3, National Library of Ireland.

20 Journal of William Smith O'Brien, 29 October 1849, in Touhill, *William Smith O'Brien*, 36.

21 *Irish Exile and Freedom's Advocate*, 26 January 1850.

22 Kirkpatrick, "Australia Shaking Off the Shackles," 30.

23 Kirkpatrick, 30.

24 William Paul Dowling to John Mat and Ann, 10 February 1850, in Glover and MacLochlainn, eds., *Letters of an Irish Patriot*, 62.

25 *Irish Exile and Freedom's Advocate*, 26 January 1850.

26 *Irish Exile and Freedom's Advocate*, 23 March 1850; 25 May 1850.

27 *Irish Exile and Freedom's Advocate*, 23 March 1850; 25 May 1850.

28 Davis, "Patrick O'Donohoe," 257.

29 Cullen, *Young Ireland in Exile*, 41; Thomas Francis Meagher to Mrs Connell of Lake Sorrell, 15 August 1852, MS287, Irish Political Prisoners of 1848, National Library of Australia.

30 McConville, *Irish Political Prisoners*, 92.

31 "Treatment of Mr. Smith O'Brien," 14 June 1850, House of Commons Debate vol. III cc1231–4.

32 Lee, "Anstey, Thomas Chisholm"; Lee, "Anstey, Thomas."

33 "The Irish Convicts in Van Diemen's Land," 12 June 1851, House of Commons Debate vol. 117 cc634–41.

34 Patrick and Patrick, *Exiles Undaunted*, 76.

35 "Treatment of Mr. Smith O'Brien," 14 June 1850.

36 "Treatment of Mr. Smith O'Brien."

37 "Treatment of Mr. Smith O'Brien."

38 *Nation*, 11 October 1851.

39 *Kerry Evening Post*, 31 May 1851.

40 *Belfast Newsletter*, 14 May 1851.

41 *Belfast Newsletter*, 14 May 1851.

42 McMahon, *Global Dimensions of Irish Identity*, 7.

43 *Boston Pilot*, 25 May 1850.

44 *New York Times*, 3 Oct 1851.

45 Touhill, *William Smith O'Brien*, 62.

46 Touhill, "*Times* versus William Smith O'Brien," 55.

47 William Smith O'Brien to Lucy O'Brien, 27 June 1852, in Davis and Richard Davis, eds., *Rebel in His Family*, 59.

48 US Congressional Serial Set, 4 December 1851, Issue 610, 1/31 US Senate.

49 US Congressional Serial Set, 2 December 1851, Issue 610, 1/31 US Senate.

50 Israel, *Expanding Blaze*, 574.

51 US Congressional Serial Set, 28 January 1852, Issue 610, 1/31 US Senate.

52 Osterhammel, "Nationalism and Globalization," 696.

53 "Irish Convicts in Van Diemen's Land," 12 June 1851.

54 "Irish Convicts in Van Diemen's Land," 12 June 1851.

55 *Launceston Examiner*, 29 March 1853.

56 "Irish Convicts in Van Diemen's Land," 12 June 1851.

57 Jenny Mitchel to Mary, 21 July 1851, Letters from Mrs. John Mitchel, 1851–1855, New York Public Library.

58 Harling, "Trouble with Convicts," 86.

59 Quinn, *John Mitchel*, 46.

60 Curthoys, "Advent of Self-Government," 156.

61 Curthoys, 156.

62 Carey, *Empire of Hell*, 226–27.

63 West, *History of Tasmania, Vol. 1*, 296.

64 Jenny Mitchel to Mary Thompson, 15 June 1852, Letters from Mrs. John Mitchel, 1851–1855, New York Public Library.

65 Campbell, *Ireland's New Worlds*, 44.

66 Mitchel, *Jail Journal*, 284.

67 Mitchel, 285.

68 Jenny Mitchel to Mary Thompson, 6 December 1851, Letters from Mrs. John Mitchel, 1851–1855, New York Public Library.

69 Mitchel, *Jail Journal*, 284.

70 Ullathorne, *Catholic Mission in Australasia*, 4–5

71 Reid, *Gender, Crime, and Empire*, 13

72 Frost, *Letter on Transportation*, 20; Hyam, *Understanding the British Empire*, 378.

73 Woollacott, *Settler Society*, 152.

74 John Mitchel to Mary Thompson, 2 October 1852, Pinkerton Papers, D1078/M4A T413, Public Record Office of Northern Ireland.

75 *Courier*, 12 March 1851.

76 O'Brien, *Principles of Government, Vol. 1*, 297.

77 O'Brien, 297.

78 For a discussion of Balfe's time in Van Diemen's Land see Martin, *John Donnellan Balfe*.

79 *Nation*, 24 January 1852; Petrow, "Judas in Tasmania," 477.

80 Hourican, "O'Donohoe, Patrick."

81 *Irish Exile and Freedom's Advocate*, 9 February 1850.

82 *Irish Exile and Freedom's Advocate*, 2 February 1850.

83 *Irish Exile and Freedom's Advocate*, 26 October 1850.

84 McGee, "McManus, Terence Bellew."

85 Cunningham, "Meagher, Thomas Francis."

86 Jenny Mitchel to Mary Thompson, February 12 1852, Letters from Mrs. John Mitchel, 1851–1855, New York Public Library.

87 *Launceston Examiner*, 14 February 1852; *Colonial Times*, 19 February 1852; *People's Advocate and New South Wales Vindicator*, 6 March 1852; *Geelong Advertiser and Intelligencer*, 24 February 1852.

88 *Launceston Examiner*, 14 February 1852.

89 *Launceston Examiner*, 14 February 1852.

90 *Nation*, 9 October 1852.

91 Maxwell-Stewart, "And All My Great Hardships Endured?," 71.

92 Petrow, "Men of Honour?," 143.

93 Keneally, *Great Shame*, 259–60.

94 *Sydney Morning Herald*, 29 October 1853.

95 Davis, "Patrick O'Donohoe," 273.

96 Quinn, *John Mitchel*, 52.

97 Clarke, *Old Tales of a Young Country*, 204.

98 Brownrigg, "Notes on Young Ireland," 74–83.

99 *Launceston Examiner*, 30 August 1853.

100 Henry Grey to William Thomas Denison, 18 January 1851, Papers of Sir William Thomas Denison, M606-M607/M671, National Library of Australia.

101 Henry Grey to William Thomas Denison, 18 January 1851.

102 *Launceston Examiner*, 30 August 1853.

103 Reynolds, *History of Tasmania*, 164.

104 O'Brien, *Principles of Government, Vol. 1*, vi.

105 O'Brien, *Principles of Government, Vol. 2*, 98.

106 O'Brien, 98.

107 O'Brien, 98.

108 *Launceston Examiner*, 9 August 1856.

109 O'Brien, *Principles of Government, Vol. 1*, 183.

110 O'Brien, 2.

111 O'Brien, 2.

112 Biagini, "Neo-Roman Liberalism," 56.

113 O'Brien, *Principles of Government, Vol. 1*, 284.

114 O'Brien, 284.

115 O'Brien, 295.

116 Curthoys, *Taking Liberty*, 234.

117 O'Brien, *Principles of Government, Vol. 2*, 294.

118 O'Brien, 295.

119 O'Brien, 98.

120 Brownrigg, "Notes on Young Ireland," 74.

121 Davis, *William Smith O'Brien*, 319.

122 Davis, "Unpublicised Young Ireland Prisoners," 134.

123 O'Donohoe, *Commentary on Teetotalism*, 4–5.

3. THE UNITED STATES OF AMERICA, 1848–1861

1 McGee, *History of Irish Settlers*, 195.

2 *American Irish*, 97.

3 Kenny, *American Irish*, 104–6.

4 *New York Daily Times*, 28 June 1852.

5 *Citizen* (New York), 7 January 1854.

6 McGee, *History of the Irish Settlers*, 194.

7 Maizlish, "Meaning of Nativism," 167–69; Gienapp, "Nativism," 529–59.

8 Anbinder, *Nativism and Slavery*, 126.

9 Hahn, *Nation without Borders*, 123.

10 Johannsen, Haynes, and Morris, *Manifest Destiny and Empire*, 163.

11 Horsman, *Race and Manifest Destiny*, 164.

12 *United States Magazine and Democratic Review* 1 (October 1837): 14.

13 *United States Magazine and Democratic Review* 17 (July–August 1845): 5. There is some dispute over the origin of the term, and some historians have argued that Jane Storm coined it. See Howe, *What Hath God Wrought*, 703, for discussion of its origins. Nevertheless, it is certain that O'Sullivan played an important role in making the term popular.

14 Pratt, "Origin of Manifest Destiny," 795–98.

15 Widmer, *Young America*, 161; Eyal, *Young America Movement*, 97.

16 Bruce, *Harp and the Eagle*; Samito, *Becoming American Under Fire*.

17 Doheny, *Felon's Track*, 282 (first published in 1849).

18 *Boston Pilot*, 12 November 1853.

19 McMahon, *Global Dimensions of Irish Identity*, 7.

20 *Republic*, 31 May 1852, *Miners' Express*, June 16, 1852, *Southern Sentinel*, 29 May 1852; *Weekly Minnesotian*, 12 June 1852; *Mountain Sentinel*, 8 July 1852.

21 *Chicago Daily Tribune*, 15 Oct 1853.

22 R. McElderry to David Boyd, 12 December 1853, McElderry Papers, T2414/12, Public Record Office of Northern Ireland.

23 John F. Crampton to Clarendon, 14 November 1853 in Barnes and Barnes, *Private and Confidential*, 89.

24 Burchell, *San Francisco Irish*, 7.

25 Burchell, 7.

26 Mitchel, *Jail Journal*, 370.

27 Quinn, *Young Ireland*, 103.

28 McLuhan, *Understanding Media*, 7.

29 Winston, *Misunderstanding Media*. See also Williams, *Keywords*, 98; and Jacob, "Why Bother with Marshall McLuhan?," 123–35.

30 Carey, "Harold Innis and Marshall McLuhan," 5–39.

31 Ó Cathaoir, "Dillon, John Blake," 303.

32 Beidleman, *California's Frontier Naturalists*, 283.

33 *Citizen* (New York), 7 January 1854, which told its readers that "Dr. Antisell has removed his office to 203 Prince Street, near McDougal, west side of Broadway."

34 Roberts, *Distant Revolutions*, 147.

35 Mitchel, *Jail Journal*, 165.

36 Henderson, "Broadway Theatre," 76; *Putnam's Monthly*, nos. 13–18 (1854).

37 Tuchinsky, *Horace Greeley's* New-York Tribune, 2.

38 *New York Daily Times*, 20 December 1853.

39 *New York Daily Times*, 20 December 1853.

40 Israel, *Expanding Blaze*, 285–320; Morley, *Irish Opinion and the American Revolution*.

41 Ashworth, *Republic in Crisis*, 80.

42 Ostendorf, *Sounds American*, 173. See also Fitz, *American Revolution Remembered*; and McDonnell Corbould, Clarke, and Brundage, *Remembering the Revolution*.

43 Bancroft, *History of the United States*, 466.

44 Emerson, "Concord Hymn," in von Frank, *Ralph Waldo Emerson*, 130.

45 Longfellow, "Paul Revere's Ride," *Atlantic Monthly*, January 1860.

46 Crider, "De Bow's Revolution," 317–32; For further discussion on the memory of the American revolution, see Hobsbawm *On Empire*, 80; and Mason, "Sacred Ashes."

47 Parry, *Politics of Patriotism*, 233.

48 Langely, *Americas in the Age of Revolution*, 218.

49 *New York Daily Times*, 20 December 1853.

50 *New York Daily Times*, 20 December 1853.

51 Andrews, *Newspapers and Newsmakers*, 57.

52 *Nation*, 26 June 1847.

53 Israel, *Expanding Blaze*, 320.

54 Quinn, *Young Ireland*, 53–59.

55 Doheny, *History of the American Revolution*, x.

56 Doheny, x.

57 Thomas D'Arcy McGee to his aunt, 6 July 1842, Personal Papers of Thomas D'Arcy McGee, M1549, Library and Archives Canada; Wilson, *Thomas D'Arcy McGee*, 102.

58 *Nation* (New York), 25 November 1848.

59 *Nation* (New York), 28 October 1848.

60 *Nation* (New York), 28 October 1848.

61 McGee, *Memoir of Charles Gavan Duffy*.

62 By "pre-paid" letters, Duffy is referring, dismissively, to the idea that rebellion in Ireland could be brought about from outside of Ireland, in the United States. Charles Gavan Duffy to Thomas D'Arcy McGee, 23 February 1849, in Wilson, *Thomas D'Arcy McGee*, 253.

63 *Nation* (New York), 29 September 1849, in Wilson, 255.

64 Wilson, 271.

65 McGee, *History of the Irish Settlers*.

66 McGee, 35.

67 McGee, 106.

68 McGee, 114.

69 McGee, 70.

70 McGee, 53, 73, 98.

71 McGee, 185.

72 Balmez, *Protestantism and Catholicity*, 419, in Wilson, *Thomas D'Arcy McGee*, 288.

73 Wilson, 288.

74 *American Celt and Adopted Citizen*, 31 May 1851, in J. J. O'Gorman Papers, MG 30 D20, vol. 2, Library and Archives Canada.

75 *American Celt and Adopted Citizen*, 31 May 1851.

76 John Stuart Mill highlights exactly this idea in a letter to the historian Pascale Villari. See John to Pascale Villari, 26 January 1862, in Mill, *The Collected Works of John Stuart Mill, Volume XV—The Later Letters of John Stuart Mill 1849–1873 Part II*, https://oll.libertyfund.org/titles/mill-the-collected-works-of-john-stuart-mill-volume-xv-the-later-letters-1849-1873-part-ii/simple#lf0223-15_head_288 (16 January 2020).

77 *American Celt and Adopted Citizen*, 31 May 1851.

78 Doheny, *Felon's Track*, 297.

79 Barr, "Imperium in Imperio," 612.

80 Wilson, *Thomas D'Arcy McGee*, 358.

81 Oxx, *Nativist Movement in America*, 90.

82 Dinnerstein and Reimers, *Ethnic Americans*, 49.

83 Anbinder, *Nativism and Slavery*, xiii.

84 Farrelly, *Anti-Catholicism in America*, 166; Flewelling, *Two Irelands beyond the Sea*, 92.

85 Verhoeven, "Neither Male Nor Female," 17.

86 Hirota, *Expelling the Poor*, 28.

87 Cohn, "Nativism and the End," 368.

88 Cohn, 368.

89 Foner, *Free Soil, Free Labor*, 259.

90 McGee, *History of Irish Settlers*, 233.

91 Wilson, *Thomas D'Arcy McGee*, 331.

92 McGee, *Irish Position*, 6–7.

93 Greenblat, *Renaissance Self-Fashioning*, 1–9.

94 *Baton-Rouge Gazette*, 12 June 1852.

95 *Burlington Free Press*, 18 June 1852.

96 *Baton-Rouge Gazette*, 12 June 1852.

97 *Weekly National Intelligencer*, 19 June 1852.

98 *Illustrated News*, 19 March 1853.

99 *New York Times*, 6 July 1853.

100 *Portsmouth Inquirer*, 19 November 1852.

101 *New York Times*, 6 July 1853.

102 *Louisville Journal*, republished in *Chicago Daily Tribune*, 13 May 1853.

103 *Chicago Daily Tribune*, 18 April 1853.

104 *Weekly Placer Herald*, 3 September 1853.

105 Wright, *Lecturing the Atlantic*, 39; Warner, "Publics and Counterpublics," 81.

106 Wright, 39.

107 Gemme, *Domesticating Foreign Struggles*, 73; Eyal, *Young America Movement*, 94.

108 Matthews, *Americanism*, 15–18; see also Widmer, *Young America*, 57.

109 "Prospectus of the Nation," in Sillard, *Life of John Mitchel*, 3.

110 Eyal, *Young America Movement*, 5.

111 Emerson, *Young American*, 3.

112 McGee, *History of the Irish Settlers*, 194.

113 Stafford, *Literary Criticism of Young America*, 17; Bancroft and Reynolds, "Its Wood Could Only Be American!," 94; Danto, *Encounters and Reflections*, 13.

114 Widmer, *Young America*, 66.

115 *Democratic Review*, 31 July 1852.

116 *Democratic Review*, 31 July 1852.

117 *Democratic Review*, 31 July 1852.

118 *United States Magazine and Democratic Review* 17 (July–August 1845): 5; Howe, *What Hath God Wrought*, 703.

119 Dahl, *Empire of the People*, 101–26.

120 Widmer, *Young American*, 40.

121 Snay, *Horace Greeley*, 45.

122 *New York Tribune*, 13 July 1865.

123 *New York Morning News*, 27 December 1845.

124 *New York Daily Times*, 28 June 1852. The newspaper later becomes the *New York Times*.

125 *New York Daily Times*, 26 May 1853.

126 *New York Daily Times*, 26 May 1853.

127 *New York Daily Times*, 26 May 1853.

128 Allen, *Republic in Time*, 17.

129 Marginalia, Charles Gavan Duffy Newsprint Collection, P8417, National Library of Ireland.

130 Horsman, *Race and Manifest Destiny*, 1.

131 Lause, *Young America*, 22.

132 Johannsen, Haynes, and Morris, *Manifest Destiny and Empire*, 163.

133 Anderson, *Ethnic Cleansing and the Indian*, 7.

134 Widmer, *Young America*, 56.

135 McGee, *History of the Irish Settlers*, 209–10; *Native American*, 12 January 1839.

136 Thomas Francis Meagher to John F. Boyle, 13 October 1859, Thomas Francis Meagher Papers, MSS655, Library of Congress.

137 Copy of report of Caleb B. Smith, secretary of the Interior Colonization in Chirqui and other places, 9 May 1862, Ambrose W. Thompson Papers, Library of Congress.

138 Minister of foreign relations of Costa Rica to Ambrose Thompson, 31 October 1859, Ambrose W. Thompson Papers, Library of Congress.

139 Minister of foreign relations of Costa Rica to Ambrose Thompson, 31 October 1859.

140 *Irish News*, 24 January 1857, in Gobat, *Empire by Invitation*, 131.

141 Thomas Francis Meagher, "The New Route Through Chiriqui," *Harper's New Monthly Magazine* 22 (1861): 208.

142 Greenburg, *Manifest Manhood*, 61.

143 Woollacott, *Gender and Empire*, 65–66.

144 Thomas Francis Meagher, "Holidays in Costa Rica," *Harper's Monthly Magazine* 20 (1860): 306.

145 Greenblat, *Renaissance Self-Fashioning*, 1–9.

146 Thomas Francis Meagher to Mary Anne Kelly, 25 September 1854, Thomas Madigan Collection, New York Public Library.

147 *Citizen* (New York), 7 January 1854.

148 *Columbia Gazette*, 25 November 1854.

149 *Citizen* (New York), 7 January 1854.

150 *Citizen* (New York), 7 January 1854.

151 *Citizen* (New York), 7 January 1854.

152 *Citizen* (New York), 7 January 1854.

153 *Citizen* (New York), 7 January 1854.

154 *Citizen* (New York), 7 January 1854.

155 *Citizen* (New York), 7 January 1854.

156 *Citizen* (New York), 7 January 1854.

157 *Citizen* (New York), 7 January 1854.

158 *Weekly Placer Herald*, 2 January 1852.

159 *Citizen* (New York), 7 January 1854.

160 *Citizen* (New York), 7 January 1854.

161 *Citizen* (New York), 7 January 1854.

162 *Citizen* (New York), 12 January 1856.

163 *New York Daily Times*, 28 June 1852.

4. THE UNITED STATES OF AMERICA, 1861–1867

1 Fenian Brotherhood in Chicago to William H. Seward, 21 September 1865, Seward Papers, AS 51, University of Rochester.

2 Samito, *Becoming American under Fire*, 6.

3 Bruce, *Harp and the Eagle*, 2.

4 Lincoln, "Emancipation Proclamation."

5 Bernstein, *New York City Draft Riots*, 78. For a broader discussion of the draft, see McPherson, *Battle Cry of Freedom*, 290, 591; Gienapp, *Abraham Lincoln and Civil War America*, 101; Smith, "Let Us All Be Grateful," 2; and Glatthaar, "What Manner of Men," 234.

6 Kenny, *American Irish*, 124.

7 Bernstein, *New York City Draft Riots*, 78.

8 Bernstein, 78.

9 Harris, *In the Shadow of Slavery*, 279–88.

10 Bruce, *Harp and the Eagle*, 247.

11 Bernstein, *New York City Draft*, 113.

12 Keating, "All of That Class That Infest NY," 253.

13 Keating, 253.

14 *New York Tribune*, 20 August 1862.

15 *New York Daily Tribune*, 9 July 1863.

16 Sharrow, "John Hughes," 256; Kelly, "Sentinel(s) of our Liberties," 157.

17 O'Neill, *Famine Irish*, 78.

18 Kurtz, *Excommunicated from the Union*, 109; Loughery, *Dagger John*, 199; Kelly, "Sentinel(s) of our Liberties," 164.

19 Foner, *Second Founding*, 19.

20 Brundage, *Irish Nationalists in America*, 81; O'Connell, *Upon American Slavery*, 7. For a detailed discussion of antislavery in Ireland, see Sweeney, Dillane, Stuart, eds., *Ireland, Slavery, Anti-Slavery, and Empire*.

21 Douglass, *Life and Times*, 180, in Geoghegan, *Liberator*, 198.

22 Geoghegan, "Consistent Advocate," 22–24.

23 Nelson, *Irish Nationalists*, 109.

24 John Mitchel to Mary Thompson, 4 October 1852, Pinkerton Papers, D1078/M4A T413/ 1, Public Record Office of Northern Ireland.

25 See, for instance, Dugger, "Black Ireland's Race," 461–85; and O'Neill, "Memory and John Mitchel," 321–43.

26 Carlyle, *Occasional Discourse*, 8. When this was originally published, in 1849, it was titled *Occasional Discourse on the Negro Question* and was more of a satire about

abolitionists. However, following criticism of the original piece, Carlyle doubled down on his racist arguments and removed much of the satire. Tarr, "Emendation as Challenge," 341–45; Goldberg, 'Liberalism's Limits," 203–16.

27 Nelson, *Irish Nationalists*, 109.

28 Mitchel, *Jail Journal*, 159.

29 Mitchel, 9.

30 Hale, "Martyrs for Contending Causes," 202.

31 Lynch, "Defining Irish Nationalist Anti-Imperialism," 94.

32 *Citizen* (New York), 20 May 1854.

33 Quinn, "Southern Citizen," 30–35.

34 Mitchel, *Life and Times of Aodh O'Neill*, v (first published in 1845).

35 McMahon, *Global Dimensions of Irish Identity*, 6; Ryder, "Autobiography as Criticism," 73.

36 *Gibbons*, "Race against Time," 103.

37 Siromahov, Buhrmester, and McKay, "Beliefs in National Continuity," 2.

38 Siromahov, Buhrmester, and McKay, 2.

39 Hannaford, *Race*, 17.

40 Todorov, *On Human Diversity*, 101.

41 John Mitchel in Dillon, *Life of John Mitchel*, 106.

42 John Mitchel to Mary Thompson, 1 November 1855, Pinkerton Papers, D1078/M4A T413, Public Record Office of Northern Ireland.

43 Karp, *This Vast Southern Empire*, 143.

44 John Mitchel to Matilda, 10 April 1859, Pinkerton Papers, D1078/7/A, Public Record Office of Northern Ireland.

45 Lucy O'Brien to William Smith O'Brien, Cahirmoyle, 29 January 1854, in Davis and Davis, eds., *Rebel in His Family*, 65. See also Goldner, "Arguing with Pictures," 71–84.

46 Oxx, *Nativist Movement in America*, 22.

47 Dillon, *Life of John Mitchel*, 101; Quinn, "Southern Citizen."

48 Quigley, *Shifting Grounds*, 76.

49 Dillon, *Life of John Mitchel*, 101.

50 Mitchel to Mary Thompson, 1 November 1855.

51 Quigley, *Shifting Grounds*, 4.

52 Karp, *This Vast Southern Empire*, 5. See also Binnington, *Confederate Visions*; Thomas, *Confederation Nation*, 10; and Faust, *Creation of Confederate Nationalism*, 60.

53 McGovern, "Young Ireland and Southern Nationalism," 53.

54 *New Orleans Crescent*, February 1861; originally printed in Brenan's paper, the *New Orleans Delta*, in 1856, month unknown, in McGovern, "Young Ireland and Southern Nationalism," 55.

55 Towers, "Origins of an Anti-Modern South," 176.

56 *Nation*, 30 December 1843.

57 McMahon, *Global Dimensions of Irish Identity*, 30.

58 Davis, *Poems*, 166; McMahon, *Global Dimensions of Irish Identity*, 31.

59 Thomas Davis, "Celts and Saxons," in *Prose Writings*, 354.
60 Mitchel, *Life and Times of Aodh O'Neill*, vii.
61 *Citizen* (New York), 12 January 1856.
62 McMahon, *Global Dimensions of Irish Identity*, 109.
63 *Irish Citizen*, 9 November 1867, in Rodgers, *Ireland, Slavery and Anti-Slavery*, 300.
64 Mitchel, *Last Conquest of Ireland (Perhaps)*, 317.
65 Moreover, Mitchel, in using a term that in Britain was derisively employed against the French, was one of the first to describe Britain's engagement with empire as imperialism. See Parry, "Impact of Napoleon III," 154.
66 Freeman et al., "Fight for Equal Rights," 118–20.
67 Quinlan, *Strange Kin*, 98.
68 McGovern, *John Mitchel*, 186.
69 Thomas Francis Meagher, "Speech on American Benevolence," in Lyons, *Brigadier-General*, 224.
70 Delahanty, "Transatlantic Roots," 183.
71 Bruce, *Harp and the Eagle*, 156.
72 Doyle, *Cause of All Nations*, 174.
73 Bruce, *Harp and the Eagle*, 87.
74 Burton, *Melting Pot Soldiers*, 19.
75 Samito, *Becoming American under Fire*, 6.
76 Cavanagh, *Memoirs*, 369; *New York Herald*, 2 June 1861.
77 Bruce, *Harp and Eagle*, 2.
78 Lecture by General Thomas Francis Meagher, at the People's Theatre, Virginia City, Montana, 17 March 1866, in Bruce, *Lectures*, 27.
79 William Seward to Thomas Francis Meagher, 21 March 1866, Seward Papers, AS51, vol. 3, University of Rochester.
80 Samito, "Meaning of the Civil War," 194.
81 Bruce, *Harp and the Eagle*, 77.
82 Meagher, *Last Days of the 69th*, 6.
83 Bruce, "Ye Sons of Green Erin Assemble," 101.
84 Cavanagh, *Memoirs*, 369, in Bruce, 103–4.
85 *Irish Brigade*, 3 February 1867, in Bruce, 60.
86 Mathisen, *Loyal Republic*, 11.
87 US Constitution, Amend. XIV, Sec. 2.
88 Balogh, *Government Out of Sight*, 286.
89 Emmons, *Beyond the American Pale*, 110.
90 Thomas Ireland to Paldino, 29 January 1912, in Wylie, *Irish General*, 224.
91 *St. Paul Press*, 3 August 1865.
92 Frederick Douglass, "Should the Negro Enlist?," 6 July 1863, National Hall, Philadelphia, in *Douglass' Monthly*, August 1863, n.p.
93 Feinman, *Citizenship Rites*, 92; Isenberg, *Sex and Citizenship*, 104.
94 General T. F. Meagher before the Young Men's Literary Association of Virginia City, Montana, 15 January 1865, in Bruce, *Lectures*, 16.

95 Meagher, *Speeches*, xviii.

96 O'Neill, "Mitchel's Appropriation of the Slave Narrative," 328; Hale, "Martyrs for Contending Causes," 204.

97 Thomas Francis Meagher to Thomas Meagher, 15 June 1867, Thomas Madigan Collection, New York Public Library.

98 Pocock, *Barbarism and Religion, Vol. 4*, 11.

99 Thomas Francis Meagher to Thomas Meagher, 15 June 1867.

100 Civil Rights Act 1866, 4 Stat. 27–30.

101 Maltz, "Fourteenth Amendment," 563–67.

102 Dwan, "Civic Virtue," 36.

103 Doheny, *Felon's Track*, 212.

104 Comerford, "O'Mahony, John."

105 McCaffrey, *Textures of Irish America*, 141.

106 Comerford, "Stephens, James."

107 Whelehan, *Dynamiters*, 14.

108 *Manchester Times*, 18 August 1866.

109 Doolin, *Transnational Revolutionaries*, 40; Carey, *Communication as Culture*, 222.

110 Gross Statement of Receipts and Expenditures of the Fenian Brotherhood, September 1, 1866–August 24, 1867, Add Mss No. 43742, British Library.

111 John Mitchel to Horace Greeley, 22 October 1858, Horace Greeley Papers ZL294, New York Public Library.

112 John Mitchel to Horace Greeley, 22 October 1858.

113 McGovern, *John Mitchel*, 104.

114 *New York Tribune*, 3 October 1848.

115 John Mitchel to Horace Greeley, 22 October 1858.

116 Steward and McGovern, *Fenians*, 1.

117 Kelly, *Ireland's Great Famine*, 49.

118 John Mitchel to John O'Mahony, 8 May 1861, Fenian Brotherhood Records and O'Donovan Rossa Personal Papers, box 3, folder ACUA 014, Catholic University of America Archive.

119 Doolin, *Transnational Revolutionaries*, 93.

120 Richardson, "Failure of the Men,'" 126.

121 Irish National Fair, February 1864, printed advertisement, Abraham Lincoln Papers, Series 1, General Correspondence, 1833–1916 Manuscript/Mixed Material, Library of Congress.

122 Steward and McGovern, *Fenians*, 29–30.

123 Brundage, *Irish Nationalists in America*, 101.

124 Savage, *Fenian Heroes and Martyrs*, 60.

125 Savage, 58.

126 Samito, *Becoming American under Fire*, 27.

127 Fenian Brotherhood Chicago to Hon. W. H. Seward, 21 September 1865, Seward Papers, AS51, vol. 3, University of Rochester.

128 Salyer, *Under the Starry Flag*, 80.

129 Salyer, 2.

130 Charles Adams to Edward Stanley, 11 September 1867, Fenian Correspondence, MR/14/K/16, 1868, Royal Irish Academy.

131 Ryan, *Civic Wars*, 273.

132 Cline, *Rebels on the Niagara*, 4.

133 Documents Relating to the Fenian Brotherhood, P 1294 Add MSS No 43742, National Library of Ireland.

134 *Fenian's Progress*, 66.

135 Guelzo, *Fateful Lightning*, 489.

136 *Fenian's Progress*, 66.

137 Guelzo, *Fateful Lightning*, 490.

138 *Fenian's Progress*, 66–67.

139 Bruce, *Harp and the Eagle*, 241; Sim, *Union Forever*, 93.

140 Gleeson, *Irish in the South*, 155.

141 Gleeson, *Green and the Gray*, 195.

142 *New York Herald*, 25 February 1867.

143 *New York Herald*, 25 February 1867.

144 Fenian Brotherhood in Chicago to William H. Seward, 21 September 1865, Seward Papers, AS 51, University of Rochester.

145 Mulholland, "Political Violence," 386.

146 Sim, *Union Forever*, 94.

147 Doolin, "Exploring Textures of Irish America," 157.

148 Doolin, *Transnational Revolutionaries*, 1.

149 John O'Mahony to John Mitchel, 10 November 1865, Fenian Brotherhood Records and O'Donovan Rossa Personal Papers, box 1, folder 8014, Catholic University of America Archive.

150 Bruce, *Harp and the Eagle*, 239–40.

151 Comerford, *Fenians in Context*, 131.

152 Senior, *Last Invasion of Canada*, 56.

153 Vronsky, *Ridgeway*, 46–47.

154 T. W. Sweeny in MacDonald, *Troublous Times in Canada*, 30.

155 Doolin, *Transnational*, 235.

156 William B. West to William H. Seward, 14 October 1865, Fenian Correspondence, MR/14/K/16, 1868, Royal Irish Academy.

157 William B. West to William H. Seward, 14 October 1865.

158 William B. West to William H. Seward, 14 October 1865.

159 Salyer, *Under the Starry Flag*, 3.

160 Salyer, 6.

161 McGee, "Cantwell, James."

162 McGee.

163 Keegan, *US Consular Representation*, 128.

164 McGee, "Cantwell, James."
165 Thomas Francis Meagher to John Dillon, 22 September 1863, Thomas Madigan Collection, Thomas Francis Meagher Papers, New York Public Library.
166 Thomas Francis Meagher to John Dillon, 22 September 1863.
167 State Department Appointments Gabon–Ireland (1861–69), Seward Papers, Box 79, Folder 3, University of Rochester.
168 William H. Seward to Charles Adams, 9 December 1867, Fenian Correspondence, MR/14/K/16, 1868, Royal Irish Academy.
169 William H. Seward to Charles Adams, 9 December 1867.
170 Salyer, *Under the Starry Flag*, 214.
171 *Convention between the United States and Great Britain*, 406.
172 Gerstle, *American Crucible*, 4.
173 Gates, *Stony the Road*, 4–7.
174 Foner, *Reconstruction*, 33.
175 Bernstein, *New York City Draft Riots*, 4.
176 McMahon, *Global Dimensions of Irish Identity*, 177.
177 Obsequies of Thos. Francis Meagher by Richard O'Gorman, n.d., Obsequies of Thomas Francis Meagher, American Irish Historical Society Archive.
178 Mitchel, *Memoir*, 39.

5. CANADA, 1857–1867

1 The Province of Canada was commonly referred to as "Canada" by contemporaries such as McGee; "Canada" is thus the term used in this chapter. "British North America" refers to Canada and the Maritime Provinces of Nova Scotia and New Brunswick before Confederation, which became the Dominion of Canada after July 1867.
2 McGee, *Canadian Ballads and Occasional Verses*, vii.
3 See the end of this chapter for discussion of the assassination.
4 Wilton, *Popular Politics and Political Culture*, 8; Schrauwers, *Union Is Strength*; Armstrong, "Oligarchy,'" 513.
5 Wilton, 8; Greer, "1837–38," 17; Ducharme, *Idea of Liberty in Canada*, 186.
6 Silver, *French-Canadian Idea of Confederation*, 218; Dickinson and Young, *Short History of Quebec*, xxii.
7 Belich, *Replenishing the Earth*, 285.
8 Heaman, *Inglorious Arts of Peace*, 52; Heaman, *Tax, Order, and Good Government*, 22.
9 Muise, "1860s," 14.
10 Sir É.-P. Taché, Premier, Lower Canada, 3 February 1865 in *Parliamentary Debates*, 6.
11 Buckner, "Creation of the Dominion," 67.
12 Wilson, *Irish in Canada*, 5.
13 McGowan and Clarke, "Two Views," 293.
14 Akenson, *Small Differences*, 90.
15 Fougères, "Introduction," 294.
16 Bradbury and Myers, "Introduction," 10.

17 McGaughey, *Violent Loyalties*, 139; Dickinson and Young, *Short History of Quebec*, 148.

18 Gauvreau, "Population, Social Identities," 654.

19 Thomas D'Arcy McGee to John O'Donohue, 15 September 1859, Charles Murphy Fonds, MG 27III B 8 35, Library and Archives Canada.

20 Jenkins, *Irish Nationalism*, 307; Barr, *Ireland's Empire*, 269.

21 Fay, "Catholic Christians," 53.

22 *New Era*, 25 May 1857.

23 *New Era*, 25 May 1857.

24 Oliver, "Moylan, James George."

25 Shanahan, "Irish Catholic Journalists," 45.

26 Thomas D'Arcy McGee to James George Moylan, 13 April 1857, George Moylan Fonds, MG 29 D15 Vol. 1, Library and Archives Canada.

27 Wilson, *Thomas D'Arcy McGee, Vol. 2*, 60.

28 Thomas D'Arcy McGee to James George Moylan, 3 June 1861, Charles Murphy Fonds, MG 27III B8 Vol. 48, Library and Archives Canada.

29 Thomas D'Arcy McGee to James George Moylan, 3 June 1861.

30 *New Era*, 25 May 1857.

31 *New Era*, 25 May 1857.

32 Thomas D'Arcy McGee to John O'Donohue, 15 October 1857, Charles Murphy Fonds, MG 27III B 8 35, Library and Archives Canada.

33 Fay, *History of Canadian Catholics*, 85.

34 *New Era*, 28 November 1857.

35 Wilson, *Thomas D'Arcy McGee, Vol. 2*, 31.

36 *New Era*, 25 May 1857.

37 *New Era*, 25 May 1857.

38 McGee, *Internal Condition of American Democracy*, 11; Livingston, "Thomas D'Arcy McGee's Civic Paidea," 95.

39 *True Witness and Catholic Chronicle*, 29 April 1859.

40 Wilson, *Thomas D'Arcy McGee, Vol. 2*, 63.

41 Wilson, 114.

42 *Globe*, 26 May 1858, in Wilson, 58.

43 Diary of George Clerk, 28 May 1858, George Clerk Fonds, P701 S2 SSI D20, Bibliothèque et Archives Nationales du Québec, in Wilson, 58.

44 *Globe*, 26 May 1858.

45 *New Era*, 4 January 1858, in Wilson, *Thomas D'Arcy McGee, Vol. 2*, 49, 61.

46 Wilson, 177.

47 Heaman, *Tax, Order, and Good Government*, 38.

48 Thomas D'Arcy McGee to James George Moylan, 3 June 1861, George Moylan Fonds, MG 29 D15 Vol. 1, Library and Archives Canada.

49 Conrad, *Concise History of Canada*, 146.

50 Conrad, 146.

51 Wilson, *Thomas D'Arcy McGee, Vol. 2*, 196.

52   *New Era*, 8 August 1857.

53   Waite, *Life and Times of Confederation*, 20; Waite and Martin, "Introduction," xxiv.

54   Black, *Divided Loyalties*, 4.

55   Thomas D'Arcy McGee, "The Policy of Conciliation," March 1861, in McGee, *Speeches and Addresses*, 8.

56   Heaman, *Tax, Order, and Good Government*, 41.

57   Laforest and Mathieu, "Trustee, Financier, and Poet," 137.

58   "The Cause of the Quebec Conference Speech by Thomas D'Arcy McGee at the Déjeûner Given to the Members of the Quebec Conference, October 29th, 1864," in McGee, *Speeches and Addresses*, 113.

59   Minutes of the Quebec Conference, Macdonald Fonds, vol. 46, f .108010, Library and Archives Canada, in Wilson, *Thomas D'Arcy McGee, Vol. 2*, 207.

60   *Montreal Gazette*, 9 December 1865.

61   Thompson, "Modern Liberty Redefined," 733.

62   McKay, "Liberal Order Framework," 633.

63   Heaman, *Tax, Order, and Good Government*, 59.

64   Thomas D'Arcy McGee, "The Common Interests of British North America—Address by Thomas D'Arcy McGee Delivered at the Temperance Hall, July 21st, 1863," in McGee, *Speeches and Addresses*, 61.

65   McGee, 61.

66   Curtis, *Politics of Population*, 235.

67   Thomas D'Arcy McGee, "Common Interests of British North America," in McGee, *Speeches and Addresses*, 62.

68   Buckner, "Maritimes and Confederation," 23.

69   Thomas D'Arcy McGee, "Common Interests of British North America," in McGee, *Speeches and Addresses*, 62.

70   McGee, *Internal Condition of American Democracy*, 16.

71   Thomas D'Arcy McGee, "American Relations And Canadian Duties—Address by Thomas D'Arcy McGee to the Irish Protestant Benevolent Society, May 10, 1862," in McGee, *Speeches and Addresses*, 35.

72   Warner, *Idea of Continental Union*, 49.

73   Winks, *Civil War Years*, 12–22.

74   Wilson, *Thomas D'Arcy McGee, Vol. 2*, 121.

75   Stacey, "Defense Problem and Canadian Confederation," 171.

76   Francis, Jones, and Smith, *Journeys*, 246; Martin, *Origins of Canadian Confederation*, 22.

77   *Fenian's Progress*, 25–30.

78   Jenkins, *Between Raid and Rebellion*, 5.

79   Charles Stanley Monck, 4th Viscount Monck to Edward Cardwell MP, 14 June 1866, in *Correspondence Respecting the Recent Fenian Aggression upon Canada*, 7–9.

80   Charles Stanley Monck, 4th Viscount Monck to Richard Plantagenet Campbell, 3rd Duke of Buckingham, and Chandos, secretary of state for the colonies, 13 June 1868, Monck Papers, MS 27,022, National Library of Ireland.

81 Bannister, "Liberty, Loyalty, and Sentiment," 78–92.

82 Conrad, *Concise History of Canada*, 150.

83 *Parliamentary Debates*, 146.

84 *Parliamentary Debates*, 146.

85 *Parliamentary Debates*, 129.

86 *Parliamentary Debates*, 146.

87 Thomas D'Arcy McGee, "The Irish in Canada: The Importation of Fenianism—An Address by Thomas D'Arcy McGee Delivered before the St. Patrick's Society, January 11th, 1865," in McGee, *Speeches and Addresses*, 147.

88 Wilson, "Fenians in Montréal," 110.

89 Thomas D'Arcy McGee, "The Policy of Conciliation—Thomas D'Arcy McGee's Remarks at Montréal, March 1861," in McGee, *Speeches and Addresses*, 7.

90 *Montreal Gazette*, 26 August 1867.

91 *Montreal Gazette*, 26 August 1867.

92 *Montreal Gazette*, 26 August 1867.

93 Thomas D'Arcy McGee to James George Moylan, 27 October 1865, George Moylan Fnds, MG 29 D15 Vol. 1, Library and Archives Canada.

94 Thomas D'Arcy McGee to James George Moylan, 27 October 1865.

95 Jenkins, *Irish Nationalism and the British State*, 307.

96 Barr, *Ireland's Empire*, 204–81.

97 Clarke, *Piety and Nationalism*, 184.

98 Rafferty, *Church, the State*, 64.

99 Thomas D'Arcy McGee to the Earl of Mayo, 4 April 1868, Charles Murphy Fonds, MG 27III B8 vol. 48, Library and Archives Canada.

100 Hanagan, "Irish Transnational Social Movements," 62.

101 *Montreal Gazette*, 5 November 1867.

102 Carrese, *Democracy in Moderation*, 79.

103 Barr, *Ireland's Empire*, 260.

104 Thomas D'Arcy McGee, "American Relations and Canadian Duties—Address by Thomas D'Arcy McGee to the Irish Protestant Benevolent Society, May 10, 1862," in McGee, *Speeches and Addresses*, 35.

105 Choudhry, "Canadian Constitution and the World," 1087.

106 Gerstle, *Liberty and Coercion*, 24–26.

107 Noël, "Democratic Deliberation," 436; For a more abstract discussion of the political thought associated with such an approach, see Hansen, "Mixed Constitution," 509–31.

108 Thomas D'Arcy McGee, Speech in the Confederation Debates, February 9, 1865, Legislative Assembly, Province of Canada, Confederation Debates Province of Canada, in *Parliamentary Debates*, 146.

109 Wilson, *Thomas D'Arcy McGee*, 205.

110 McGee, *Internal Condition of American Democracy*, 19. The pamphlet was first published in London in 1863 but was widely available in Canada and received much press coverage there in magazines such as the the *British American Magazine*, 208.

111 McGee, *Internal Condition of American Democracy*, 19.

112 McGee, 19.

113 McGee, 11.

114 Thomas D'Arcy McGee to John A. Macdonald, 18 Oct 1867, Charles Murphy Fnds, MG 27III B 8 35, Library and Archives Canada.

115 McGee, *Internal Condition of American Democracy*, 2.

116 Tocqueville, *Democracy in America, Vol. 1*, 330.

117 McGee, Speech in the Confederation Debates, February 9, 1865, 143.

118 McGee, 143.

119 McGee, 143.

120 Buckner, "Maritimes and Confederation," 23.

121 Ajzenstat, *Once and Future Canadian Democracy*, 71.

122 Ajzenstat et al., *Canada's Founding Debates*, 190.

123 LaSelva, *Moral Foundations of Canadian Federalism*, 126.

124 Thomas D'Arcy McGee, "American Relations and Canadian Duties—Address by Thomas D'Arcy McGee to the Irish Protestant Benevolent Society, May 10, 1862," in McGee, *Speeches and Addresses*, 356.

125 *Dublin Evening Mail*, 16 May 1865.

126 *Dublin Evening Mail*, 16 May 1865.

127 *Montreal Gazette*, 5 November 1867.

128 Ballstadt, "Thomas D'Arcy McGee."

129 *Montreal Gazette*, 5 November 1867.

130 *Montreal Gazette*, 5 November 1867.

131 McGee, *Canadian Ballads and Occasional Verses*, viii.

132 McGee, vii.

133 Jess, "Rubbing Away Their Roughness," 157.

134 *Montreal Gazette*, 5 November 1867.

135 *Dublin University Magazine*, February 1847, 199.

136 McGee, *Canadian Ballads and Occasional Verses*, 12.

137 Urschel, "From the 'White Lily,'" 49.

138 Mitchel, *Last Conquest of Ireland (Perhaps)*, 317

139 *Parliamentary Debates*, 139.

140 *Parliamentary Debates*, 139.

141 Thomas D'Arcy McGee, "The Policy of Conciliation—Thomas D'Arcy McGee's Remarks at Montréal, March 1861," in McGee, *Speeches and Addresses*, 8.

142 McGee, *Canadian Ballads and Occasional Verses*, 29; Wilson, *Thomas D'Arcy McGee: The Extreme Moderate, 1857–1868*, 27.

143 Toorn, "Aboriginal Writing," 28.

144 Phillips and McDougall, "Baldoon Mysteries," 123.

145 McGee, *Canadian Ballads and Occasional Verses*, 29.

146 McGee, 29.

147 Wilson, "Time and Space," 109–23.

148 Thomas D'Arcy McGee, "Constitutional Difficulties between Upper and Lower Canada," in McGee, *Speeches and Addresses*, 175–76.

149 McGee, *Poems*, 249, 255, 309.

150 "O Canada!"

151 *Montreal Gazette*, 5 November 1867.

152 Wilson, *Thomas D'Arcy McGee: The Extreme Moderate, 1857–1868*, 100.

153 McGee, "Constitutional Difficulties," 175–76.

154 Burns, "McGee, Thomas D'Arcy," 489–94.

155 Russell, *Canada's Odyssey*, 127.

156 McGee, *Internal Condition of American Democracy*, 12.

157 *Montreal Gazette*, November 5 1867.

158 *Montreal Gazette*, November 5 1867.

159 McGee, "Probable Capital," 60–64.

160 Grannan, "Thomas D'Arcy McGee," 95.

161 McGee, "Common Interests of British North America," 61.

162 Quebec Resolutions, October 1864, in *Documents on Confederation*, 165.

163 Otter, *Philosophy of Railways*, 124.

164 Huurdeman, *Worldwide History of Telecommunications*, 602.

165 *New York Times*, 29 July 1866.

166 Osterhammel, *Transformation of the World*, 720.

167 Bell, *Reordering the World*, 98.

168 Burbank and Cooper, *Empires in World History*, 458.

169 *Ottawa Times*, 9 August 1866.

170 *Ottawa Times*, 9 August 1866.

171 Steward and McGovern, *Fenians*, 134.

172 Bumsted, "Consolidation of British North America," 64.

173 Russell, *Canada's Odyssey*, 148.

174 Wilson, "Wexford Speech of 1865," 12.

175 *Dublin Evening Mail*, 16 May 1865.

176 Thomas D'Arcy McGee, "The Irish in Canada: The Importation of Fenianism—An Address by Thomas D'Arcy McGee Delivered before the St. Patrick's Society, January 11th, 1865," in McGee, *Speeches and Addresses*, 145.

177 J. J Sullivan to Thomas D'Arcy McGee, 23 November 1865, Thomas D'Arcy McGee Fonds, MG27 IE 9, Library and Archives Canada.

178 J. J Sullivan to Thomas D'Arcy McGee, 23 November 1865.

179 J. J Sullivan to Thomas D'Arcy McGee, 23 November 1865.

180 *New Era*, 10 October 1857; Thomas D'Arcy McGee to John A. McDonald, 15 February 1868, John A. McDonald Papers, MG 26 A, vol. 231, Library and Archives Canada, in Wilson, "Orange Influences of the Right Kind," 90.

181 McCarroll, *Letters of Terry Finnegan*, 8.

182 Senior, *Orangeism*, 69.

183 Wilson, "Orange Influences of the Right Kind," 107.

184 Wilson, *Thomas D'Arcy McGee: The Extreme Moderate, 1857–1868*, 387.

185 Canada, House of Commons, 6 April 1868.
186 Canada, House of Commons, 6 April 1868.

6. AUSTRALIA, 1856–1872

1 Duffy, *Civil and Religious Liberty*, 7–8.
2 Pitts, *Turn to Empire*, 2; Bell, *Reordering the World*, 366.
3 Bell, 20.
4 *Census of Victoria, 1854*, v.
5 Russell, "Gender and Colonial Society," 485.
6 *Irish Examiner*, 12 April 1852.
7 *Waterford News and Star*, 7 October 1853.
8 *Nation*, 22 May 1852.
9 *Nation*, 22 May 1852.
10 *Nation*, 22 May 1852.
11 *Melbourne Daily News*, 27 May 1851.
12 Galbally, *Redmond Barry*, 88; Goold, *Diary*, 46.
13 Catalogue of the Melbourne Public Library–1862, Presented by the Tustees of the Melbourne Public Library to the Honourable Chief Secr. John O'Shanassy Esq., History of the Library Collection, box 4385/11 MS10128, State Library of Victoria; Davison, "Gold Rush Melbourne," 63.
14 Curthoys and Mitchell, "Advent of Self-Government," 161.
15 Duffy, *My Life in Two Hemispheres*, 141.
16 Duffy, 163.
17 Blainey, *History of Victoria*, 50.
18 Boucher, "Victorian Liberalism," 35.
19 *Age*, 2 February 1858.
20 Sunter and Williams, "Eureka's Impact on Victorian Politics," 17.
21 Clark and Cathcart, *History of Australia*, 256.
22 Molony, *Eureka*, 28.
23 Carboni, *Eureka Stockade*, 2.
24 Carboni, 47.
25 Blainey, *Rush That Never Ended*, 56; Taylor, "1848 Revolutions," 174.
26 Geoghegan and Quinn, "O'Doherty, Kevin Izod."
27 John Martin to Mrs. Connell, 15 December 1858, Irish Political Prisoners of 1848, National Library of Australia.
28 *Australasian Medical Gazette*, 21 August 1905.
29 Patrick and Patrick, *Exiles Undaunted*, 156.
30 Patrick and Patrick, 176.
31 Rudé, "O'Doherty, Kevin Izod."
32 Malcolm, *Ireland's Farthest Shores*, 152.
33 Vries and Vries *Historic Brisbane*, 118.
34 Buckridge, "Irish Poets in Colonial Brisbane," 33–34.
35 O'Doherty, "Queensland," in *Poems*, 92.

36 O'Doherty, "In The West," 51.

37 Russell, "Gender and Colonial Society," 485.

38 O'Doherty, "Ad Astra," in *Poems*, 102.

39 O'Doherty, 102.

40 O'Doherty, *Poems by "Eva."*

41 "On Behalf of the Hibernian Australian Catholic Benefit Society," Charles Gavan Duffy Papers, MS 7001, National Library of Australia.

42 "On Behalf."

43 Central Committee to Charles Gavan Duffy, n.d., Charles Gavan Duffy Papers, MS 7001/7, National Library of Australia.

44 Central Committee to Charles Gavan Duffy, n.d.

45 *Geelong Advertiser and Intelligencer*, 11 March 1856; *Age*, 30 April 1856; *Age*, 22 February 1856.

46 *Empire*, 21 July 1856.

47 *Empire*, 22 October 1855.

48 *Empire*, 22 October 1855.

49 *Empire*, 22 October 1855.

50 *Empire*, 5 April 1856.

51 Noone, "Irish Rebel in Victoria," 110.

52 *Empire*, 22 October 1855.

53 Duffy, "Civil and Religious Liberty."

54 Lang, *Freedom and Independence*, 14.

55 Ward, *State and the People*, 31.

56 Victoria Report from the Select Committee on Military and Naval Forces and Defences Together with the Proceedings of the Committee and Minutes of Evidence and Appendix, 1861–62, Friday 23rd May 1862, Victorian Collection, Nq 328.945 VIC, National Library of Australia.

57 *Leader*, 11 May 1867.

58 Parry, *Politics of Patriotism*, 282.

59 *Argus*, 27 December 1853.

60 Richard Baker to Charles Gavan Duffy Adelaide, 19 December 1870, MS 7957, box 662, State Library of Victoria.

61 Victoria Report from the Select Committee on Military and Naval Forces and Defences Together with the Proceedings of the Committee and Minutes of Evidence and Appendix, 1861–62, 19 March 1862, Victorian Collection, Nq 328.945 VIC, National Library of Australia.

62 Edward Butler to Charles Gavan Duffy, 1 January 1871, Correspondence of Sir Charles Gavan Duffy, MS 7957, box 662, State Library of Victoria.

63 Edward Butler to Charles Gavan Duffy, 1 January 1871.

64 Edward Butler to Charles Gavan Duffy, 1 January 1871.

65 Edward Butler to Charles Gavan Duffy, 1 January 1871.

66 Duffy, "Civil and Religious Liberty."

67 Ford and Roberts, "Expansion," 135.

68 Ford and Roberts, 134.

69 Woods, "Gray, Moses Wilson."

70 Sinclair, "Gray, Moses Wilson."

71 *Moreton Bay Courier*, 11 September 1860; *Argus*, 5 November 1869.

72 Connolly, "Limits of Democracy in Ireland," 179.

73 Duffy, *Guide to the Land Law of Victoria*, 7.

74 Land Bill of the Government!, "Out of Their Own Mouths Shall Ye Judge Them," 1859, Rare Books and Pamphlets, f 333.16 G781L, Monash University Library.

75 Weaver, *Great Land Rush*, 316.

76 Ireland, "Victorian Land Act 1862 Revisited," 136.

77 Duffy, *Land Societies in Victoria*, 16.

78 Belich, *Replenishing the Earth*, 147–48.

79 Woollacott, *Settler Society*, 39–40; Wakefield, *View of the Art*, 29–32.

80 Stewart, "Britain's Australia," 14.

81 Kawana, "John Stuart Mill," 44; Zastoupil, "Moral Government," 709.

82 Mill, "'The Condition of Ireland, 10 October 1846," in Mill, *Collected Works, Vol. 14*, 889.

83 Duffy, *Land Societies in Victoria*, 3.

84 Duffy, 3.

85 Duffy, 4.

86 Duffy, 4.

87 Bate, "Ballarat," 21.

88 Duffy, *Land Societies in Victoria*, 4.

89 Kelson and McQuilton, *Kelly Country*, 48.

90 O'Farrell, *Irish in Australia*, 296

91 Kelson and McQuilton, *Kelly Country*, 47.

92 Belich, *Replenishing the Earth*, 23.

93 Darwin, "Imperialism and the Victorians," 616.

94 McKenna, *Captive Republic*, 111.

95 Banner, *Possessing the Pacific*, 13.

96 Edmonds, "Canada and Australia," 125.

97 Lake and Reynolds, *Drawing the Global Colour Line*, 27.

98 Duffy, *Land Societies*, 4.

99 Stephens, *White without Soap*, 132.

100 Noone, "Irish Rebel in Victoria," 113.

101 Malcolm and Hall, *New History of the Irish*, 66.

102 Curthoys and Mitchell, *Taking Liberty*, 274.

103 Fawcett, *Liberalism*, 293.

104 Wilson, *Irish and Scottish Encounters*, 18.

105 *Irish Exile and Freedom's Advocate*, 26 January 1850, in McMahon, "Transnational Dimensions," 102.

106 *Irish Exile and Freedom's Advocate*, 28 September 1850, in McMahon, 102.

107 Duffy, *Australian Policy Speech*, 14.

108 Duffy, *My Life in Two Hemispheres*, 157.

109 Goodman, *Gold Seeking*, 129.

110 Malcolm and Hall, *New History of the Irish*, 285.

111 Duffy, *My Life in Two Hemispheres*, 331.

112 Duffy, 332.

113 Scalmer, "Charles Gavan Duffy's Ministerial Tour," 158.

114 *Bendigo Advertiser*, 22 July 1871.

115 *Bendigo Advertiser*, 22 July 1871.

116 Biagini, *Liberty Retrenchment and Reform*, 371.

117 *Daily Telegraph*, 28 December 1871, in Scalmer, "Charles Gavan Duffy's Ministerial Tour," 165.

118 *Argus*, 14 November 1871.

119 Duffy, *Australian Policy Speech*, 14; *People's Charter*.

120 *Argus*, 14 November 1871.

121 Jackson, *Religious Education and the Anglo-world*, 39.

122 Duffy, "Civil and Religious Liberty."

123 Dowd, *Rome in Australia*, 21.

124 Rudé, "O'Doherty, Kevin Izod."

125 *Victorian Hansard*, 31 August 1869.

126 Knowlton, "Enigma of Sir Charles Gavan Duffy," 191.

127 Charles Gavan Duffy to Moriarty, 12 April 1856, Monsell Papers, MS8319, National Library of Ireland.

128 Mayrl, *Secular Conversions*, 74.

129 Barr, *Ireland's Empire*, 17.

130 Biagini, *British Democracy and Irish Nationalism*, 116.

131 Henry Parkes to Charles Gavan Duffy, 23 December 1870, Papers of Sir Henry Parkes, A915/140, State Library of New South Wales.

132 Parkes to Charles Gavan Duffy, 23 December 1870.

133 For instance, in 1891, Duffy wrote to Parkes telling him that "if you succeed in federating the young nation you will have good reason to be gratified with your position." Charles Gavan Duffy to Henry Parkes, 13 October 1891, Papers of Sir Henry Parkes, A921/138, State Library of New South Wales.

134 Charles Gavan Duffy to Henry Parkes, 14 April 1874, Papers of Sir Henry Parkes, A921/44, State Library of New South Wales.

135 Parkes, *Federal Government of Australasia*, 83.

136 Duffy, *Land Societies in Victoria*, 4.

137 Distribution of Patronage by the Duffy Government: Speech of the Honorable Chief Secretary on the Motion of No Confidence, Legislative Assembly, 22 May 1872, Charles Gavan Duffy papers, MS 7001, National Library of Australia.

CONCLUSION

1 Yeats, "September 1913," in *Variorum Poems*, 819.

2 Much as John Stuart Mill had argued in 1861: Mill, *Considerations on Representative Government*, 11.

3 Duffy, *Young Ireland*, 1.

4 Duffy, 48.

5 Gerstle, *American Crucible*, 4.

6 Eyal, *Young America Movement*, 94.

7 Belich, *Replenishing the Earth*, 23.

8 *Nation*, 15 October 1842.

9 Duffy, *Land Societies in Victoria*, 4.

10 Dwan, "Civic Virtue,'" 736.

11 Curthoys and Mitchell, "Advent of Self-Government," 161; Blainey, *History of Victoria*, 50.

12 Heaman, *Tax Order and Good Government*, 7, 32; Buckner, "Creation of the Dominion of Canada," 67.

13 Wenzlhuemer, *Connecting the Nineteenth-Century World*, 56.

14 Carey, *Communication as Culture*, 222.

15 Quinn, *Young Ireland*, 103.

16 Wilson, "Wexford Speech of 1865," 11.

17 Foster, *Words Alone*, 50–52.

18 Duffy, "Civil and Religious Liberty."

BIBLIOGRAPHY

MANUSCRIPTS

Abraham Lincoln Papers, Library of Congress.

Ambrose W. Thompson Papers, Library of Congress.

Autograph Letters, Daniel O'Connell, British Library.

Charles Gavan Duffy Newsprint Collection, National Library of Ireland.

Charles Gavan Duffy Papers, National Library of Australia.

Charles Murphy Fonds, Libraries and Archives Canada.

Correspondence of Sir Charles Gavan Duffy, State Library of Victoria.

Davis, Marianne, Richard Davis, ed. *The Rebel in His Family: Selected Papers of William Smith O'Brien*. Cork: Cork University Press, 1998.

Documents Relating to the Fenian Brotherhood, National Library of Ireland.

Fenian Brotherhood Records and O'Donovan Rossa Personal Papers, American Catholic University Archive.

Fenian Correspondence, 1866–67, Royal Irish Academy.

George Clerk Fonds, Bibliothèque et Archives Nationales du Québec.

George Moylan Fonds, Libraries and Archives Canada.

Glover, Margaret, and Alf MacLochlainn, eds. *Letters of an Irish Patriot: William Paul Dowling in Tasmania*. Sandy Bay: Tasmanian Historical Research Association, 2005.

Gross Statement of Receipts and Expenditures of the Fenian Brotherhood, British Library.

History of the Library Collection, State Library of Victoria.

Horace Greely Papers, New York Public Library.

Irish Political Prisoners of 1848, National Library of Australia.

J. J. O'Gorman papers, Libraries and Archives Canada.

John Mitchel Correspondence, State Library of Victoria.

Letterbook of Richard O'Gorman, National Library of Ireland.

Letters and Papers of the Irish Political Prisoners of the 1848 Insurrection, National Library of Australia.

Letters from Mrs. John Mitchel, 1851–1855, New York Public Library.

Macdonald Fonds, Library and Archives Canada.

McElderry Papers, Public Record Office of Northern Ireland.

Monck Papers, National Library of Ireland.

Monsell Papers, National Library of Ireland.

Obsequies of Thomas Francis Meagher, American Irish Historical Society Archive.

Papers of Lord John Russell, Personal Collections, National Archives of the United Kingdom.

Papers of Sir Henry Parkes, State Library of New South Wales.

Papers of Sir John A. Macdonald, Library and Archives Canada.

Papers of Sir William Thomas Denison, National Library of Australia.

Papers of William Smith O'Brien, National Library of Ireland.

Personal Papers of Thomas D'Arcy McGee, Libraries and Archives Canada.

Pinkerton Papers, Public Record Office of Northern Ireland.

Seward Papers, University of Rochester.

Thomas D'Arcy McGee Fonds, Library and Archives Canada.

Thomas Francis Meagher Papers, Library of Congress.

Thomas Madigan Collection, Thomas Francis Meagher Papers, New York Public Library.

Victorian Collection, National Library of Australia.

OFFICIAL PUBLICATIONS

"1841 Census Ireland Reports and Abstract, 1841." Online Historical Population Reports. Colchester, University of Essex, 2007. www.histpop.org.

Australian Convict Records. Tasmania in the State Library of South Australia. Accessed 3 January 2023. guides.slsa.sa.gov.au.

Canadian Hansard.

Census of Victoria, 1854: Population Tables. Melbourne: Ferres, 1855.

Civil Rights Act 1866 4 Stat. 27–30.

Convention between the United States and Great Britain, Relative to Naturalization. Concluded May 13, 1870; Ratifications Exchanged August 10, 1870; Proclaimed September 16, 1870, in Treaties and Conventions Concluded between the United States of America and Other Powers since July 4, 1776. Washington, DC: Government Printing Office 1873.

Duffy, Charles Gavan. *Guide to the Land Law of Victoria.* Melbourne: John Ferres Government Printer, 1862.

Hansard Parliamentary Debates, 3d series (1830–91).

Higgins, Michael D. Higgins, President of Ireland, Speech to the Parliament of Western Australia, Perth, 10 October 2017.

Lincoln, Abraham. "Emancipation Proclamation." 1 January 1863. National Archives of the United States.

O Canada! Government of Canada. canada.ca.

Parliamentary Debates on the Subject of the Confederation of the British North America Provinces, 3rd Session, 8th Provincial Parliament of Canada. Quebec: Hunter, Rose, 1865.

Quebec Resolutions, October 1864. In *Documents on Confederation of British North America.* Montreal: McGill-Queen's University Press, 2015.

Queensland Parliamentary Debates, Legislative Council.

Remarks by the President at Irish Celebration in Dublin, Ireland. White House Office of the Press Secretary, 23 May 2011.

"Reports, Abstract, Ireland, 1841." Online Historical Population Reports. Colchester, University of Essex, 2007. www.histpop.org.

Trudeau, Justin, Prime Minister of Canada. Speech at Dublin Castle, 4 July 2017.
US Congressional Serial Set, Issue 610, 1/31 US Senate, 1851–52.
US Const. Amend. 14, Sec. 2.
Victorian Hansard.

NEWSPAPERS

The Age.
American Celt and Adopted Citizen.
The Argus.
Atlantic Monthly.
Australasian Medical Gazette.
Baton-Rouge Gazette.
Belfast Newsletter.
Bendigo Advertiser.
Boston Pilot.
British American Magazine.
British Magazine.
Burlington Free Press.
The Citizen.
The Citizen (New York).
Chicago Daily Tribune.
Colonial Times.
Columbia Gazette.
The Courier.
Daily Telegraph.
Democratic Review.
Douglass' Monthly.
Dublin Evening Mail.
Dublin Penny Journal.
Dublin University Magazine.
The Empire.
Freeman's Journal.
Geelong Advertiser and Intelligencer.
The Globe.
Harper's Monthly Magazine.
Illustrated News.
Irish Citizen.
Irish Examiner.
Irish Exile and Freedom's Advocate.
Irish Felon.
Irish News.
Irish Penny Journal.
Kerry Evening Post.

Launceston Examiner.
The Leader.
Living Age.
Louisville Journal.
Manchester Times.
Melbourne Daily News.
Miners' Express.
Montreal Gazette.
Moreton Bay Courier.
Mountain Sentinel.
The Nation.
The Nation (New York).
Native American.
New Era.
New Orleans Crescent.
New Orleans Delta.
New York Daily Times.
New York Daily Tribune.
New York Herald.
New York Morning News.
New York Times.
New York Tribune.
Ottawa Times.
People's Advocate and New South Wales Vindicator.
Portsmouth Inquirer.
Putnam's Monthly.
Southern Sentinel.
The Republic.
St. Paul Press.
Sydney Morning Herald.
True Witness and Catholic Chronicle.
United States Magazine and Democratic Review.
Weekly Minnesotan.
Waterford News and Star.
Weekly Placer Herald.
Weekly National Intelligencer.
Young America.

PRINTED PRIMARY SOURCES

Balmez, Jaime Luciano. *Protestantism and Catholicity Compared in Their Effects on the Civilisation of Europe.* Baltimore, MD: John Murray, 1851.

Bancroft, George. *History of the United States, from the Discovery of the American Continent.* Boston: Little, Brown, 1860.

Barnes, James J., and Patience P. Barnes. *Private and Confidential: Letters from British Ministers in Washington to the Foreign Secretaries in London, 1844–67.* Selinsgrove: Susquehanna University Press, 1993.

Barrett, Richard. *History of the Irish Confederation.* Dublin: George Mason, 1849.

Bruce, John P. *Lectures of Gov. Thomas Francis Meagher, in Montana, Together with His Messages, Speeches.* Virginia City: Bruce & Wright, 1867.

Carboni, Raffaello. *The Eureka Stockade: The Consequence of Some Pirates Wanting on Quarter-deck a Rebellion by Raffaello Carboni by the Grace of Spy "Goodenough," Captain of Foreign Anarchists but by the Unanimous Choice of His Fellow-Miners Member of the Local Court, Ballaarat.* Melbourne: J. P. Atkinson, 1855.

Carlyle, Thomas. *Occasional Discourse on the Nigger Question. Reprinted, with Additions, from* Fraser's Magazine. London: Thomas Bosworth, 1853.

Cavanagh, Michael. *Memoirs of Gen. Thomas Francis Meagher.* Worchester, MA: Messenger, 1892.

Clarke, Marcus. *Old Tales of a Young Country.* Melbourne: Mason, Firth & M'Cutcheon, 1871.

Davis, Thomas, ed. *Literary and Historical Essays.* Dublin: James Duffy, 1846.

———. *The Poems of Thomas Davis.* New York: P. J. Kennedy, n.d.

———. *The Poems of Thomas Davis: Now First Collected.* Edited by Thomas Wallis. Dublin: James Duffy, 1857.

———. *The Prose Writings of Thomas Davis.* Edited by T. W. Rollenston. London: W. Scott, 1890.

———. *The Spirit of the Nation: Ballads and Songs by the Writers of The Nation, with Original and Ancient Music, Arranged for the Voice and Piano Forte.* Dublin: The Nation, 1845.

Doheny, Michael. *History of the American Revolution.* Dublin: James Duffy, 1846.

———. *The Felon's Track: Or, History of the Attempted Outbreak in Ireland, Embracing the Leading Events in the Irish Struggle from the Year 1843 to the Close of 1848.* Dublin: M. H. Gill, 1918.

Douglass, Frederick. *Life and Times of Frederick Douglass.* New York: Cowell, 1966.

Duffy, Charles Gavan. *An Australian Policy Speech.* Melbourne: Stillwell & Knight, 1872.

———. *Ballad Poetry of Ireland.* 40th ed. Dublin: James Duffy, 1869.

———. *Civil and Religious Liberty: Speech of Charles Gavan Duffy at Melbourne on the Presentation of a Property Qualification to Him, 20 August 1856.* Melbourne: Michael T. Gason, 1856.

———. *Conversations with Carlyle.* New York: Charles Scribner, 1892.

———. *Land Societies in Victoria by the Hon. Charles Gavan Duffy President of the Board of Land and Works.* Melbourne: Wilson & MacKinnon, 1862.

———. *My Life in Two Hemispheres.* London: T. Fisher Unwin, 1898.

———. *Thomas Davis: The Memoirs of an Irish Patriot, 1840–1846.* London: Kegan Paul, 1890.

———. *The Voice of the Nation: A Manual of Nationality.* Dublin: James Duffy, 1844.

————. *Young Ireland: A Fragment of Irish History, 1840–1845.* Dublin: M. H. Gill & Son, 1884.

————. *Young Ireland: A Fragment of Irish History, 1840–1850.* 2nd ed. London: Cassell, Petter, Galpin, 1880.

Emerson, Ralph Waldo. *The Young American: A Lecture Read before the Mercantile Library Association, Boston, February 7, 1844.* London: John Chapman, 1844.

The Fenian's Progress: A Vision. New York: J. Bradburn, 1865.

Fitzpatrick, W. J. *Correspondence of Daniel O'Connell.* London: John Murray, 1888.

Frost, Robert. *A Letter to the People of Great Britain & Ireland on Transportation, Showing the Effects of Irresponsible Power on the Physical and Moral Conditions of Convicts.* London: n.p., 1856.

Goold, James. *The Diary of James Alipius Goold Osa First Catholic Bishop and Archbishop of Melbourne, 1848–1886, 2 June 1853.* Melbourne: Melbourne Diocesan Historical Commission, 2009.

Herder, Johann Gottfried. *Herder's Sämmtliche Werke.* Berlin: Weidmann, 1877–1913. In *Three Critics of the Enlightenment: Vico, Hamann, Herder,* by Isaiah Berlin. Vol 27. Princeton, NJ: Princeton University Press, 2000.

————. *Outlines of a Philosophy of the History of Man.* Translated by T. Churchill. New York: Bergman, 1966.

————. "This Too a Philosophy of History for the Formation of Humanity (1774)." In *Herder: Philosophical Writings,* edited by Michael N. Forster, 272–358. Cambridge: Cambridge University Press, 2002.

————. "Treatise on the Origin of Language (1772)." In *Herder: Philosophical Writings,* edited by Michael N. Forster, 65–164. Cambridge: Cambridge University Press, 2002.

Huish, Robert. *The Memoirs, Private and Political, of Daniel O'Connell, Esq., from the Year 1776 to the Close of the Proceedings in Parliament for the Repeal of the Union: Compiled from Official Documents.* London: W. Johnston, 1836.

The Irish Confederation: Proceedings of the Young Ireland Party, at the Great Meeting in the Music Hall, Belfast, on the 15th November, 1847: With a Correct Report of the Speeches Delivered by the Deputation from Dublin. Belfast: John Henderson, 1848.

Lalor, James Fintan, and James Connolly. *The Rights of Ireland: And The Faith of a Felon.* New York: Donnelly, 1900.

Lang, John Dunmore. *Freedom and Independence for the Golden Lands of Australia: The Right of the Colonies and the Interest of Britain and of the World.* 2nd ed. Sydney: Cunninghame, 1857.

List, Friedrich. *The National System of Political Economy.* London: Longmans, Green, 1909.

Lyons, W. F. *Brigadier-General Thomas Francis Meagher: His Political and Military Career, With Selections from His Speeches and Writings.* New York: D. J. Sadler, 1870.

Madden, Daniel Owen. *Ireland and Its Rulers since 1829.* London: T. C. Newby, 1843.

Matthews, Cornelius. *Americanism: An Address Delivered before the Eucleian Society of the New York University, 30th June, 1845.* New York: Paine & Burgess, 1845.

McCarroll, James. *Letters of Terry Finnegan, Author of Several Imaginary Works*. Vol. 1. Toronto: n.p., 1863.

McGee, Thomas D'Arcy. *Canadian Ballads and Occasional Verses*. Toronto: W. C. F. Caverhill, 1858.

—. *Historical Sketches of O'Connell and His Friends*. Boston: Donohoe & Ronan, 1845.

—. *A History of the Irish Settlers in North America, from the Earliest Period to the Census of 1850*. Boston: American Celt Office, 1851.

—. *History of the Irish Settlers in North America, from the Earliest Period to the Census of 1850*. Boston: Patrick Donohoe, 1855.

—. *The Internal Condition of American Democracy*. London: R. Hardwick, 1863.

—. *The Irish Position in British and Republican North America: A Letter to the Editors of the Irish Press Irrespective of Party*. Montreal: M. Longmore, 1866.

—. *The Irish Writers of the Seventeenth Century*. Dublin: James Duffy, 1846.

—. *Memoir of Charles Gavan Duffy, Esq., as a Student, Journalist, and Organizer: With Selections from His Poems and Essays*. Dublin: W. Hogan, 1849.

—. *The Poems of Thomas D'Arcy McGee: With Copious Notes*. New York: J. D. Sadlier, 1869.

—. *Speeches and Addresses Chiefly on the Subject of British-American Union*. London: Chapman & Hall, 1865.

Meagher, Thomas Francis. *The Last Days of the 69th In Virginia: A Narrative in Three Parts*. New York: Published at the Office of the Irish-American. New York: The Irish American, 1861.

—. *Speeches on the Legislative Independence of Ireland*. New York: Redfield, 1853.

Mill, John Stuart. *The Collected Works of John Stuart Mill, Vol. 14: Newspaper Writings, January 1835–June 1847*. Edited by Ann Robson and John Robinson. Toronto: University of Toronto Press, 1986.

—. *The Collected Works of John Stuart Mill, Vol. 15: The Later Letters of John Stuart Mill, 1849–1873, Part 2*. Edited by Francis E. Mineka and Dwight N. Lindley. Toronto: University of Toronto Press, 1972.

Mitchel, John. *The History of Ireland from the Treaty of Limerick to the Present Time*. Vol. 2. James Duffy: Dublin, 1866.

—. *Irish Political Economy by Jonathan Swift and George Berkeley*. Dublin: Irish Confederation, 1847.

—. *The Last Conquest of Ireland (Perhaps)*. Dublin: Irishman Office, 1861.

—. *The Life and Times of Aodh O'Neill, Prince of Ulster*. New York: P. M. Haverty, 1868.

—. *The Jail Journal*. Dublin: M. H. Gill & Son, 1921.

—. *Jail Journal: Or Five Years in British Prisons*. New York: Offices of the Citizen, 1854.

—. *Memoir of Thomas Devin Reilly: A Lecture Delivered by John Mitchel, in the Tabernacle, New-York, on Dec. 29th, 1856*. New York: P. M. Haverty, 1857.

Moore, M. B. *The Geographical Reader, for the Dixie Children*. Raleigh: Branson Farrar, 1863.

O'Brien, William Smith. *Principles of Government, or Meditations in Exile, Vol. 1.* Dublin: James Duffy, 1856.

———. *Principles of Government, or Meditations in Exile, Vol. 2.* Dublin: James Duffy, 1856.

———. *Reproductive Employment: A Series of Letters to the Landed Proprietors of Ireland, With a Preliminary Letter to Lord John Russell.* Dublin: James McGlashan, 1847.

O'Connell, Daniel. "Catholic Association Meeting 13th January 1828 Dublin." In UCC Multitext Project In Irish History, Gillian M. Doherty and Tomás A. O'Riordan, University College Cork, 2014. http://multitext.ucc.ie/d/The_campaign_for_Catholic_Emancipation_1823ndash1829 (accessed 7 October 2022).

———. "In Favour of the Repeal of the Union, Delivered at Mullaghmast, Ireland, in September, 1843." In *The World's Famous Orations*, vol. 6, edited by William Jennings Bryan, 195–208. New York: Funk & Wagnalls, 1906.

———. *Upon American Slavery: With Other Irish Testimonies, Vol. 3.* New York: American Anti-Slavery Society, 1860.

O'Connell, John. *The Select Speeches of Daniel O'Connell, M.P.* Dublin: James Duffy, 1854.

O'Doherty, Mary Anne. *Poems by "Eva."* San Francisco: P. J. Thomas, 1877.

———. *Poems: Eva of* The Nation. Dublin: M. H. Gill, 1909.

O'Donohoe, Patrick. *A Commentary on Teetotalism: Its Principles Vindicated, and Its Abuses Exposed.* Launceston: J. S. Waddell, 1852.

O'Sullivan Beare, Philip, *Historiae Catholicae Iberniae Compendium.* Lisbon: n.p., 1621.

———. *Ireland under Elizabeth: Chapters towards a History of Ireland in the Reign of Elizabeth, Being a Portion of the History of Catholic Ireland by Philip O'Sullivan Beare.* Dublin: Sealy, Bryers & Walker, 1903.

———. *Patritiana Decas.* Madrid: n.p., 1629.

O'Sullivan, T. F. *The Young Irelanders.* Tralee: Kerryman, 1944.

Parkes, Henry. *The Federal Government of Australasia, Speeches Delivered on Various Occasions (November 1889–May 1890) by Sir Henry Parkes, G.C.M.G.* Sydney: Turner & Henderson 1890.

The People's Charter; Being an Outline of an Act to Provide for the Just Representation of the People of Great Britain in the Common House of Parliament. London: Working Man's Association, 1838.

Prospectus of The Nation.

Prospectus of the United Irishman.

Savage, John. *Fenian Heroes and Martyrs.* Boston: P. Donahoe, 1868.

The Spirit of the Nation by the Writers of The Nation *Newspaper.* Dublin: James Duffy, 1845.

Tocqueville, Alexis De. *Democracy in America, Vol. 1.* Cambridge: Sever & Francis, 1863.

Ullathorne, William Bernard. *The Catholic Mission in Australasia.* Liverpool: Rockliff & Duckworth, 1837.

West, John. *The History of Tasmania, Vol. 1.* Launceston: Henry Dowling, 1852.

Wilson, Moses Gray. *The Land Bill of the Government! "Out of Their Own Mouths Shall Ye Judge Them."* 1859. Monash Rare Books and Pamphlets.

Yeats, W. B., *The Variorum Edition of the Poems of W. B. Yeats*, edited by Peter Allt and Russell K. Alspach. New York: Macmillan, 1957.

SECONDARY SOURCES

Ajzenstat, Janet, Paul Romney, Ian Gentles, and William D. Gairdner. *Canada's Founding Debates*. Toronto: University of Toronto Press, 2003.

———. *Once and Future Canadian Democracy: An Essay in Political Thought*. Montreal: McGill-Queen's University Press, 2003.

Akenson, Donald Harman. *The Irish Diaspora: A Primer*. Toronto: Dufour Editions, 1997.

———. *Small Differences: Irish Catholics and Irish Protestants, 1815–1922*. Montreal: McGill-Queen's University Press, 2000.

Alison, Johnathan. "Yeats and His Politics." In *The Cambridge Companion to W. B. Yeats*, edited by Marjorie Howes and John Kelly, 185–205. Cambridge: Cambridge University Press, 2006.

Allen, Thomas M. *A Republic in Time: Temporality and Social Imagination in Nineteenth-Century America*. Chapel Hill: University of North Carolina Press, 2008.

Anbinder, Tyler. *Nativism and Slavery: The Northern Know Nothings and the Politics of the 1850s*. Oxford: Oxford University Press, 1992.

Anderson, Benedict. *Imagined Communities: Reflections on the Origin and Spread of Nationalism*. London: Verso, 1991.

Andrews, Ann. *Newspapers and Newsmakers: The Dublin Nationalist Press in the Mid-Nineteenth Century*. Liverpool: Liverpool University Press, 2014.

Armstrong, Frederick H. "The Oligarchy of the Western District of Upper Canada, 1788–1841." In *Historical Essays on Upper Canada: New Perspectives*, edited by J. K. Johnson and Bruce G. Wilson, 513–36. Montreal: McGill-Queen's University Press, 1989.

Ashworth, John. *The Republic in Crisis, 1848–1861*. Cambridge: Cambridge University Press, 2012.

Aughey, Arthur, and John Oakland. *Irish Civilization: An Introduction*. Oxon: Routledge, 2013.

Ballstadt, C. "Thomas D'Arcy McGee as a Father of Canadian Literature." *Studies in Canadian Literature* 1 (1976): 85–95.

Balogh, Brian. *A Government Out of Sight: The Mystery of National Authority in Nineteenth-Century America*. Cambridge: Cambridge University Press, 2012.

Banner, Stuart. *Possessing the Pacific*. Cambridge, MA: Harvard University Press, 2009.

Bannister, Jerry. "Liberty, Loyalty, and Sentiment in Canada's Founding Debates, 1864–1873." In *Violence, Order, and Unrest: A History of British North America, 1749–1876*, edited by Elizabeth Mancke, Jerry Bannister, Denis McKim, and Scott W. See, 78–92. Toronto: University of Toronto Press, 2019.

Barr, Colin. "'Imperium in Imperio': Irish Episcopal Imperialism in the Nineteenth Century." *English Historical Review* 123, no. 502 (2008): 611–50.

————. *Ireland's Empire: The Roman Catholic Church in the English-Speaking World.* Cambridge: Cambridge University Press, 2020.

Barr, Colin, and Hilary M. Carey, eds. *Religion and Greater Ireland: Christianity and Irish Global Networks, 1750–1969.* Montreal: McGill-Queen's Press, 2015.

Bartlett, Thomas. *Ireland: A History.* Cambridge: Cambridge University Press, 2010.

Bate, Weston. "Ballarat: Built for Federation." In *Becoming Australians: The Movement towards Federation in Ballarat and the Nation,* edited by Kevin T. Livingston, Richard Jordan, and Gay Sweely, 20–24. Kent Town, MA: Wakefield, 2001.

Baycroft, Timothy. "Introduction." In *Folklore and Nationalism in Europe during the Long Nineteenth Century,* edited by Timothy Baycroft and David Hopkins, 1–10. Leiden: Brill, 2012.

Beidleman, Richard G. *California's Frontier Naturalists.* Berkeley: University of California Press, 2006.

Bélanger, Damien-Claude, Sophie Coupal, and Michel Ducharme eds. *Les Idées En Mouvement: Perspectives en Histoire Intellectuelle et Culturelle du Canada.* Sainte-Foy: Laval, 2004.

Belich, James. *Replenishing the Earth: The Settler Revolution and the Rise of the Angloworld.* Oxford: Oxford University Press, 2009.

Bell, Duncan. *Reordering the World: Essays on Liberalism and Empire.* Princeton, NJ: Princeton University Press, 2016.

Belshaw, John Douglas. *Canadian History: Post-Confederation.* Vancouver: BC Campus OpenEd, 2016.

Benatti, Francesca. "Irish Patriots and Scottish Adventurers: The *Irish Penny Journal,* 1840–1841." *Canadian Journal of Irish Studies* 35, no. 2 (2009): 36–41.

Benner, Erica. "Nationalism Intellectual Origins." In *The Oxford Handbook of the History of Nationalism,* edited by John Breuilly, 36–55. Oxford: Oxford University Press, 2013.

Bernstein, George L. "Special Relationship and Appeasement: Liberal Policy towards America in the Age of Palmerston." *Historical Journal* 41, no. 3 (1998): 725–50.

Bernstein, Iver. *The New York City Draft Riots: Their Significance for American Society and Politics in the Age of the Civil War.* New York: Oxford University Press, 1990.

Bew, Paul. *Ireland: The Politics of Enmity, 1789–2006.* Oxford: Oxford University Press, 2007.

Biagini, Eugenio. "Neo-Roman Liberalism: 'Republican' Values and British Liberalism, ca. 1860–1875." *History of European Ideas* 29, no. 1 (2003): 55–72.

Bielenberg, Andy. *British Democracy and Irish Nationalism, 1876–1906.* Cambridge: Cambridge University Press, 2007.

————. *Ireland and the Industrial Revolution: The Impact of the Industrial Revolution on Irish Industry, 1801–1922.* London: Routledge, 2009.

————. *Liberty, Retrenchment, and Reform: Popular Liberalism in the Age of Gladstone, 1860–1880.* Cambridge: Cambridge University Press, 1992.

Binnington, Ian. *Confederate Visions: Nationalism, Symbolism, and the Imagined South in the Civil War.* Charlottesville: University of Virginia Press, 2013.

Black, E. R. *Divided Loyalties: Canadian Concepts of Federalism*. Montreal: McGill-Queen's University Press, 1975.

Blainey, Geoffrey. *A History of Victoria*. Cambridge: Cambridge University Press, 2013.

———. *The Rush That Never Ended*. Melbourne: Melbourne University Press, 1963.

Boucher, Leigh. "Victorian Liberalism and the Effect of Sovereignty: A View from the Settler Periphery." *History Australia* 13, no. 1 (2016): 35–51.

Bradbury, Bettina, and Tamara Myers. "Introduction." In *Negotiating Identities in Nineteenth- and Twentieth-Century Montreal*, edited by Bettina Bradbury and Tamara Myers, i–vi. Vancouver: University of British Columbia Press, 2005.

Brand, Ian. *The Convict Probation System: Van Diemen's Land, 1839–1854; a Study of the Probation System of Convict Discipline; Together with C. J. La Trobe's 1847 Report on Its Operation, and the 1845 Report of James Boyd on the Probation Station at Darlington*. Maria Island: Blubber Head, 1990.

Briggs, Asa, and Peter Burke. *A Social History of Media, from Gutenberg to the Internet*. Cambridge: Polity, 2009.

Brown, Malcolm. *The Politics of Irish Literature from Thomas Davis to W. B. Yeats*. London: George Allen & Unwin, 1972.

Brownrigg, Jeff. "Notes on 'Young Ireland' in Australia and the United States." *Australasian Journal of American Studies* 19, no. 2 (2000): 74–83.

Bruce, Samantha Ural. *The Harp and the Eagle: Irish American Volunteers in the Union Army, 1861–1865*. New York: New York University Press, 2006.

———. "'Ye Sons Of Green Erin Assemble': Northern Irish American Catholics and the Union War Effort, 1861–1865." In *Civil War Citizens: Race, Ethnicity, and Identity in America's Bloodiest Conflict*, edited by Samantha Ural Bruce, 99–132. New York: New York University Press, 2010.

Brundage, David. *Irish Nationalists in America: The Politics of Exile, 1798–1998*. Oxford: Oxford University Press, 2016.

Buckner, Phillip. "The Creation of the Dominion of Canada." In *Canada and the British Empire*, edited by Philip Buckner, 66–86. Oxford: Oxford University Press, 2008.

———. "The Maritimes and Confederation: A Reassessment." *Canadian Historical Review* 81, no. 1 (1990), 1–30.

Buckridge, Patrick. "Irish Poets in Colonial Brisbane: Mary Eva O'Doherty and Cornelius Moynihan." *Queensland Review* 8, no. 2 (2001): 29–40.

Bumsted, J. M. "Consolidation of British North America." In *Canada and the British Empire*, edited by Phillip Buckner, 44–65. Oxford: Oxford University Press, 2008.

Burbank, Jürgen Frederick Cooper. *Empires in World History: Power and the Politics of Difference*. Princeton, NJ: Princeton University Press, 2010.

Burchell, Robert Arthur. *The San Francisco Irish, 1848–1880*. Berkeley: University of California Press, 1980.

Burns, Robin B. "McGee, Thomas D'Arcy." In *Dictionary of Canadian Biography*, vol. 9. Edited by Francess G. Halpenny and Jean Hamelin, 489–94. Toronto: University of Toronto Press, 1976.

Burton, William L. *Melting Pot Soldiers: The Union's Ethnic Regiments*. New York: Fordham University Press, 1998.

Cairns, David, and Shaun Richards. *Writing Ireland; Colonialism, Nationalism, and Culture*. Manchester: Manchester University Press, 1988.

Campbell, Malcolm. *Ireland's Farthest Shores, Mobility, Migration, and Settlement in the Pacific World*. Madison: University of Wisconsin Press, 2022.

———. *Ireland's New Worlds: Immigrants, Politics, and Society in the United States and Australia, 1815–1922*. Madison: University of Wisconsin Press, 2008.

Carey, Hilary M. *Empire of Hell*. Cambridge: Cambridge University Press, 2019.

Carey, James W. *Communication as Culture: Essays on Media and Society*. Boston: Unwin Hyman, 1989.

———. "Harold Innis and Marshall McLuhan." *Antioch Review* 27, no. 1 (1967): 5–39.

Carrese, Paul O. *Democracy in Moderation: Montesquieu, Tocqueville, and Sustainable Liberalism*. Cambridge: Cambridge University Press, 2016.

Carroll, Francis M. "McGee, Thomas D'Arcy." In *Dictionary of Irish Biography*, edited by James McGuire and James Quinn. Cambridge: Cambridge University Press, 2009. dib.cambridge.org.

Choudhry, Sujit. "The Canadian Constitution and the World." In *The Oxford Handbook of the Canadian Constitution*, edited by Peter Oliver, Patrick Macklem, and Nathalie Des Rosiers, 1076–100. Oxford: Oxford University Press, 2017.

Cíosáin, Niall Ó. "Famine Memory and the Popular Representation of Scarcity." In *History and Memory in Modern Ireland*, edited by Ian McBride, 95–117. Cambridge: Cambridge University Press, 2001.

Clark, Christopher. *Iron Kingdom: The Rise and Downfall of Prussia, 1600–1947*. Cambridge, MA: Bellknap Press of Harvard University Press, 2009.

Clarke, Brian P. *Piety and Nationalism: Lay Voluntary Associations and the Creation of an Irish-Catholic Community in Toronto, 1850–1895*. Montreal: McGill-Queen's University Press, 1993.

Clarke, Manning, and Michael Cathcart. *Manning Clarke's History of Australia*. Melbourne: Melbourne University Press, 1997.

Cline, Lawrence E. *Rebels on the Niagara: The Fenian Invasion of Canada*. Albany: State University of New York Press, 2018.

Cohn, Raymond L. "Nativism and the End of the Mass Migration of the 1840s and 1850s." *Journal of Economic History* 60, no. 2 (2000): 361–83.

Comerford, R. V. *The Fenians in Context: Irish Politics and Society, 1848–82*. Dublin: Wolfhound, 1998.

———. "O'Mahony, John (1815–1877), Irish Nationalist." In *Oxford Dictionary of National Biography*. Oxford: Oxford University Press, 2004. www-oxforddnb.com.

———. "Stephens, James (1824–1901), Fenian Leader." In *Oxford Dictionary of National Biography*. Oxford: Oxford University Press, 2004. www-oxforddnb.com.

Comte, Auguste. *Cours de Philosophie Positive*. Paris: Bachelier, 1830.

Connolly, Sean. "The Limits of Democracy in Ireland, 1778–1848." In *Re-Imagining Democracy in the Age of Revolutions: America, France, Britain, Ireland, 1750–1850*, edited by Joanna Innes and Mark Philp, 174–90. Oxford: Oxford University Press, 2013.

Conrad, Margaret. *A Concise History of Canada*. Cambridge: Cambridge University Press, 2012.

Constant, Jean François, and Michel Ducharme, eds. *Liberalism and Hegemony Debating the Canadian Liberal Revolution*. Toronto: University of Toronto Press, 2009.

Conway, Stephen. *War, State, and Society in Mid-Eighteenth-Century Britain and Ireland*. Oxford: Oxford University Press, 2006.

Craven, Avery. *The Growth of Southern Nationalism, 1848–1861*. Baton Rouge: Louisiana State University Press, 1953.

Crider, Jonathan B. "De Bow's Revolution: The Memory of the American Revolution in the Politics of the Sectional Crisis, 1850–1861." *American Nineteenth-Century History* 10, no. 33 (2009): 317–32.

Cullen, John H. *Young Ireland in Exile: The Story of the Men of '48 in Tasmania*. Dublin: Talbot, 1928.

Cunningham, E. P. "Meagher, Thomas Francis." In *Dictionary of Irish Biography*, edited by James McGuire and James Quinn. Cambridge: Cambridge University Press, 2009. dib.cambridge.org.

Curthoys, Ann, and Jessie Mitchell. "The Advent of Self-Government, 1840s–90." In *The Cambridge History of Australia, Vol. 1*, edited by Alison Bashford and Stuart Macintyre, 149–69. Cambridge: Cambridge University Press, 2013.

———. *Taking Liberty: Indigenous Rights and Settler Self-Government in Colonial Australia, 1830–1890*. Cambridge: Cambridge University Press, 2018.

Curtis, Bruce. *The Politics of Population: State Formation, Statistics, and the Census of Canada, 1840–1875*. Toronto: University of Toronto Press, 2002.

Dahl, Adam. *Empire of the People: Settler Colonialism and the Foundations of Modern Democratic Thought*. Lawrence: University Press of Kansas, 2018.

Daly, Mary E. *Industrial Development and Irish National Identity, 1922–1939*. Syracuse, NY: Syracuse University Press, 1992.

Danto, Arthur C. *Encounters and Reflections: Art in the Historical Present*. Berkeley: University of California Press, 1997.

Darwin, John. "Imperialism and the Victorians: The Dynamics of Territorial Expansion." *English Historical Review* 112, no. 447 (1997): 614–42.

Davis, John R. *The Victorians and Germany*. Oxford: Peter Lang, 2007.

Davis, Richard. "Patrick O'Donohoe: Outcast of the Exiles." In *Exiles from Erin Convict Lives in Ireland and Australia*, edited by Bob Reece, 246–83. London: Macmillan, 1991.

———. "Unpublicised Young Ireland Prisoners in Van Diemen's Land." In *Tasmanian Historical Research Association, Papers and Proceedings* 38, nos. 3–4 (December 1991): 131–37.

———. *William Smith O'Brien: Ireland–1848–Tasmania*. Dublin: Geography, 1989.

———. *William Smith O'Brien, Revolutionary Imperialist*. Dublin: Lilliput, 1998.

Davison, Graeme. "Gold Rush Melbourne." In *Gold: Forgotten Histories and Lost Objects of Australia*, edited by Iain McCalman, Alexander Cook, and Andrew Reeves, 52–66. Cambridge: Cambridge University Press, 2001.

Dearinger, Ryan L. "Violence, Masculinity, Image, and Reality on the Antebellum Frontier." *Indiana Magazine of History* 100, no. 1 (2004): 26–55.

Delahanty, Ian. "The Transatlantic Roots of Irish American Anti-Abolitionism, 1843–1859." *Journal of the Civil War Era* 6, no. 2 (2016): 164–92.

Delaney, Enda. *The Curse of Reason: The Great Irish Famine*. Dublin: Gill & Macmillan, 2012.

———. "The Irish Diaspora." *Irish Economic and Social History* 33 (2006): 35–45.

Dickinson, John, and Brian Young. *A Short History of Quebec* 4th ed. Montreal: McGill-Queen's Press, 2008.

Dickson, David. *Dublin: The Making of a Capital City*. London: Profile, 2014.

Dillon, William. *The Life of John Mitchel*. London: Kegan Paul, Trench, 1888.

Dinnerstein, Leonard, and David M. Reimers. *Ethnic Americans: A History of Immigration*. New York: Columbia University Press, 2009.

Doolin, David. "Exploring Textures of Irish America: A New Perspective on the Fenian Invasion of Canada." *Irish Studies Review* 23, no. 2 (2015): 154–65.

———. *Transnational Revolutionaries: The Fenian Invasion of Canada, 1866*. Bern: Peter Lang, 2016.

Dowd, Christopher. *Rome in Australia: The Papacy and Conflict in the Australian Catholic Missions, 1834–1884*. Leiden: Brill, 2008.

Doyle, Aidan: *A History of the Irish Language: From the Norman Invasion to Independence*. Oxford: Oxford University Press, 2005.

———. "Language and Literacy in the Eighteenth and Nineteenth Centuries." In *The Cambridge History of Ireland, Vol. 3*, edited by James Kelly, 353–79. Cambridge: Cambridge University Press, 2018.

Doyle, Don H. *The Cause of All Nations: An International History of the American Civil War*. New York: Basic Books, 2015.

Ducharme, Michel. *The Idea of Liberty in Canada during the Age of Atlantic Revolutions, 1776–1838*. Montreal: McGill-Queen's University Press, 2014.

Dudink, Stefan, Karen Hagemann, and Josh Tosh. *Masculinities in Politics and War: Gendering Modern History*. Manchester: Manchester University Press, 2009.

Dugger, Julie M. "Black Ireland's Race: Thomas Carlyle and the Young Ireland Movement." *Victorian Studies* 48, no. 3 (2006): 461–85.

Dwan, David. "Civic Virtue in the Modern World: The Politics of Young Ireland." *Irish Political Studies*, 22, no. 1 (2007): 35–60.

———. *The Great Community: Culture and Nationalism in Ireland*. Dublin: Field Day Review, 2008.

———. "Romantic Nationalism: History and Illusion in Ireland." *Modern Intellectual History* 14, no. 3 (2017): 717–45.

Elding, Max. *A Revolution in Favor of Government: Origins of the US Constitution and the Making of the American State*. Oxford: Oxford University Press, 2003.

Edmonds, Penelope. "Canada and Australia: An Interconnected Pacific World." In *Within and Without the Nation: Canadian History as Transnational History*, edited by Karen Dubinsky, Adele Perry, and Henry Yu, 115–42. Toronto: University of Toronto Press, 2015.

Edmunds, Jane, and Byran S. Turner. "Introduction: Generational Consciousness, Narrative, and Politics." In *Generational Consciousness, Narrative, and Politics*, edited by Jane Edmunds and Byran S. Turner, 1–13. Oxford: Rowman & Littlefield, 2002.

Egan, Timothy. *The Immortal Irishman: The Irish Revolutionary Who Became an American Hero*. Boston: Houghton Mifflin Harcourt, 2016.

Ellis, Joseph, *The Founding Brothers: The Revolutionary Generation*. New York: Random House, 2001.

Emerson, Ralph Waldo. "Concord Hymn." In *Ralph Waldo Emerson: The Major Poetry*, edited by Albert von Frank, 129–32. Cambridge, MA: Belknap Press of Harvard University Press, 2015.

Emmons, David. *Beyond the American Pale: The Irish in the West, 1845–1900*. Norman: University of Oklahoma Press, 2020.

Eyal, Yonatan. *The Young America Movement and the Transformation of the Democratic Party, 1828–1861*. Cambridge: Cambridge University Press, 2007.

Farrell, Sean. "Irish Rebel, Imperial Reformer Charles Gavan Duffy." In *Ireland in an Imperial World: Citizenship, Opportunism, and Subversion*, edited by Timothy G. McMahon, Michael de Nie, and Paul Townsend, 69–89. London: Palgrave Macmillan, 2017.

Farrelly, Maura Jane. *Anti-Catholicism in America, 1620–1860*. Cambridge: Cambridge University Press, 2017.

Faust, Drew Gilpin. *Creation of Confederate Nationalism: Ideology and Identity in the Civil War South*. Baton Rouge: Louisiana State University Press, 1989.

Fawcett, Edmund. *Liberalism: The Life of an Idea*. Princeton, NJ: Princeton University Press, 2015.

Fay, Terrence. "Catholic Christians." In *The Religion of Canadians*, edited by Jamie Scott, 33–74. Toronto: University of Toronto Press, 2012.

———. *A History of Canadian Catholics*. Montreal: McGill-Queen's University Press, 2002.

Feinman, Ilene. *Citizenship Rites: Feminist Soldiers and Feminist Antimilitarists*. New York: New York University Press, 2000.

Fenton, Elizabeth. *Religious Liberties: Anti-Catholicism and Liberal Democracy*. Oxford: Oxford University Press, 2011.

Fergus, Sinclair. "Gray, Moses Wilson." In *Dictionary of Irish Biography*, edited by James McGuire and James Quinn. Cambridge: Cambridge University Press, 2009. dib.cambridge.org.

Fitz, Karsten. *The American Revolution Remembered, 1830s to 1850s: Competing Images and Conflicting Narratives*. Heidelberg: Universitätsverlag C. Winter, 2010.

Fitzgerald, John. "Irish Demography since 1740." In *The Cambridge Social History of Modern Ireland*, edited by Eugenio Biagini and Mary E. Daly, 7–24. Cambridge: Cambridge University Press, 2017.

Fitzpatrick, David. *Oceans of Consolation: Personal Accounts of Irish Immigration to Australia*. Ithaca, NY: Cornell University Press, 1994.

Flewelling, Lindsey. *Two Irelands beyond the Sea: Ulster Unionism and America, 1880–1920*. Liverpool: Liverpool University Press, 2018.

Foner, Eric. *Free Soil, Free Labor, Free Men: The Ideology of the Republican Party before the Civil War*. Oxford: Oxford University Press, 1995.

———. *Reconstruction: America's Unfinished Revolution, 1863–1877*. New York: Perennial, 2002.

———. *The Second Founding: How the Civil War Made and Remade the Constitution*. New York: W. W. Norton, 2019.

Ford, Lisa, and David Andrew Roberts. "Expansion, 1820–1850." In *The Cambridge History of Australia*, edited by Alison Bashford and Stuart Macintyre, 121–48. Cambridge: Cambridge University Press, 2015.

Forster, Michael. "Johann Gottfried von Herder." In *The Stanford Encyclopedia of Philosophy*, edited by Edward N. Zalta, 2019. plato.stanford.edu.

Foster, R. F. *Vivid Faces: The Revolutionary Generation in Ireland, 1890–1923*. London: Penguin, 2014.

———. *Words Alone: Yeats and His Inheritances*. Oxford: Oxford University Press, 2012.

———. *Yeats: A Life, Vol. 1*. Oxford: Oxford University Press, 1998.

Fougères, Dany. "Introduction." In *Montreal: The History of a North American City*, edited by Dany Fougères and Roderick MacLeod, 3–4. Montreal: McGill-Queen's Press, 2018.

Francis, R., Douglas Richard Jones, and Donald B. Smith. *Journeys: A History of Canada*. Toronto: University of Toronto Press, 2010.

Freeman, Elsie, Wynell Burroughs Schamel, and Jean West. "The Fight for Equal Rights: A Recruiting Poster for Black Soldiers in the Civil War." *Social Education* 56, no. 2 (1992): 118–20.

Freifeld, Alice, *Nationalism and the Crowd in Liberal Hungary, 1848–1914*. Washington, DC: Woodrow Wilson Center, 2000.

Galbally, Ann. *Redmond Barry: An Anglo-Irish Australian*. Melbourne: Melbourne University Press, 1995.

Garvin, Tom. "An Irish Republican Tradition." In *Republicanism in Ireland: Confronting Theory and Practice*, edited by Iseult Honohan, 23–30. Manchester: Manchester University Press, 2008.

———. *Nationalist Revolutionaries in Ireland, 1858–1928*. London: Gill & Macmillan, 2005.

Gat, Azar, and Alexander Yakobson. *Nations: The Long History and Deep Roots of Political Ethnicity and Nationalism*. Cambridge: Cambridge University Press, 2013.

Gates, Henry Louis, Jr. *Stony the Road: Reconstruction, White Supremacy, and the Rise of Jim Crow*. New York: Penguin, 2019.

Gauvreau, Danielle. "Population, Social Identities, and Daily Life." In *Montreal: The History of a North American City*, edited by Dany Fougères and Roderick MacLeod, 638–69. Montreal: McGill-Queen's University Press, 2018.

Gellner, Ernest. *Nations and Nationalism*. Oxford: Clarendon, 1983.

Gemme, Paola. *Domesticating Foreign Struggles: The Italian Risorgimento and Antebellum American Identity*. Athens: University of Georgia Press, 2005.

Geoghegan, Patrick. "A Consistent Advocate of Nigger Emancipation: Daniel O'Connell and the Campaign against Slavery." *History Ireland* 18, no. 5 (2010): 22–24.

———. *Liberator: The Life and Death of Daniel O'Connell, 1830–1847*. Dublin: Gill & Macmillan, 2010.

Geoghegan, Patrick, and James Quinn. "O'Doherty, Kevin Izod." In *Dictionary of Irish Biography* edited by James McGuire and James Quinn Cambridge: Cambridge University Press, 2009. dib.cambridge.org.

Gerstle, Gary. *American Crucible: Race and the Nation in the Twentieth Century*. Princeton, NJ: Princeton University Press, 2004.

———. *Liberty and Coercion: The Paradox of American Government from the Founding to the Present*. Princeton, NJ: Princeton University Press, 2015.

Gibbons, Luke. "Race against Time: Racial Discourse and Irish History." *Oxford Literary Review* 13, nos. 1–2 (1991): 95–117.

Gienapp, William E. *Abraham Lincoln and Civil War America: A Biography*. Oxford: Oxford University Press, 2002.

———. "Nativism and the Creation of a Republican Majority in the North before the Civil War." *Journal of American History* 72, no. 3 (1985): 529–59.

Glatthaar, Joesph T. "Leaving Their Mark on the Battlefield." In *The Civil War Soldier: A Historical Reader*, edited by Michael Barton and Larry M. Logue, 228–60. New York: New York University Press, 2002.

Gleeson, David T. *The Green and the Gray: The Irish in the Confederate States of America*. Chapel Hill: University of North Carolina Press, 2013.

———. *Irish in the South, 1815–1877*. Chapel Hill: University of North Carolina Press, 2001.

Gobat, Michael. *Empire by Invitation: William Walker and Manifest Destiny in Central America*. Cambridge, MA: Harvard University Press, 2018.

Goldberg, David Theo. "Liberalism's Limits: Carlyle and Mill on 'The Negro Question.'" *Nineteenth-Century Contexts* 22, no. 2 (2000): 203–16.

Goldner, E. J. "Arguing with Pictures: Race, Class, and the Formation of Popular Abolitionism through *Uncle Tom's Cabin*." *Journal of American & Comparative Cultures* 24, nos. 1–2 (2001): 71–84.

Goodman, David. *Gold Seeking: Victoria and California in the 1850s*. Stanford, CA: Stanford University Press, 1994.

Goodway, David. *London Chartism, 1838–1848*. Cambridge: Cambridge University Press, 1982.

Grannan, Richmond L. "Thomas D'Arcy McGee and Confederation in the Maritimes." *Canadian Catholic History Association*, 20 (1953): 93–100.

Gray, Peter. "The Great Famine, 1845–1850." In *The Cambridge History of Ireland, Vol. 3, 1730–1880*, edited by James Kelly, 639–65. Cambridge: Cambridge University Press, 2018.

Greenblatt, Stephen. *Renaissance Self-Fashioning from More to Shakespeare*. Chicago: University of Chicago Press, 2005.

Greenburg, Amy S. *Manifest Manhood and the Antebellum American Empire*. Cambridge: Cambridge University Press, 2005.

Greer, Allan. "1837–38: Rebellion Reconsidered." *Canadian Historical Review* 76, no. 1 (1995): 1–18.

Guelzo, Allen C. *Fateful Lightning: A New History of the Civil War and Reconstruction*. Oxford: Oxford University Press, 2012.

Habermas, Jürgen. *The Structural Transformation of the Public Sphere: An Inquiry into a Category of Bourgeois Society*. Cambridge, MA: MIT Press, 1991.

Hahn, Stephen. *A Nation without Borders: The United States and Its World in an Age of Civil Wars, 1830–1910*. New York: Penguin, 2016.

Hale, Anthony R. "Martyrs for Contending Causes: John Mitchel, David Walker, and the Limits of Liberation." In *The Black and Green Atlantic*, edited by Peter O'Neill and David Lloyd, 197–212. Basingstoke: Palgrave Macmillan, 2009.

Hall, Catherine. "Of Gender and Empire: Reflections on the Nineteenth Century." In *Gender and Empire*, edited by Philippa Levine, 46–76. Oxford: Oxford University Press, 2007.

Hall, John A., and G. John Ikenberry. *The State*. Minneapolis: University of Minnesota Press, 1989.

Hamilton, Mark. "New Imaginings: The Legacy of Benedict Anderson and Alternative Engagements of Nationalism." *Studies in Ethnicity and Nationalism* 6, no. 3 (2006): 73–89.

Hanagan, Michael. "Irish Transnational Social Movements, Migrants, and the State System." In *Globalization and Resistance: Transnational Dimensions of Social Movements*, edited by Jackie G. Smith, Jackie Smith, and Hank Johnston, 53–74. Lanham, MD: Rowman & Littlefield, 2002.

Hannaford, Ivan. *Race: The History of an Idea in the West*. Washington, DC: Woodrow Wilson Center, 1996.

Hansen, Mogens Herman. "The Mixed Constitution versus the Separation of Powers: Monarchical and Aristocratic Aspects of Modern Democracy." *History of Political Thought* 31, no. 3 (2010): 509–31.

Harling, Philip. "The Trouble with Convicts: From Transportation to Penal Servitude, 1840–67." *Journal of British Studies* 53, no. 1 (2014): 80–110.

Harris, Cole. *A Bounded Land: Reflections on Settler Colonialism in Canada*. Vancouver: University of British Columbia Press, 2020.

Harris, Leslie. *In the Shadow of Slavery: African Americans in New York City, 1626–1863*. Chicago: University of Chicago Press, 2003.

Hart, Peter. *The IRA and Its Enemies*. Oxford: Oxford University Press, 1999.

Hayley, Barbara. "A Reading and Thinking Nation: Periodicals as the Voice of Nineteenth-Century Ireland." In *Three Hundred Years of Irish Periodicals*, edited by Barbara Hayley and Enda McKay, 29–48. Mullingar: Association of Irish Learned Journals/Lilliput, 1987.

Heaman, E. A. *The Inglorious Arts of Peace: Exhibitions in Canadian Society during the Nineteenth Century*. Toronto: University of Toronto Press, 1999.

———. *A Short History of the State in Canada*. Toronto: University of Toronto Press, 2015.

———. *Tax, Order, and Good Government: A New Political History of Canada, 1867–1917*. Montreal: McGill-Queen's University Press, 2017.

Hearne, John M., and Rory T. Cornish. *Thomas Francis Meagher: The Making of an Irish American*. Dublin: Irish Academic Press, 2006.

Henderson, Mary C. "Broadway Theatre." In *The Cambridge Guide to American Theatre*, edited by B. Wilmeth and Tice L. Miller, 76. Cambridge: Cambridge University Press, 1996.

Hewitt, Martin. *The Dawn of the Cheap Press in Victorian Britain: The End of the "Taxes on Knowledge," 1849–1869*. London: Bloomsbury, 2014.

Hirota, Hidetaka. *Expelling the Poor Atlantic Seaboard States and the Nineteenth-Century Origins of American Immigration Policy*. Oxford: Oxford University Press, 2017.

Hobsbawm, Eric. *On Empire, America, War, and Global Supremacy*. New York: New Press, 2009.

Hogan, Ciara, "'Lost Hero of the Past': Ruin, Wound, and the Failure of Idealism in the Poetry of James Clarence Mangan." *Études irlandaises* 35, no. 1 (2010): 131–46.

Hoppen, K. Theodore. *Governing Hibernia: British Politicians and Ireland, 1800–1921*. Oxford: Oxford University Press, 2016.

Horsman, Reginald. *Race and Manifest Destiny: The Origins of American Racial Anglo-Saxonism*. Cambridge, MA: Harvard University Press, 1986.

Hourican, Bridget. "O'Donohoe, Patrick." In *Dictionary of Irish Biography*, edited by James McGuire and James Quinn. Cambridge: Cambridge University Press, 2009. dib.cambridge.org.

Howe, Daniel. *What Hath God Wrought: The Transformation of America, 1815–1848*. Oxford: Oxford University Press, 2007.

Howe, Stephen. *Ireland and Empire: Colonial Legacies in Irish History and Culture*. Oxford: Oxford University Press, 2002.

Howes, Marjorie. "Introduction." In *The Cambridge Companion to W. B. Yeats*, edited by Marjorie Howes and John Kelly, 1–18. Cambridge: Cambridge University Press, 2006.

Huggins, Michael. "A Strange Case of Hero-Worship: John Mitchel and Thomas Carlyle." *Studi Irlandesi: A Journal of Irish Studies* 2, no. 2 (2012): 329–52.

Hutchinson, John. "Cultural Nationalism." In *The Oxford Handbook of the History of Nationalism*, edited by John Breuilly, 75–96. Oxford: Oxford University Press, 2013.

———. *Dynamics of Cultural Nationalism: The Gaelic Revival and the Creation of the Irish Nation State*. Abingdon: Routledge, 2012.

Huurdeman, Anton A. *The Worldwide History of Telecommunications*. Hoboken, NJ: Wiley, 2003.

Hyam, Ronald. *Understanding the British Empire*. Cambridge: Cambridge University Press, 2010.

Ignatiev, Noel. *How The Irish Became White*. New York: Routledge, 1995.

Innis, Harold Adams. *The Bias of Communication*. Toronto: University of Toronto Press, 1991.

———. *Empire and Communications*. Toronto: University of Toronto Press, 2014.

Ireland, John. "The Victorian Land Act 1862 Revisited." In *Victorian Historical Journal* 65, no. 2 (1994): 130–44.

Isenberg, Nancy. *Sex and Citizenship in Antebellum America*. Chapel Hill: University of North Carolina Press, 1998.

Israel, Johnathan. *The Expanding Blaze: How the American Revolution Ignited the World, 1775–1848*. Princeton, NJ: Princeton University Press, 2017.

Jackson, Alvin. *Ireland, 1798–1998: War, Peace, and Beyond*. Oxford: Blackwell, 1998.

Jackson, Stephen. *Religious Education and the Anglo World*. Leiden: Brill, 2020.

Jacob, Alan. "Why Bother with Marshall McLuhan?' *New Atlantis* 31, no.1 (2011): 123–35.

Jaeger, Hans. "Generations in History: Reflections on a Controversial Concept." *History and Theory* 24, no. 3 (1985): 273–92.

Jenkins, Brian. *Irish Nationalism and the British State: From Repeal to Revolutionary Nationalism*. Montreal: McGill-Queen's University Press, 2006.

Jenkins, W. *Between Raid and Rebellion: The Irish in Buffalo and Toronto, 1867–1916*. Montreal: McGill-Queen's University Press, 2013.

Jess, Raymond. "'Rubbing Away Their Roughness by Mutual Contact': Post-Confederation Irish Writers and Canadian National Identity." *Études irlandaises* 41, no. 1 (2016): 155–66.

Johannsen, Robert Walter, Sam W. Haynes, and Christopher Morris. *Manifest Destiny and Empire: American Antebellum Expansionism, Vol. 1*. College Station: Texas A&M University Press, 1997.

Jupp, James. *The English in Australia*. Cambridge: Cambridge University Press, 2004.

Karp, Matthew. *This Vast Southern Empire*. Cambridge, MA: Harvard University Press, 2016.

Kawana, Yuichiro. "John Stuart Mill and the Politics of the Irish Land Question." *Kyoto Economic Review* 79, no. 2 (2010): 34–54.

Keating, Ryan W. "'All of That Class That Infest N.Y.': Perspectives on Irish American Loyalty and Patriotism in the Wake of the New York City Draft Riot." In *Contested Loyalty: Debates over Patriotism in the Civil War North*, edited by Robert M. Sandow, Gary W. Gallagher, Judith Giesberg, Ryan W. Keating, Melinda Lawson, and Julie A. Mujic, 239–67. New York: Fordham University Press, 2018.

Keegan, Nicholas M. *US Consular Representation in Britain since 1790*. London: Anthem, 2018.

Kelly, Mary C. *Ireland's Great Famine in Irish American History: Enshrining a Fateful Memory*. Lanham, MD: Rowman & Littlefield, 2014.

———. "A Sentinel of Our Liberties: Archbishop John Hughes and Irish American Intellectual Negotiation in the Civil War Era." *Irish Studies Review* 18 no. 2 (2010): 155–72.

Kelly, Matthew. "Irish Nationalist Opinion and the British Empire in the 1850s and 1860s." In *Past and Present* 204, no. 1 (2009): 127–54.

Kelson, Brendon, and John McQuilton. *Kelly Country: A Photographic Journey*. St. Lucia: University of Queensland Press, 2001.

Keneally, Thomas. *The Great Shame: A Story of the Irish in the Old World and the New.* London: Vintage, 1999.

Kenealy, Christine. *The Great Irish Famine: Impact, Ideology, and Rebellion.* New York: Palgrave Macmillan, 2002.

Kenny, Kevin. *The American Irish: A History.* New York: Longman Pearson, 2000.

Kerber, Linda E. "The Revolutionary Generation: Ideology, Politics, and Culture in the Early Republic." In *The New American*, edited by Eric Foner, 25–50. Philadelphia: Temple University Press, 1990.

Kiberd, Declan. *Inventing Ireland: The Literature of a Modern Nation.* London: Vintage, 1995.

Kiberd, Declan, and P. J. Mathews. "A Thought Revival." In *Handbook of the Irish Revival*, edited by Declan Kiberd and P. J. Mathews, 56–80. Dublin: Abbey Theatre, 2015.

Kiernan, Ben. *Blood and Soil: Modern Genocide, 1500–2000.* New Haven, CT: Yale University Press, 2007.

Kiernan, Victor. "The British Isles: Celt and Saxon." In *The National Question in Europe in Historical Context*, edited by Mikuláš Teich and Roy Porter, 1–34. Cambridge: Cambridge University Press, 1993.

Kilfeather, Siobháin. *Dublin: A Cultural and Literary History.* Oxford: Signal, 2005.

Kirkpatrick, Rod. "Australia Shaking Off the Shackles to Earn the Badge of Independence." In *The Rise of Western Journalism, 1815–1914*, edited by Ross F. Collins and E. M. Palmegiano, 11–41. Jefferson NC: McFarland, 2007.

Knowlton, Christopher. "The Enigma of Sir Charles Gavan Duffy: Looking for Clues in Australia." *Éire-Ireland* 31, no. 3 (1996): 189–208.

Koditschek, Theodore. *Liberalism, Imperialism, and the Historical Imagination: Nineteenth-Century Visions of a Greater Britain.* Cambridge: Cambridge University Press, 2011.

Kriegel, Annie, and Elisabeth Hirsch. "Generational Difference: The History of an Idea." *Daedalus* 107, no. 4 (1978): 23–38.

Kurtz, William B. *Excommunicated from the Union: How the Civil War Created a Separate Catholic America.* New York: Fordham University Press, 2015.

Kymlicka, Will. *Multicultural Citizenship: A Liberal Theory of Minority Rights.* Oxford: Oxford University Press, 1996.

Laforest, Guy, and Félix Mathieu. "The Trustee, The Financier, and the Poet: Cartier, Galt, and D'Arcy McGee." In *The Quebec Conference of 1864: Understanding the Emergence of the Canadian Federation*, edited by Alain-G. Gagnon, Guy Laforest, and Eugénie Brouillet, 117–41. Montreal: McGill-Queen's University Press, 2018.

Lake, Marilyn, and Henry Reynolds. *Drawing the Global Colour Line.* Cambridge: Cambridge University Press, 2008.

Langely, Lester D. *The Americas in the Age of Revolution, 1750–1850.* New Haven, CT: Yale University Press, 1996.

LaSelva, Samuel Victor. *The Moral Foundations of Canadian Federalism: Paradoxes, Achievements, and Tragedies of Nationhood.* Montreal: McGill-Queen's University Press, 1996.

Lause, Mark. *Young America: Land, Labor, and the Republican Community.* Urbana: University of Illinois Press, 2005.

Lawrence, Jon. "Political History." In *Writing History: Theory and Practice*, edited by Stefan Berger Heiko Feldner and Kevin Passmore, 183–202. London: Bloomsbury, 2003.

———. *Speaking for the People: Party, Language, and Popular Politics in England, 1867–1914*. Cambridge: Cambridge University Press, 1998.

Lawson, Tom. *The Last Man: A British Genocide in Tasmania*. London: I. B. Taurus, 2014.

Lee, Sidney, and K. D. Reynolds. "Anstey, Thomas (1777–1851)." In *Australian Dictionary of Biography*. National Centre of Biography, Australian National University, Canberra, 1966. adb.anu.edu.au.

———. "Anstey, Thomas Chisholm (1816–1873), Lawyer and Politician." In *The Oxford Dictionary of National Biography*. Oxford: Oxford University Press, 2004. www-oxforddnb.com.

Leerssen, Joep. *National Thought in Europe*. Amsterdam: Amsterdam University Press, 2006.

———. *Remembrance and Imagination: Patterns in the Historical and Literary Imaginations of Ireland in the Nineteenth Century*. Cork: Cork University Press/Field Day, 1996.

Levine, Philippa. "Introduction: Why Gender and Empire?" In *Gender and Empire*, edited by Philippa Levine, 1–13. Oxford: Oxford University Press, 2007.

Levinger, Matthew Bernard. *Enlightened Nationalism: The Transformation of Prussian Political Culture, 1806–1848*. Oxford: Oxford University Press, 2010.

Lewis, Milton James. *The People's Health: Public Health in Australia, 1788–1950*. Westport CT: Greenwood, 2003.

Livingston, David W. "Thomas D'Arcy McGee's Civic Paidea." in *Liberal Education, Civic Education, and the Canadian Regime*, edited by David W. Livingston, 90–113. Montreal: McGill-Queen's University Press, 2015.

Lloyd, David. *Irish Culture and Colonial Modernity, 1800–2000: The Transformation of Oral Space*. Cambridge: Cambridge University Press, 2011.

Losurdo, Domenico. *Liberalism: A Counter-History*. London: Verso, 2011.

Loughery, John. *Dagger John: Archbishop John Hughes and the Making of Irish America*. Ithaca, NY: Cornell University Press, 2018.

Lynch, Niamh. "Defining Irish Nationalist Anti-Imperialism: Thomas Davis and John Mitchel." *Éire-Ireland* 42, nos. 1–2 (2007): 82–107.

MacCarthy, Anne. *Definitions of Irishness in the "Library of Ireland" Anthologies*. Bern: Peter Lang, 2012.

MacDonagh, Oliver. "The Age of O'Connell, 1830–45." In *A New History Of Ireland, Vol. 5: Ireland under the Union, 1: 1801–1870*, edited by W. E. Vaughan, 158–68. Oxford: Oxford University Press, 2010.

MacDonald, John A. *Troublous Times In Canada: A History of the Fenian Raids of 1866 and 1870*. Toronto: W. S. Johnston, 1910.

Madley, Benjamin. "From Terror to Genocide: Britain's Tasmanian Penal Colony and Australia's History Wars." *Journal of British Studies* 47, no. 1 (2008): 77–106.

Maizlish, Stephen E. "The Meaning of Nativism and the Crisis of the Union: The Know-Nothing Movement in the Antebellum North." In *Essays on American Antebellum*

Politics, 1840–1860, edited by Stephen E. Maizlish, William E. Gienapp, Thomas B. Alexander, and Michael F. Holt, 166–98. College Station: Texas A&M University Press, 1982.

Malcolm, Elizabeth, and Dianne Hall. *A New History of The Irish in Australia.* Cork: Cork University Press, 2019.

Maltz, Earl M. "The Fourteenth Amendment and Native American Citizenship." *Constitutional Commentary* 289 (2000): 563–67.

Mannheim, Karl. "The Problem of Generations." In *Karl Mannheim: Essays*, edited by Paul Kecskemeti, 276–322. London: Routledge, 1952.

Martin, Ged. *Britain and the Origins of Canadian Confederation, 1837–67.* Vancouver: University of British Colombia Press, 1995.

———. "Introduction to the 2006 Edition." In *Confederation Debates in the Province of Canada, 1865*, edited by Ged Martin, vii–xxxix, Montreal: McGill-Queen's University Press, 2006.

Martin, John. *John Donnellan Balfe and the Collective Experience of the Huon, 1850–1858.* Bachelor's thesis, University of Tasmania, 1968.

Mason, M. "'The Sacred Ashes of the First of Men': Edward Everett, the Mount Vernon Ladies Association of the Union, and Late Antebellum Unionism." In *Remembering the Revolution: Memory, History, and Nation Making from Independence to the Civil War* edited by M. McDonnell, C. Corbould, F. Clarke, and W. Brundage, 265–79. Amherst: University of Massachusetts Press, 2013.

Mathisen, Eric. *The Loyal Republic: Traitors, Slaves, and the Remaking of Citizenship in Civil War America.* Chapel Hill: University of North Carolina Press, 2018.

Maxwell, Constantia. *A History of Trinity College Dublin.* Dublin: University Press, Trinity College, 1946.

Maxwell-Stewart, Hamish. "'And All My Great Hardships Endured'? Irish Convicts in Van Diemen's Land." In *Transnational Perspectives on Modern Irish History: Beyond the Island*, edited by Niall Whelehan, 67–87. London: Routledge, 2015.

Mayrl, Damon. *Secular Conversions: Political Institutions and Religious Education in the United States and Australia, 1800–2000.* Cambridge: Cambridge University Press, 2016.

McCabe, Desmond, and James Quinn. "Doheny, Michael." In *Dictionary of Irish Biography*, edited by James McGuire and James Quinn. Cambridge: Cambridge University Press, 2009. dib.cambridge.org.

McCaffrey, Lawrence John. *Daniel O'Connell and the Repeal Year.* Lexington: University Press of Kentucky, 2015.

———. *The Irish Catholic Diaspora in America.* Washington, DC: Catholic University of America Press, 1976.

———. *Textures of Irish America.* Syracuse, NY: Syracuse University Press, 1992.

McConville, Seán. "Gentlemen Convicts, Dynamitards, and Paramilitaries: The Limits of Criminal Justice." In *Ideology, Crime, and Criminal Justice*, edited by Anthony Bottoms and Michael Tonry, 55–73. Cullompton: Willan, 2002.

———. *Irish Political Prisoners, 1848–1922: Theatres of War.* London: Routledge, 2003.

McDonnell, Michael A., Clare Corbould, Frances M. Clarke, and William Fitzhugh Brundage. *Remembering the Revolution: Memory, History, and Nation Making from Independence to the Civil War*. Amherst: University of Massachusetts Press, 2013.

McGaughey, Jane G. V. *Violent Loyalties: Manliness, Migration, and the Irish in the Canadas, 1798–1841*. Oxford: Oxford University Press, 2020.

McGee, Owen. "Cantwell, James." In *Dictionary of Irish Biography*, edited by James McGuire and James Quinn. Cambridge: Cambridge University Press, 2009. dib. cambridge.org.

———. "McManus, Terence Bellew." In *Dictionary of Irish Biography*, edited by James McGuire and James Quinn Cambridge: Cambridge University Press, 2009. dib. cambridge.org.

McGovern, Bryan *John Mitchel: Irish Nationalist, Southern Secessionist*. Knoxville: University of Tennessee Press, 2009.

———. "Young Ireland and Southern Nationalism." *Irish Studies South* 2, no. 5 (2016): 45–60.

McGowan, Mark, and Brian Clarke. *Death or Canada: The Irish Migration to Toronto, 1847*. Toronto: Novalis, 2019.

———. "Two Views—the Historian and the Archdiocese of Toronto." In *Catholics at the Gathering Place*, edited by Mark McGowan and Brian Clarke, 293–97. Toronto: Canadian Historical Association, 1993.

———. *The Waning of the Green: Catholics, the Irish, and Identity in Toronto, 1887–1922*. Montreal: McGill-Queen's. University Press, 1999.

McKay, Ian. "The Liberal Order Framework: A Prospectus for a Reconnaissance of Canadian History." *Canadian Historical Review* 81 (2000): 617–45.

McKenna, Mark. *The Captive Republic: A History of Republicanism in Australia, 1788–1996*. Cambridge: Cambridge University Press, 1996.

McLuhan, Marshall. *Understanding Media: The Extensions of Man*. London: Routledge & Kegan Paul, 1964.

McMahon, Cian. *The Global Dimensions of Irish Identity: Race, Nation, and the Popular Press, 1840–1880*. Chapel Hill: University of North Carolina Press 2015.

———. "Transnational Dimensions of Irish Anti-Imperialism, 1842–54." In *Irish and Scottish Encounters with Indigenous Peoples*, edited by Graeme Morton and David A. Wilson, 92–108. Montreal: McGill-Queen's University Press, 2013.

McPherson, James M. *Battle Cry of Freedom: The American Civil War*. Oxford: Oxford University Press, 1990.

———. *Emigrants and Exiles: Ireland and the Irish Exodus to North America*. Oxford: Oxford University Press, 1988.

Miller, Kerby A. *Ireland and Irish America: Culture, Class, and Transatlantic Migration*. Derry: Field Day, 2008.

Molony, John. "Davis, Thomas Osborne." In *Dictionary of Irish Biography*, edited by James McGuire and James Quinn. Cambridge: Cambridge University Press, 2009. dib.cambridge.org.

———. *Eureka*. Melbourne: Melbourne University Press, 2001.

Moody, T. W. *Davitt and Irish Revolution, 1846–82.* Oxford: Clarendon, 1981.

Morash, Christopher. "The Rhetoric of Right in Mitchel's Jail Journal." In *Forging in the Smithy: National Identity and Representation in Anglo-Irish Literary History*, edited by Joep Leersen, A. H. van der Weel, and Bart Westerwell, 207–18. Amsterdam: Rodopi, 1995.

Morgan, Thaïs. "The Poetry of Victorian Masculinities." In *The Cambridge Companion to Victorian Poetry*, edited by Joseph Bristow, 203–27. Cambridge: Cambridge University Press, 2000.

Morley, Vincent. *Irish Opinion and the American Revolution, 1760–1783.* Cambridge: Cambridge University Press, 2002.

Morrow, John. "Thomas Carlyle, 'Young Ireland,' and the 'Condition of Ireland Question.'" *Historical Journal* 51, no. 3 (2008): 643–67.

Morton, Graeme, and David A. Wilson, eds. *Irish and Scottish Encounters with Indigenous Peoples: Canada, the United States, New Zealand, and Australia.* Montreal: McGill-Queen's University Press, 2013.

Moyn, Samuel, and Andrew Sartori. "Approaches to Global Intellectual History." In *Global Intellectual History*, edited by Samuel Moyn and Andrew Sartori, 3–33. New York: Colombia University Press, 2015.

Muise, D. A. "The 1860s: Forging the Bonds of Union." In *The Atlantic Provinces in Confederation*, edited by E. R. Forbes and D. A. Muise, 13–47. Toronto: University of Toronto Press, 2016.

Mulholland, Marc. "Political Violence." In *The Princeton History of Modern Ireland*, edited by Richard Bourke and Ian McBride, 382–402. Princeton, NJ: Princeton University Press, 2016.

Murphy, Maureen, and James Quinn. "O'Mahony, John." In *Dictionary of Irish Biography*, edited by James McGuire and James Quinn. Cambridge: Cambridge University Press, 2009. dib.cambridge.org.

Nelson, Bruce. *Irish Nationalists and the Making of the Irish Race.* Princeton, NJ: Princeton University Press, 2012.

Ní Úrdail, Meidhbhín. "A Cork Scribe in Victorian London." In *Traveling Irishness in the Long Nineteenth Century*, edited by Marguérite Corporaal and Christina Morin, 225–45. London: Palgrave MacMillan, 2017.

Noël, Alain. "Democratic Deliberation in a Multinational Federation." *Critical Review of International Social and Political Philosophy* 9, no. 3 (2006): 419–44.

Noone, Val. "An Irish Rebel in Victoria: Charles Gavn Duffy, Selectors, Squatters, and Aborigines." In *Echoes of Irish Australia: Rebellion to Republic*, edited by Jeff Brownrigg, Cheryl Morgan, and Richard Reid, 108–17. Galong: St. Clements's Retreat & Conference Centre, 2007.

North, John S. *The Waterloo Directory of Irish Newspapers and Periodicals, 1800–1900.* Waterloo: North Waterloo Academic Press, 1986.

Ó Cathaoir, Brendan. "Dillon, John Blake." In *Dictionary of Irish Biography*, edited by James McGuire and James Quinn, 309. Cambridge: Cambridge University Press, 2009. dib.cambridge.org.

O'Farrell, Patrick. *The Irish in Australia*. Sydney: University of New South Wales Press, 1993.

Ó Gráda, Cormac. *The Great Irish Famine*. Cambridge: Cambridge University Press, 1995.

———. *Ireland: A New Economic History, 1780–1939*. Oxford: Oxford University Press, 1995.

———. *Ireland before and after the Famine: Explorations in Economic History, 1800–1925*. Manchester: Manchester University Press, 1988.

O'Neill, Ciaran. "Bourgeois Ireland, or, On the Benefits of Keeping One's Hands Clean." In *The Cambridge History of Ireland, Vol. 3*, edited by James Kelly, 517–41. Cambridge: Cambridge University Press, 2018.

O'Neill, Peter D. *Famine Irish and the American Racial State*. New York: Routledge, 2017.

———. "Memory and John Mitchel's Appropriation of the Slave Narrative." *Atlantic Studies* 11, no. 3 (2014): 321–43.

Oliver, Peter. "Moylan, James George." In *Dictionary of Canadian Biography*, vol. 13. Quebec City: University of Toronto/Université Laval, 1994. www.biographi.ca.

Ostendorf, Ann. *Sounds American: National Identity and the Music Cultures of the Lower Mississippi River Valley, 1800–1860*. Athens: University of Georgia Press, 2011.

Osterhammel, Jürgen. "Nationalism and Globalization." In *The Oxford History of Nationalism*, edited by John Breuilly, 694–712. Oxford: Oxford University Press, 2013.

———. *The Transformation of the World: A Global History of the Nineteenth Century*. Princeton, NJ: Princeton University Press, 2014.

Otter, A. A. Den. *The Philosophy of Railways: The Transcontinental Railway Idea in British North America*. Toronto: University of Toronto Press, 1997.

Oxx, Katie. *The Nativist Movement in America: Religious Conflict in the Nineteenth Century*. Oxon: Routledge, 2013.

Parry, Jonathan. "The Impact of Napoleon III on British Politics, 1851–1880." *Transactions of the Royal Historical Society* 11 (2001): 147–75.

———. *The Politics of Patriotism: English Liberalism, National Identity, and Europe, 1830–1886*. Cambridge: Cambridge University Press, 2006.

Patrick, Heather, and Ross Patrick. *Exiles Undaunted: The Irish Rebels, Kevin and Eva O'Doherty*. Brisbane: University of Queensland Press, 1989.

Patrick, Ross. "Young Irelanders in Australia." *Journal of the Galway Archaeological and Historical Society* 38 (1981/82): 73–78.

Pearl, Cyril. *The Three Lives of Gavan Duffy*. Sydney: New South Wales University Press, 1979.

Penet, Jean-Christophe. "Thomas Davis, *The Nation*, and the Irish Language." *Studies: An Irish Quarterly Review* 96, no. 384 (2007): 433–43.

Petrow, Stefan. "Judas in Tasmania, John Donellan Balfe 1850–80." In *Irish-Australian Conference, Hobart*, edited by Richard Davis, Jennifer Livett, Anne-Maree Whitaker, and Peter Moore, 474–85. Sydney: Crossing, 1996.

———. "Men of Honour? The Escape of the Young Irelanders from Van Diemen's Land." *Journal of Australian Colonial History* 7 (2005): 139–60.

Phillips, Lisa, and Allan McDougall. "The Baldoon Mysteries." In *Phantom Past, Indigenous Presence: Native Ghosts in North American Culture and History*, edited by Colleen Boyd and Coll Thrush, 117–50. Lincoln: University of Nebraska Press, 2011.

Pilcher, Jane. "Mannheim's Sociology of Generations: An Undervalued Legacy." *British Journal of Sociology* 45, no. 3 (1994): 481–95.

Pitts, Jennifer. *A Turn to Empire: The Rise of Imperial Liberalism in Britain and France.* Princeton, NJ: Princeton University Press, 2005.

Pocock, J. G. A. *Barbarism and Religion.* Vol. 4. Cambridge: Cambridge University Press, 2005.

Pratt, Julius W. "The Origin of 'Manifest Destiny.'" *American Historical Review* 32, no. 4, (1927): 795–98.

Quigley, Paul. *Shifting Grounds: Nationalism and the American South, 1848–1865.* Oxford: Oxford University Press, 2011.

Quinlan, Kieran. *Strange Kin: Ireland and the American South.* Baton Rouge: Louisiana State University Press, 2005.

Quinn, James. "Southern Citizen: John Mitchel, the Confederacy and Slavery." *History Ireland* 15, no. 3 (2007): 30–35.

Quinn, James. *John Mitchel.* Dublin: University College Dublin Press, 2008.

———. *Young Ireland and the Writing of Irish History.* Dublin: University College Dublin Press, 2015.

Rafferty, Oliver. *The Church, the State, and the Fenian Threat, 1861–75.* New York: Palgrave, 1999.

———. "Fenianism in North America in the 1860s: The Problems for Church and State." *History* 84 (1999): 257–77.

Rao, Gautham. "The New Historiography of the Early Federal Government: Institutions, Contexts, and the Imperial State." *William and Mary Quarterly* 77, no. 1 (2020): 97–128.

Rapport, Mike, *1848: A Year of Revolution.* New York: Basic Books, 2009.

Reid, Kirsty. *Gender, Crime, and Empire: Convicts, Settlers, and the State in Early Colonial Australia.* Manchester: Manchester University Press, 2012.

Reynolds, David S. "'Its Wood Could Only Be American!': *Moby-Dick* and Antebellum Popular Culture." In *Herman Melville's* Moby-Dick, edited by Harold Bloom, 93–116. New York: Bloom's, 2007.

Reynolds, Henry. *A History of Tasmania.* Cambridge: Cambridge University Press, 2012.

Riall, Lucy. *Garibaldi: Invention of a Hero.* New Haven, CT: Yale University Press, 2008.

Richardson, Caleb. "'The Failure of the Men to Come Up': The Reinvention of Irish Nationalism." In *Reconstruction in a Globalizing World*, edited by David Prior, 121–44. New York: Fordham University Press, 2018.

Roberts, Matthew. *Chartism, Commemoration, and the Cult of the Radical Hero.* London: Routledge, 2019.

Roberts, Timothy Mason. *Distant Revolutions, 1848, and the Challenge to American Exceptionalism.* Charlottesville: University of Virginia Press, 2009.

Rodgers, Nini. *Ireland, Slavery, and Anti-Slavery: 1612–1865.* Basingstoke: Palgrave, 2007.

Rudé, G. "O'Doherty, Kevin Izod (1823–1905)." In *Australian Dictionary of National Biography.* National Centre of Biography, Australian National University, Canberra, 1974. adb.anu.edu.au.

Russell, Penny. "Gender and Colonial Society." In *The Cambridge History of Australia,* edited by Alison Bashford and Stuart Macintyre, 426–86. Cambridge: Cambridge University Press, 2015.

Russell, Peter H. *Canada's Odyssey: A Country Based on Incomplete Conquests.* Toronto: University of Toronto Press, 2017.

Ryan, Mary P. *Civic Wars: Democracy and Public Life in the American City during the Nineteenth Century.* Berkeley: University of California Press, 1997.

Ryder, Sean. "Male Autobiography and Irish Cultural Nationalism: John Mitchel and James Clarence Mangan." *Irish Review,* no. 13 (Winter 1992/93): 70–77.

Rynne, Frank. "Young Ireland and Irish Revolutions." *Revue Française de Civilisation Britannique* 19, no. 2 (2014): 105–24.

Salyer, Lucy E. *Under the Starry Flag: How a Band of Irish Americans Joined the Fenian Revolt and Sparked a Crisis over Citizenship.* Cambridge, MA: Belknap Press of Harvard University Press, 2018.

Samito, Christian. *Becoming American under Fire: Irish Americans, African Americans, and the Politics of Citizenship during the Civil War Era.* Ithaca, NY: Cornell University Press, 2009.

———. "The Meaning of the Civil War for Irish America." In *So Conceived and So Dedicated,* edited by Lorien Foote and Kansiorn Wongsrichanalai, 193–286. New York: Fordham University Press, 2015.

Sawer, Marian. *Elections: Full, Free, and Fair.* Annadale: Federation, 2001.

Scalmer, Sean. "Charles Gavan Duffy's Ministerial Tour: Oratory, Electioneering, and the Meaning of Colonial Democracy." *Australian Journal of Politics & History* 57, no. 2 (2011): 153–73.

Schrauwers, Albert. *Union Is Strength: W. L. Mackenzie, The Children of the Peace, and the Emergence of Joint Stock Democracy.* Toronto: University of Toronto Press, 2009.

Senior, Hereward. *The Last Invasion of Canada: The Fenian Raids, 1866–1870.* Toronto: Dundurn, 1991.

———. *Orangeism: The Canadian Phase.* Toronto: McGraw-Hill Ryerson, 1972.

Shanahan, David. "Irish Catholic Journalists and the New Nationality in Canada." PhD diss., Lakehead University, 1984.

Sharrow, Walter G. "John Hughes and a Catholic Response to Slavery in Antebellum America." *Journal of Negro History* 57, no. 3 (1972): 254–69.

Sillard, P. A. *Life of John Mitchel.* Dublin: James Duffy, 1908.

Silver, A. I. *The French-Canadian Idea of Confederation, 1864–1900.* Toronto: University of Toronto Press, 1997.

Sim, David. *A Union Forever: The Irish Question and US Foreign Relations in the Victorian Age.* Ithaca, NY: Cornell University Press, 2013.

Simes, Douglas. "Ireland, 1760–1820." In *Press, Politics, and the Public Sphere in Europe*, edited by Hannah Barker, Simon Burrows, 113–39. Cambridge: Cambridge University Press, 2002.

Siromahov, Metodi, Michael Buhrmester, and Ryan McKay. "Beliefs in National Continuity Are Related to Essentialist Thinking and to Perceptions of the Nation as a Family." *Nations and Nationalism* (2020): 1–19.

Smith, John David. "Let Us All Be Grateful That We Have Colored Troops That Will Fight." In *Black Soldiers in Blue: African American Troops in the Civil War Era*, edited by John David Smith, 1–77. Charleston: University of North Carolina Press, 2002.

Snay, Mitchell. *Horace Greeley and the Politics of Reform in Nineteenth-Century America*. Lanham, MD: Rowman & Littlefield, 2011.

Stacey, C. P. "The Defense Problem and Canadian Confederation." *Revista De Historia De América*, no. 138 (2007): 169–75.

Stafford, John. *The Literary Criticism of Young America*. Berkeley: University of California Press, 1952.

Stephens, Marguerita. *White without Soap: Philanthropy, Caste, and Exclusion in Colonial Victoria, 1835–1888: A Political Economy of Race*. Melbourne: University of Melbourne Custom Book Centre, 2010.

Steward, Patrick, and Bryan P. McGovern. *The Fenians: Irish Rebellion in the North Atlantic World, 1858–1876*. Knoxville: University of Tennessee Press, 2013.

Stewart, Ken. "Britain's Australia." In *The Cambridge History of Australian Literature*, edited by Peter Pierce, 7–33. Cambridge: Cambridge University Press, 2009.

Stöter, Eva. "'Grimmige Zeiten': The Influence of Lessing, Herder, and the Grimm Brothers on the Nationalism of the Young Irelanders." In *Ideology and Ireland in the Nineteenth Century*, edited by Tadgh Foley and Sean Ryder, 173–80. Dublin: Four Courts, 1998.

Sullivan, Eileen P. "Liberalism and Imperialism: J. S. Mill's Defense of the British Empire." *Journal of the History of Ideas* 44, no. 4 (1983): 599–617.

Sunter, Anne Beggs, and Paul Williams. "Eureka's Impact on Victorian Politics." In *Labour Traditions: Proceedings of the Tenth National Labour History Conference*, edited by Julie Kimber, Peter Love, and Phillip Deery, 15–21. Melbourne: Australian Society for the Study of Labour History, 2008.

Tarr, Rodger L. "Emendation as Challenge: Carlyle's 'Negro Question' from Journal to Pamphlet." *Papers of the Bibliographical Society of America* 75, no. 3 (1981): 341–45.

Tatz, Colin Martin. *With Intent to Destroy: Reflecting on Genocide*. London: Verso, 2003.

Taylor, Miles. "The 1848 Revolutions and the British Empire." *Past and Present* 166, no. 1 (2000): 166–80.

Thomas, Emory M. *The Confederation Nation: 1861–1865*. New York: Harper, 1979.

Thompson, James. "Modern Liberty Redefined." In *The Cambridge History of Nineteenth-Century Political Thought*, edited by Gareth Stedman Jones and Gregory Claeys, 720–47. Cambridge: Cambridge University Press, 2011.

Tilly, Charles. "Reflections on the History of European State Making." In *The Forma-tion of National States in Western Europe*, edited by Charles Tilly, 3–83. Princeton, NJ: Princeton University Press, 1975.

Ting, Helen. "Social Construction of Nation—A Theoretical Exploration." *Nationalism and Ethnic Politics* 14, no. 3 (2008): 453–82.

Todorov, Tzvetan. *On Human Diversity: Nationalism, Racism, and Exoticism in French Thought*. Translated by Catherine Power. Cambridge, MA: Harvard University Press, 1993.

Toorn, Penny Van. "Aboriginal Writing." In *The Cambridge Companion to Canadian Literature*, edited by Eva-Marie Kröller, 22–48. Cambridge: Cambridge University Press, 2004.

Touhill, Blanche M. "The *Times* versus William Smith O'Brien." *Victorian Periodicals Review* 15, no. 2 (1982): 52–63.

———. *William Smith O'Brien and His Irish Revolutionary Companions in Exile*. Colum-bia: University of Missouri Press, 1981.

Towers, Frank. "The Origins of an Anti-Modern South: Romantic Nationalism and the Secession Movement in the American South." In *Secession as an International Phenom-enon: From America's Civil War to Contemporary Separatist Movements*, edited by Don H. Doyle, 174–92. Athens: University of Georgia Press, 2010.

Tuchinsky, Adam-Max. *Horace Greeley's* New-York Tribune: *Civil War–Era Socialism and the Crisis of Free Labor*. Ithaca, NY: Cornell University Press, 2009.

Urschel, Katrin. "From the 'White Lily' to the 'King Frog in a Puddle': A Comparison of Confederation and Multiculturalism in Irish-Canadian Literature." *International Journal of Canadian Studies/Revue internationale d'études canadiennes* 43, no. 1 (2011): 45–65.

Verhoeven, Timothy. "Neither Male nor Female: Androgyny, Nativism and International Anti-Catholicism." *Australasian Journal of American Studies* 24, no. 1 (2005): 5–19.

Vries, Susanna de, and Jake de Vries. *Historic Brisbane: Convict Settlement to River City*. Brisbane: Pandanus, 2003.

Vronsky, Peter. *Ridgeway: The American Fenian Invasion and the 1866 Battle That Made Canada*. Toronto: Penguin-Allen Lane, 2011.

Waite, P. B. *The Life and Times of Confederation, 1864–1867: Politics, Newspapers, and the Union of British North America*. Toronto: University of Toronto Press, 1962.

Walker, Brian M. *Parliamentary Election Results in Ireland, 1801–1922*. Dublin: Royal Irish Academy, 1978.

Wall, Maureen. "The Rise of a Catholic Middle Class in Eighteenth-Century Ireland." *Irish Historical Studies* 11, no. 42 (1958): 91–115.

Ward, John Manning. *The State and the People: Australian Federation and Nation-Making, 1870–1901*. Annadale: Federation, 2001.

Warner, Donald F. *Idea of Continental Union: Agitation for the Annexation of Canada to the United States, 1849–1893*. Lexington: University of Kentucky Press, 1960.

Warner, Michael. "Publics and Counterpublics." *Public Culture* 14, no. 1 (2002): 49–90.

Weaver, John C. *The Great Land Rush and the Making of the Modern World, 1650–1900*. Montreal: McGill-Queen's University Press, 2003.

Wells, Cory. "'Tie the Flags Together': Migration, Nativism, and the Orange Order in the United States, 1840–1930." PhD diss., University of Texas at Arlington, 2018.

Wenzlhuemer, Roland. *Connecting the Nineteenth-Century World: The Telegraph and Globalization.* Cambridge: Cambridge University Press, 2012.

Whelehan, Niall. *The Dynamiters: Irish Nationalism and Political Violence in the Wider World, 1867–1900.* Cambridge: Cambridge University Press, 2012.

Whyte, William Hadden. *Redbrick: A Social and Architectural History of Britain's Civic Universities.* Oxford: Oxford University Press, 2015.

Widmer, Edward. *Young America: The Flowering of Democracy in New York City.* Oxford: Oxford University Press, 1999.

Wilentz, Sean. *The Rise of American Democracy: Jefferson to Lincoln.* New York: W. W. Norton, 2005.

Williams, Raymond. *Keywords: A Vocabulary of Culture and Society.* London: Fourth Estate, 2014.

Wilson, David A. "The Fenians in Montreal, 1862–68: Invasion, Intrigue, and Assassination." *Éire-Ireland* 38 no. 3 (2003): 109–33.

———. "Introduction." In *Irish and Scottish Encounters with Indigenous Peoples,* edited by Graeme Morton and David A. Wilson, 3–21. Montreal: McGill-Queen's University Press, 2013.

———. *The Irish in Canada.* Ottawa: Canadian Historical Society, 1998.

———. "Introduction." In *Irish Nationalism in Canada,* edited by David A. Wilson, 3–21. Montreal: McGill-Queen's. University Press, 2009.

———. "'Orange Influences of the Right Kind': Thomas D'Arcy McGee, the Orange Order, and the New Nationality." In *The Orange Order in Canada,* edited by David A. Wilson, 89–108. Dublin: Four Courts, 2007.

———. *Thomas D'Arcy McGee, Vol. 1: Passion, Reason, and Politics, 1825–1857.* Montreal: McGill-Queen's University Press, 2014.

———. *Thomas D'Arcy McGee, Vol. 2: The Extreme Moderate, 1857–1868.* Montreal: McGill-Queen's University Press, 2012.

———. "Thomas D'Arcy McGee's Wexford Speech of 1865: Reflections on Revolutionary Republicanism and the Irish in North America." *Canadian Journal of Irish Studies* 26–27 (2000): 9–24.

———. "Time and Space in the Nationalism of Thomas D'Arcy McGee." In *Landscapes and Landmarks of Canada: Real, Imagined, (Re)Viewed,* edited by Maeve Conrick, Munroe Eagles, Jane Koustas, and Caitríona Ní Chasaide, 109–23. Waterloo: Wilfrid Laurier University Press, 2017.

Wilton, Carol. *Popular Politics and Political Culture in Upper Canada, 1800–1850.* Montreal: McGill-Queen's University Press, 2000.

Winks, Robin W. *The Civil War Years: Canada and the United States.* Montreal: McGill-Queen's University Press, 1998.

Winston, Brian. *Misunderstanding Media.* London: Routledge, 1986.

Woods, Carole. "Gray, Moses Wilson (1813–1875)." In *Australian Dictionary of National Biography*. National Centre of Biography, Australian National University, Canberra, 1972. adb.anu.edu.au.

Woollacott, Angela. *Gender and Empire*. Basingstoke: Palgrave Macmillan, 2006.

———. *Settler Society in the Australian Colonies Self-Government and Imperial Culture*. Oxford: Oxford University Press, 2015.

Wright, Tom F. *Lecturing the Atlantic: Speech, Print, and an Anglo-American Commons, 1830–1870*. New York: Oxford University Press, 2017.

Wylie, Paul R. *The Irish General: Thomas Francis Meagher*. Norman: University of Oklahoma Press, 2011.

Yaffey, Michael. "Friedrich List and the Causes of Irish Hunger." in *A World without Famine?*, edited by H. O'Neill and J. Toye, 84–106. London: Palgrave Macmillan, 1998.

Yeats, W. B. *Tribute to Thomas Davis*. Cork: Cork University Press, 1947.

Zastoupil, Lynn. "Moral Government: J. S. Mill on Ireland." *Historical Journal* 26, no. 3 (1986): 707–17.

INDEX

1848: Europe in, 22, 44, 46, 171; Ireland in, 2–3, 23, 74, 113, 171, 175, 199; Kossuth, Louis, 58, 77; legacy of, 78, 172; Mazzini, Giuseppe, 79

abolitionism, 101–2, 104, 109, 110, 120. *See also* O'Connell, Daniel; slavery
aboriginal, 9, 51, 63, 69, 157, 168, 183–85; Kulin Nation, 184; and land distribution, 183–85; Nak-krom allocation, 184
African American, 9, 92, 117–18
The Age. See newspapers and periodicals
Ajzenstat, Janet, 153
American Celt and Adopted Citizen. See newspapers and periodicals
American Revolution, 75, 78–82, 129; as model, 80
American South, 107, 126, 146; compared to Ireland, 109–11, 115, 126. *See also* Confederate States of America
American West, 83, 86, 92, 94, 117
Andrews, Ann, 80
Anglo-American Treaty, 131
Anglophobia, 75; vs. anti-Englishness, 37, 98, 121
Anglophone, 135–37, 142, 153, 162–63
Anglo-Saxon, 72–73, 94, 110, 183
antebellum US, influences of, 12
anti-Englishness. *See* Anglophobia
Antisell, Thomas, 16, 47, 75–76
Anstey, Thomas Chisholm, 16, 22, 55
aristocracy, 40, 51, 91, 128, 151–52
Australia, 1–2, 4, 8–13, 48–51, 60–63, 69–70, 73–74, 94, 119, 138, 150, 167–99; cultural

institutions, 170, 172; gold rush in, 48, 167, 169–72; Irish Diaspora in, 4, 54. *See also* Federation of Australia; Van Diemen's Land
Australian Catholic Benefit Society, 175

Baker, Richard, 177
Balfe, John Donnellan, 63
ballads, 35–36, 41, 110, 134, 155–56, 158. See also *Canadian Ballads and Occasional Verses*
Ballingarry County Tipperary, 2, 45
Balmez, Jaime Luciano, influence on McGee, 84
Bancroft, George, 79, 90
barrister, 17, 55. *See also* lawyer
Barry, Michael J., 32
Belfast, 19, 38, 40, 161, 164
Belfast Newsletter. See newspapers and periodicals
Bell, Duncan, 9, 161, 168
Biagini, Eugenio, 189
Black, 2, 102, 106, 108, 111–12, 117–18, 126. *See also* African American
Black, E. R., 143
Boston, 71, 74, 81–82, 90
Boston Pilot. See newspapers and periodicals
Boyle, John F., 95
Brazil, 103
Brenan, Joseph, 110
Brisbane, 172–74, 188
Britain, 8, 10, 64, 79, 82, 89, 99, 110, 124, 127–28, 131, 152, 161, 170, 177; British Government, 20, 56, 63, 98. *See also* British Empire; United Kingdom

newspapers and periodicals: *The Age,* 171; *American Celt and Adopted Citizen,* 83–85; *Belfast Newsletter,* 57; *Boston Pilot,* 57, 85; *Canadian Freeman,* 138; *Catholic Citizen,* 138; *Citizen,* 19, 97–98, 107, 113; *The Empire,* 175, 178; *Freeman's Journal,* 138; *Harper's Magazine,* 96–97; *Irish Citizen,* 111; *Irish Exile and Freedom's Advocate,* 53–54, 57, 184; *Irish Felon,* 56; *The Irishman,* 110; *Kerry Evening Post,* 57; *Launceston Examiner,* 66; *Montreal Gazette,* 149, 154; *New Era,* 138–39, 143, 163–64; *New York Times,* 57, 88, 161; *New-York Tribune,* 78, 103; *Southern Citizen,* 109; *True Witness,* 141; *United Irishman,* 56, 110, 172; *United States Magazine and Democratic Review,* 91. *See also* Canada: press culture in; Dublin: press culture in; *The Nation*

newspapers and periodicals, global reach of, 56, 59

New-York Tribune. See newspapers and periodicals

Nicaragua, 96

Nova Scotia, 134, 136, 143, 154, 160–61, 164

Obama, Barack, 1

O'Brien, Lucius, 55–56

O'Connell, Daniel, 6, 15, 19–25, 104. *See also* Catholic Emancipation; Repeal

O'Conor, Charles, 78

O'Doherty, Kevin Izod, 16, 62, 70, 169, 172, 174, 175, 188

O'Donnell, John, 74–75

O'Donohoe, John, 139–40

O'Donohoe, Patrick, 48–49, 53–54, 57, 62–65, 74–75, 184–85; escape from Van Diemen's Land, 65, 74

O'Gorman, Richard, 16, 22, 74–76, 78, 112, 126, 132

O'Leary, John, 17

O'Loghlen, Bryan, 16

O'Loghlen, Colman, 55

O'Mahony, John, 16, 47, 75, 120–21, 124, 128, 130, 147, 193

O'Neill, Aodh, 33, 35, 173

O'Shanassy, John, 65, 175, 179, 188

O'Sullivan Beare, 33, 158

O'Sullivan, John, 73, 91–94

Ontario, 128, 134–135

Orange Order, 40, 139–41, 153, 164

Osterhammel, Jürgen, 59

Ottawa, 158, 162–63, 165

pardons, 49, 50, 55, 62, 68, 70, 74

Paris, 47, 63, 70, 112, 121–22

Parkes, Henry, 175–76, 178, 189–90

Parliament, 175–76; Canada, 158, 167; Ireland, 16, 28, 55; Victoria, 172, 177, 190; Westminster, 52, 55, 80

"pastoral" monopoly, 179, 185

patriotism, 58, 131, 145, 149, 154

Pearse, Pádraig, 8, 46

Phillips, Lisa, 157

pluralism, 137, 140, 159, 163, 199

plurinational, 151

political thought, 4, 7–8, 193, 199; in Australia, 48, 68, 190; in Canada, 95, 150, 154; in Ireland, 75, 101; in the United States, 71, 73

Polk, James K., 90–91

Premier of Victoria, 1, 65, 168, 175, 185

press culture. *See* Canada; Dublin

Prince Edward Island, 143

property qualification, 21, 171, 175, 184

prosperity, 15, 96, 144, 149, 169, 180–82, 196

protectionism, 38, 45, 88, 145, 159, 164

Protestant, 28, 33, 72–73, 82, 84, 94, 135, 137, 141–42, 170, 188–89; Presbyterians, 82, 207n128. *See also* Irish Protestant Benevolent Society

Prussia, 30

public sphere, 5, 24–27, 75, 89, 104, 121, 139, 198–99

ABOUT THE AUTHOR

CHRISTOPHER MORASH holds a PhD in History from the University of Cambridge, where he held a prestigious National University of Ireland Travelling Studentship. He has contributed chapters about Young Ireland to edited collections published by Liverpool University Press and the University of Pavia. He is currently an Irish diplomat.